Overcoming
Middle Class Rage

OVERCOMING
MIDDLE CLASS RAGE

Edited by MURRAY FRIEDMAN

THE WESTMINSTER PRESS
Philadelphia

BOOK DESIGN BY
DOROTHY ALDEN SMITH

301.44/
F91/o

Published by The Westminster Press®
Philadelphia, Pennsylvania

PRINTED IN THE UNITED STATES OF AMERICA

To David Danzig

Friend, colleague,
and student of the "New Pluralism"

Contents

III. MIDDLE AMERICA VS. THE LIBERAL CULTURE

IV. THE "NEW PLURALISM"

List of Contributors

Murray Friedman is Pennsylvania-Delaware-Maryland Regional Director of the American Jewish Committee and lecturer in urban sociology and minority groups at La Salle College.

Richard Rogin is a free-lance writer.

Jerome M. Rosow is Assistant Secretary of Labor.

Peter Binzen is Urban Affairs Editor of *The Evening Bulletin,* Philadelphia.

Lewis Carliner is Professor of Labor Studies at Rutgers University.

Michael Lerner is Assistant Professor of Political Science and Psychology at Yale.

Rudolph J. Vecoli is Professor of History, University of Minnesota, and Director, Center for Immigration Studies.

Daniel Patrick Moynihan was a member of the Subcabinet of Presidents Kennedy and Johnson and, until his return to Harvard early in 1971, of the Cabinet of President Nixon.

Eric Hoffer is the San Francisco longshoreman-philosopher.

Milton Himmelfarb is a contributing editor to *Commentary.*

Haskell L. Lazere is New York Regional Director of the American Jewish Committee.

Andrew M. Greeley is a sociologist and Program Director of the National Opinion Research Center, University of Chicago.

David Danzig was Associate Professor of Social Work at Columbia University's School of Social Work at his death. Earlier, he served as Program Director and later Associate Director of the American Jewish Committee.

11

Irving M. Levine is Director of the National Project on Ethnic America of the American Jewish Committee.

Judith M. Herman is Assistant Director of the National Project on Ethnic America.

Kevin P. Phillips is a syndicated columnist. He has served as special assistant to Attorney General John Mitchell.

Spiro Agnew is Vice-President of the United States.

Edmund S. Muskie is U.S. Senator from Maine.

Bayard Rustin is Executive Director of the A. Philip Randolph Institute.

Nathan Glazer is Professor of Education and Social Structure at Harvard University.

By Hubert H. Humphrey

Foreword

O UR NATION has properly given prime attention in recent years to the problems of our most disadvantaged groups—the very poor and the victims of racial discrimination. Even while we have been trying to bridge the gap between promise and performance for these groups, we have become increasingly aware of the very real problems facing an even larger group of Americans—the near-poor, the lower middle class, the "ethnics," the "blue-collar" worker. And we are beginning to understand that we cannot improve the lot of the first group at the expense of the second. We must listen to and learn from all of the different ethnic and economic groups that make up America. We need to know their problems and to understand their points of view.

Dr. Murray Friedman's new book, OVERCOMING MIDDLE CLASS RAGE, can do much to help us in that understanding. He has brought together a wide range of contributors to this much-needed inquiry. One does not have to agree with every one of the contributions—and I do not—to recognize the value of a searching review of the problems, the values, the frustrations, and the hopes of a crucial segment of our society. I recommend this book for its insights and its helpfulness toward greater understanding.

13

By Murray Friedman

Introduction:
Middle America
and the "New Pluralism"

IN RECENT YEARS we have become aware of the emergence of Middle Americans. They have been described as "troubled," "angry," "forgotten," and the "silent majority." Newspaper and magazine articles have been written about them, social scientists are beginning to study this group, and politicians have developed elaborate strategies in an effort to use them to gain or keep power. Like poverty, Middle Americans have been "discovered," although, like the poor, they have always been with us.

In spite of the growing interest in Middle America, no clear picture has emerged as to who Middle Americans are and what they really stand for. Frequently, they are labeled "hardhats" and bigots and represented as an obstacle to be overcome rather than an authentic group with real needs and problems. It is important, therefore, to gain a clearer insight into the nature of this group, the forces that have made them into a major factor in American life, and how to deal with their anger and frustration.

In its January, 1970, cover story naming them "Man and Woman of the Year," *Time* estimated that there are some 100 million Middle Americans. This would mean that just under half the American population are Middle Americans. In a speech late in 1967, which was one of the starting points in the public discussion of this group, Robert C. Wood, then Under Secretary of the U.S. Department of Housing and Urban Development, described the "working American" as a blue- or white-collar male earning between $5,000 and $10,000 a year.[1] Since then, inflation has raised these figures further. In a more recent discussion, Gus Tyler points out that of the 77,902,000 gainfully employed in 1969, 28,237,000 or 36 percent wore blue collars. Of the 36,844,000 white-collar workers, about 18 million were in clerical and sales jobs—an added 22 percent of the employed. In addition, there were another 9,528,000 employed in service trades—a category that earned less than the blue-collar, clerical, or sales people. "The total in these blue and bluish jobs," Tyler concludes, "comes to 69 percent of the employed."[2]

Middle Americans can be defined, also, as first- and second-generation Polish, Irish, Greek, Slovak, and other ethnic groups living, often, in ethnically homogeneous neighborhoods and possessing similar incomes, values, and styles of life. At this writing, 1970 census data is not available, but in 1960 there were 34 million persons of foreign stock background, including 4,900,000 in New York City, 1,800,000 in Los Angeles, 2,000,000 in Chicago, and 1,100,000 each in Detroit and Boston. Even though there are considerably more white ethnics than blacks, recognition of this group has come only recently.

We have little information on the income and occupation of ethnic groups as such, but it is believed that most have not been successful. A hospital planning study in Chicago—the protypical ethnic city—updating 1960 figures to 1969 found that the median income for foreign born for all ethnic groups was only $6,273 and for the second generation it was only $7,163.[3] In the 1970 Introduction to their book, *Beyond the Melting Pot*, Nathan Glazer and Daniel Patrick Moynihan report that a sample survey in New York City shows many on a level with or below Negroes in the proportion professionally employed. They suggest that the negative reaction among many of them to special assistance to blacks stems not alone from racism but from their own position and sense of the right relationship between effort and reward.[4]

As a result of lack of clarity of definition, a number of oversimplifications as to who Middle Americans are have arisen. For example, they are supposed to be white and mostly Roman Catholic. These are certainly nuclear groups, but Middle Americans include many blacks. In 1968, 34 percent of all black families had incomes between $5,000 to $10,000. They are part of a growing black middle class who, by virtue of discrimination and their own rising sense of group identity, are forced to live with or near the black and white poor. For them and those who have managed to move out of racial ghettos, there is resentment that their schools are forced to absorb large numbers of children from welfare families, at efforts to concentrate public housing in their neighborhoods, and deep fear of the growth of crime and violence. ("There is a terrible feeling of fear in Harlem," John Morsell, assistant director of the NAACP said in March, 1969. "The streets appear deserted after 7:00 P.M. Residents are more afraid of the criminals today than of the police. We must have more police protection and sterner measures to control crime and narcotics.")[5]

Although a considerable number of black youth are more militant, there is a deep conservative strain within black America today. In one of his "purloined memoranda" to President Nixon, Daniel Moynihan advised that there is a black silent majority that is politically moderate on issues other than racial equality. "The more recognition we can give to it, the better off we shall all be." [6]

To the surprise of many, also, there are a considerable

number of Jewish Middle Americans. A group that has defined itself often in terms of its liberal stand on social issues now finds that many of its teachers, lower- or middle-rung civil servants, merchants, and other small businessmen are increasingly angry and fearful at the rise of anti-Semitism on the part of black militants, preferential treatment accorded disadvantaged minorities, and the growth of crime, violence, and other disruptive trends in American life today. This has found expression in the creation of the Jewish Defense League and the heavy vote that Jews in New York gave to the two conservative candidates who ran against and were defeated by Mayor John Lindsay in the mayoral campaign in 1969. Many other Jews, especially those from upper-middle-class backgrounds, particularly in Manhattan, have remained staunchly liberal. In 1970, Jews in New York united with Negroes and Puerto Ricans in strong opposition to the Conservative Party candidate, James Buckley. Although Jews are backlashing less than other white groups, the growing restlessness within its lower middle class is symptomatic of the growing alienation of significant numbers of Americans.

If we include in our definition of Middle Americans those who grew up in second-generation homes and persons of other ethnic backgrounds and higher incomes who possess similar attitudes and values, we are stretching it out of all shape and describing virtually all Americans. Perhaps it is in the nature of this elusive concept that it is impossible to define Middle America with any conciseness. In the final analysis, Middle America is a state of mind as much as it is anything else.

The emergence of Middle America stems from certain political and social changes and shifting intellectual moods and currents during the 1960's. In the early years of the decade, working-class and white ethnic groups, generally, were firmly anchored in the "Great Society" coalition along with liberals, intellectuals, church groups, and blacks. This coalition supported and continued the social and economic reforms of the New Deal–Fair Deal period. Under President Johnson, who had begun his political career during the New Deal, a "War on Poverty" had been launched and other significant welfare and educational gains had been made.

The alliance between working-class whites, through their labor unions, and blacks extended even into the civil rights arena. A high point in cooperation was reached in the March on Washington in 1963 where Martin Luther King announced his dream of a united America. This was followed a year later by passage of the omnibus civil rights act. Although pushing for equal rights and opportunities for blacks was not the top priority for working whites, they were willing to go along with the broader goals of the liberal coalition because they saw it as working for themselves as well.

The breakup of this coalition has been attributed to post-World War II economic and status gains made by working Americans and unwillingness to share them with disadvantaged minorities. The upsurge of black militancy, reaction to the war in Vietnam, and changing cultural styles in our society added to their disaffection. But if attitudes of Middle Americans were shifting during the '60s, as they were, so too were those of many of their former allies. The American political style has been traditionally formed by its liberal upper classes and most particularly its dissenting Protestant and Jewish strains. In the '50s and '60s, these elements had been strengthened by a new class of college and university professors, young activists from upper-middle-class homes, new-rich

businessmen with time and money to devote to social issues in New York, Los Angeles, and other cities, and a
vastly enlarged educational, welfare, foundation, and
mass media bureaucracy that gravitated, generally, to
the liberal-left and "new morality" side of most political
and social issues. A sharp cleavage had now developed
between these better educated and more affluent "cosmopolitans" and the less educated, less affluent, more
tradition-minded, blue-collar-ish "provincials."

Increasingly, the "cosmopolitans," who had once seen
in the working class now transformed into a middle class
a vehicle for social change, tended to look down upon
them. Jason Epstein now wrote in the *New York Review*
of "the middle class grunting its way upward."[7] S. I.
Hayakawa, president of San Francisco State College and
himself somewhat of an intellectual highbrow, has said
of this educational and cultural gap:

> This great middle class majority didn't just spring up.
> They've been there all along, but the college-educated
> classes have been moving farther and farther away from
> the middle and lower classes. Their professors teach them
> to look down on the American Legion, Lions Club, and
> the Rotary—all the popular manifestations of everyday
> culture. The professors represent a value system that is
> foreign to the middle class.[8]

A major reason for the estrangement of the "cosmopolitans" from the "provincials," also, was that the liberal-left
began to shift its sympathies and attention to black Americans. Poverty was "discovered" but not in the sense that
it was during the New Deal when all the poor suffered
more or less equally. It was the black poor who seemed
to stimulate the idealism and capture the imagination of
the young, the media, and government itself. That many

of the programs which emerged were often poorly thought out, underfinanced, and badly implemented, ensuring little real gains for Negroes, did not matter. Insofar as struggling blue-collar workers, clerks, teachers, and service personnel were concerned, it was the blacks who were getting all the action. In the mid-'60s, a young lawyer—an aspiring politician in an extremely poor section of Boston—told psychiatrist Robert Coles:

> This is a slum . . . but it's a white slum, so no one cares about it. There's no glamour in white slums, only Negro ones. The suburban housewives and the Ivy League students, they've gone poor-crazy, but only for the colored poor. They've been pushing us around all these years before the Negroes started coming up from the South, and now they have someone to do it for them. They do a good job, too, the Negroes do. They act as if they own the world, just like their friends out there in the suburbs. It's contagious, you see. The ministers and the students come on Saturdays to tutor the Negro kids and take them to the park. They drive right by this neighborhood without blinking an eye. We have overcrowded schools. We have rotten buildings that should have been torn down years ago. We have lousy parks that aren't half the size they should be. A lot of people here have jobs that barely give them enough to get by; and the others, I'll tell you, are on relief or unemployment checks or veterans' checks, or something. We have our delinquents and our drop-outs—the works. Who cares though? Who has ever cared about this neighborhood? [9]

There was and is, of course, genuine sympathy for the unconscionable treatment of blacks in our society and an earnest desire to alleviate their plight among the "cosmopolitans." But mixed in with this, too, has been a certain amount of intellectual slumming—what Tom Wolfe called "radical chic"—among some of those who watched or occasionally interacted from a safe distance with the tragic drama being played out in the urban slums.[10] Moynihan pointed out in a book on the evolution of the poverty program that the intellectual and cultural elite were often not appalled by disorder but almost seemed to welcome it. "How grand to live in interesting times!" he wrote.[11]

To Middle Americans in the latter part of the 1960's, the suspicion grew that an informal alliance had been effected between better-educated and upper-class whites and the black poor and other minorities—directed against them. "The Protestants and better-off Jews" in New York, Glazer and Moynihan wrote, "determined that the Negroes and Puerto Ricans were deserving and in need and, on those grounds, further determined that these needs would be met by concessions of various kinds from the Italians and the Irish (or generally speaking, from the Catholic players) and worse-off Jews. The Catholics resisted, and were promptly judged to be opposed to helping the deserving and needy." [12] In effect, the ethnics were held to be less capable and should influence government processes minimally than upper-class whites who sided with the more disadvantaged.

Simultaneous with the fear and reality of loss of power by Middle Americans, a new mood and cultural style was coming into existence consistent with the attitudes and values of the "cosmopolitans," but sharply at variance with their own. Habits of discipline and self-control, honored if not always obeyed by the latter, were now deemed to be "up tight" or "straight." The actress Shirley Mac-Laine, writing in Look in January, 1971, described the family as becoming obsolete, since it was impossible, she said, to sustain a physical relationship between partners longer than three to five years. In addition, a war was being fought that called upon the traditional patriotism of Middle America but was under attack from a liberal culture that seemed to them to make a mockery of their sacrifices.

The culture had become frankly hostile to Middle Americans. Hollywood made a film, *Joe*, on a blue-collar worker in which the hero declares in a bar, "Forty-two percent of all liberals are queer" and ends up shooting a number of hippies.[13] Early in 1971, a new CBS television series, *All in the Family*, premiered, featuring a blue-collar worker in Queens, New York, who openly attacked Jews, Negroes, the church, and his "bleeding heart" son-in-law. The series is, indeed, funny and may even strike a blow against bigotry. But the real racist in the program may well be the writer, who has fashioned Archie Bunker into a blue-collar stereotype.[14] By the late '60s and early '70s, the working American and homeowner had suffered a sharp decline in status.

The dominant trends in the social sciences for more than a generation largely reinforced these cultural currents. Ethnic diversity had been largely ignored since the Chicago sociologists of the 1920's. In the intervening years, investigators had tended to focus on class and regional forces, prejudice as a form of social illness, and, of course, on the Negro. The '60s saw a vast outpouring of materials dealing with Negro history, culture, personalities, psychology, strategies, and other subjects relating to the race revolution. Most of it was sympathetic to the problems of black people. The urban riots of 1964 to 1968 were described by some social scientists and civil rights activists as racial disorders—a gentler term—and explained as a form of communication on the part of the disinherited in our society.[15] There was much truth in this analysis, but it seemed to condone racial disorders as a legitimate form of social protest.

To Middle Americans, it appears, the professors are

leaning over backward on behalf of the Negro and, in addition, not being fair to them. Crime among blacks is explained; that of Italians, denounced and emphasized. One scholar developed the concept of "working-class authoritarianism" and suggested that "the less sophisticated and more economically insecure a group is, the more likely its members are to accept the more simplistic ideology or political program offered to them." [16] Another refers in an undifferentiated way to the "white working-class racism" of Gary workers as a factor in their reluctance to finance municipal services.[17]

The climax of social scientific thought on race relations in our society came with the publication of the Report of the National Advisory Commission on Civil Disorders (the Kerner Commission) in 1968. The conclusion of this generally excellent analysis, which carried the prestige of its vice-chairman, Mayor John Lindsay, and other eminent figures and scholars, was that we were becoming two societies—one white and the other black—and the central cause for racial disorders was the national disease of "white racism." In short, white America had been tried —and the media quickly picked up on this—by some of this country's most distinguished experts and leaders and found guilty of bigotry. Obviously, Middle America knew there was much wrong with our society and, in particular, with its treatment of the Negro, but it could not and would not accept this verdict of itself.

The decline in the status of Middle Americans and attack on the heartland of their values and style of life came at a time when they were beginning to experience severe financial strains. As Gus Tyler has pointed out, if we use the Labor Department's figure of approximately $6,000 for a family of four as a cutoff poverty line, more than 29 percent of all the families in this country were living in poverty in 1968. Fifty-two percent had an income of less than $9,000 a year—a figure still below the official "modest but adequate" income. Seventy-two percent of all families were found to have an income below $12,000 a year, a sum just above what the Bureau of Labor Statistics considers adequate for a family of four in New York City. As the decade came to a close, three of every four families found themselves in economic difficulties.[18]

It was true, of course, that most Americans were enjoying a higher standard of living during the 1960's than at any time in their life and this included real income. Over the years, many had developed a style of life based on rising expectations. Home mortgages, installment-plan purchases, and perhaps even a "good" college for the children had become norms. Unions began to teach something called "debt management," and many workingmen's wives now went out to work, thereby creating other problems. As inflation and high taxes took an increasing bite out of the workingman's take-home pay and as job automation and the danger of unemployment became more prevalent, many working Americans grew increasingly fearful and harassed. It is significant that backlash voting developed after a period of intense industrial strife. The number of man hours lost in strikes in 1967 and 1968 was higher than that of any comparable period since World War II.[19]

As Americans entered upon the '70s, there had developed a growing feeling of powerlessness and alienation from the "system" on the part of Middle Americans that rivals in power and importance the race revolution and youth revolt. Much of this anger has been directed against the media, the counter culture, and, especially, the black man who seems to symbolize the constellation of problems facing them. Open confrontations developed with

expanding black communities as evidenced in the late
Martin Luther King's forays into the Chicago area and
the New York City school strikes. These were largely between Polish, Italian, and Slovak groups and blacks, and
between Jews and blacks.

In August, 1969, four thousand construction workers
in Pittsburgh took to the streets in protest against blacks
who had been demonstrating against the small number
of jobs held by them in construction unions. Many of
their signs had to do with lost wages resulting from a
two-day shutdown of fifteen construction projects, but,
significantly, the issues were widening. "We build the
city, not burn it down," and "We are the majority," other
signs read. On Wall Street the celebrated hardhats had
clashed with youthful war protesters, and a number of
the latter had been beaten. In Cleveland, white ethnic
groups were demanding and getting a voice on boards
and commissions, especially in examining textbooks "to
be sure an ethnic identity could be found in the history
books our children study." And Italian Americans throughout the country began to strike back at media stereotypes
much as the black man, earlier, had protested against efforts to make him the butt of racist humor.[20]

The political consequences of the emergence of Middle
America were also beginning to be felt. "Backlash politics," Seymour M. Lipset and Earl Rabb have written,
"may be defined as the reaction by groups which are declining in a felt sense of importance, influence and power,
as a result of secular endemic change in the society to
seek to reverse or stem the direction of change through
political means."[21] In New York City, conservative candidates won the primaries in mayoral contests in *both*
political parties, and only by splitting the vote was John
Lindsay able to win. In 1970, a Conservative Party candi-

date, James Buckley, bested incumbent Senator Charles Goodell, although, this time, the liberal forces were split. Earlier, in Minneapolis and Los Angeles, "law and order" mayoral candidates won. Explaining his victory, Charles Stenvig, a Minneapolis detective, said:

> People felt that nobody was representing them and nobody was listening. They felt alienated from the political system, and they had it up to their Adam's apples on just about everything. So they took a guy like me—four kids, an average home, working man, they could associate themselves with. They just said, "Lookit, we're sick of you politicians." [22]

The discovery of Middle America was taking shape, also, from another direction. Although the mood of more than a generation of social scientists was marked by indifference and even, at times, hostility toward the values and life-styles of Middle Americans, a new group began to appear in the '60s who operated out of a different set of theoretical premises. Many of the "new pluralists" were themselves from Jewish, Negro, Catholic, and other minority cultural backgrounds and responded affirmatively to these origins. Their research and analyses went beyond prevailing class theories of "haves" and "have nots," the conventional white-black dichotomy, an outworn political terminology of "left," "liberal," and "center" and sectional interpretations. Above all, they made a serious effort to understand the forces that lay behind the attitudes and responses of ethnic groups.

Among the founding fathers of the "new pluralism" were Nathan Glazer and Daniel Patrick Moynihan, who first published their trailblazing study of the racial, religious, and ethnic groups in New York City, *Beyond the Melting Pot*, in 1963.[23] By 1970, some three hundred thousand copies had been sold. In it, they called attention to the tribal character of the groups living in New York and, inferentially, of much of American life, the continued and often subtle tenacity of ethnicity as reflected in group interests, styles, values, and behavior long after these were supposed to have disappeared into the melting pot.

They sparked what is rapidly becoming a flood of studies and analyses of ethnicity the consequences of which are just beginning to be felt and acted upon. Edward C. Banfield and James Wilson have shown that urban politics is the art of power brokerage among the various racial, religious, and ethnic groups.[24] Gerald D. Suttles[25] and Harold J. Abramson[26] describe the territorial arrangements of these groups and the importance of friendship patterns and familial ties in neighborhoods. Gerald Lesser and Susan S. Stodolsky have pioneered in research on the special learning habits and skills of four groups of children—Chinese, Jews, Negroes, and Puerto Ricans—which suggest a distinctive profile of ethnic achievement seemingly independent of class background. (Chinese children, for example, score highest on space conceptualization, whereas Jewish youngsters do best in verbal facility.)[27] Morris Gross has shown that even within groups —Ashkenazic and Sephardic Jews—there is varying readiness to learn based on cultural and historical experiences and backgrounds that are independent of economic advantages or lack of these.[28]

Earlier, Gerhard Lenski had demonstrated that religion in various ways significantly influences the daily lives of masses of Americans:

Depending on the socio-religious group to which a person belongs, the probabilities are increased or decreased that he will enjoy his occupation, indulge in installment buying, save to achieve objectives far in the future, believe in the American Dream, vote Republican, favor the welfare state, take a liberal view on the issue of freedom of speech, oppose racial integration in the schools, migrate to another community, maintain close ties with his family, develop a commitment to the principle of intellectual autonomy, have a large family, complete a given unit of education, or rise in the class system.[29]

What was beginning to emerge was a view of our society as an intricate mosaic of racial, religious, and ethnic groups who alone and interacting with each other heavily influence and, at times, often determine the social, political, cultural, and economic arrangements of American life.

Part of what had gone wrong, the "new pluralists" seemed to be saying, also, was that there had occurred a loss of the sense of community as a result of the triumph of eighteenth-century and modern liberalism. Freeing the individual from the restraints of church, family, and neighborhood had had obviously beneficial results. With greater freedom had come, however, community disorganization and rudderlessness, especially among the most emancipated. Traditionalist Middle Americans understand almost instinctively what liberal intellectuals, focused on community improvement, often forget: the importance of continuity and the need to bolster those institutions and traditions which hold things together while we go about the business of making necessary change. What had happened, overnight, was that many of these traditions and their authority had broken down. One of his great tasks, Moynihan warned an incoming President in a private memorandum, would be "to restore the authority of American institutions. . . . What is at issue is the continued acceptance by the great mass of the people of the legitimacy and efficacy of the present arrangements of American society, and of our processes for changing these arrangements." [30]

As a result of the work of the "new pluralists" and rising group identification (out of which much of their work stems), new and complicated questions have to be asked about issues long held to be settled. How do we deal with complex issues such as separation of church and state at a time of mounting Catholic pressures to fund the secular aspects of parochial school education? [31] Is desegregation or integration the best model for a pluralist society, or is a certain amount of separation desirable and even necessary? And if so, how much? How do we deal with ethnically homogeneous neighborhoods that seek to keep out, often through the use of force, persons of other racial backgrounds? (The landless Polish peasant who came to this country found his opportunity to make something of himself through the acquisition of a home, which symbolized for him the freedom, security, and dignity he found in the New World. A threat to the neighborhood by the movement in of blacks is a threat to property which, in turn, is a threat to the core of his selfhood.) Older views such as those contained in *The Authoritarian Personality*[32] which saw prejudice and discrimination as a form of illness and a social aberration, while valid, are also incomplete. Group conflict is inevitable in a pluralistic setting where the issue has come increasingly to be how to work out collisions of group interests, values, and styles while working to move the total society forward. This does not settle the issue of a black family moving into a hostile, ethnic neighborhood. Nor can we justify its exclusion and violence. Clearly, the problem is far more complicated than denunciations of racial bigotry and exhortations to fulfill the democratic ideal suggest.

Irving M. Levine and Judith M. Herman have asked

other important questions. "Did certain groups make it easier for a young person to enter the job market, for example, because of cultural factors or the group's place in the occupational structure? . . . Why have some groups adopted entrepreneurial models of economic mobility rather than industrial models? . . . In which ethnic groups might which kinds of economic advancements occur with what initial outside stimulation?" [33] Ought programs designed to meet the needs of blue-collar Americans to be developed with sensitivity to the ethnic diversity as well as economic homogeneity of this group? The research hiatus of several decades leaves us with few answers to questions central to the revolt of Middle America and group adjustments generally in our society. One does not have to be a supporter of Vice-President Agnew to feel that our intellectuals have let us down. "New pluralists" are calling increasingly for studies of ethnicity and have expressed impatience with the cultural elite for failing to address themselves to these questions.[34]

They are seeking, also, new approaches for dealing with white and black America that go beyond the older model and assumptions of the Kerner Commission. It is not that there is any doubt about the pervasiveness of racism in American life. But the Kerner Commission had it down too pat. It utilized an almost Hollywood "good guys" and "bad guys" scenario for viewing racial conflicts. Thus it not only exaggerated or oversimplified the role of government in instituting racial change but encouraged a confrontationist strategy of pitting angry blacks and sympathetic whites against Middle America. What kind of strategy is it, anyway, that accuses almost 90 percent of the population of more than 350 years of racial guilt, especially when the grandparents of so many had barely arrived in the country?

In place of confrontation, "new pluralists" have been urging depolarization. This is not "benign neglect"—here Moynihan stumbled—of the very real problems of racial adjustments. Depolarization calls for replacing rhetoric and racial charges with newer types of alliances of white and black Americans based upon common economic and political problems and needs. These alliances would have to recognize differences among the respective groups— something the older New Deal–Fair Deal coalitions did not—and that sometimes they would each have to travel along parallel and separate routes to obtain common objectives.

Depolarization has found favorable response among moderate black leaders such as Bayard Rustin. "Working men, blue collar as well as Blacks," Rustin wrote, "must be brought together in support of a mutually beneficial platform if we are to have any social progress—or register any political gains at the polls in '72. And I think the key to accomplishing this is having as much compassion for the blue collar worker as we have for the people in the ghetto." [35] While many in the liberal-left were focusing on the failures of American institutions and denunciations of hardhats, reactionaries, and racists, there was beginning to emerge by the late '60s a strategy for attempting to work with Middle America for progressive, social change.

An important role in translating depolarization and "new pluralism" ideas into mainstream American life was played by the American Jewish Committee and *Commentary*, an independent journal published by the Committee. First under Elliot Cohen and later, Norman Podhoretz, who succeeded him as editor, *Commentary* had sought to temper the universalistic traditions of the liberal-left by publishing articles on ethnic identification and by proponents of moderate racial strategies such as Rustin.

For a time, Nathan Glazer served on its editorial staff, and chapters of *Beyond the Melting Pot* first appeared there. The late David Danzig, program director and later associate director of the American Jewish Committee, was among the first to recognize the emergence of Catholics as a growing force in American life and to attempt to build bridges between them and the liberal community.

This newer strategy began to take clearer shape with the appointment of Irving Levine, a race-relations activist, to head a newly created Urban Affairs Department in 1966. An effort was soon under way to turn on public opinion makers and institutional leadership to newer approaches for dealing with low-income, white ethnic groups and developing depolarization models outside the context of the usual liberal agenda. Conferences were held at Fordham University in New York and at the University of Pennsylvania in June, 1968. Papers were delivered by Levine, Danzig, Greeley, and other "new pluralists." In the next few years, local consultations were developed in Detroit, Chicago, St. Louis, New Haven, Providence, and other cities, each attracting increasingly wider attention and interest. Articles, including Murray Friedman's "Kensington, U.S.A." (*La Salle Quarterly*, Fall, 1967), pamphlets such as *The Reacting Americans* (October, 1968), and Andrew Greeley's *Why Can't They Be Like Us?* (May, 1969) were reprinted or published and widely disseminated in the academic community and among the mass media.

By the summer of 1969 and in subsequent months, the mass media began to focus on working-class and ethnic whites. *The New York Times* and *Newsday* in Long Island carried feature-length articles on the personality, life-style, and economic plight of lower-middle-class Americans. *Time* featured "The Middle Americans" on its front cover and analyzed them in an essay on its inside pages. *News-week* developed A Special Report on the White Majority, "The Troubled American," later expanded into a book. It quoted Eric Hoffer as warning, "You better watch out— the common man is standing up." [36] In its August, 1969, issue, *Harper's Magazine* contributed two articles to this flow of materials.[37]

In the space of a few short months, the Middle American was no longer an invisible man. A new interest in "peoplehood" was also developing. Armenians in New York began to learn the language of the old country again, Polish youth organizations were coming into existence in Brooklyn's Greenpoint section, and department stores began to feature peasant blouses and ethnic handbags.[38] *The New York Times* and the Philadelphia *Evening Bul-letin* soon began to explore in feature articles the Irish, Italian, Polish, Jewish, and other ethnic enclaves in their cities. Best-seller novels now included Chaim Potok's *The Chosen* and *The Promise* and Mario Puzo's *The Godfather*.

The reemergence of ethnicity was not simply a counter-response to growing racial assertiveness of Negroes. It was a response to a depersonalized mass society. By the '60s also, second- and third-generation ethnics no longer felt themselves poor immigrants and apologetic and unwel-come guests in a strange house. They were people who had fought in this country's wars and "made it" by their own efforts. With these accomplishments came a new sense of belonging. They felt the country had changed and they did not have to modify or surrender their special beliefs or style of life. Even though they were not able to articulate it clearly, they recognized that in a post-WASP society, *their* perceptions of reality were every bit as good as anybody else's.

With growing self-assurance came the recognition, too,

that their communities were confronted with serious problems. In almost every part of the country grass-roots efforts were shortly under way, often aided by community organizers formerly active in civil rights and poverty efforts, to grapple with their special problems. In ten cities as 1970 came to an end—Boston, Providence, Newark, Philadelphia, Baltimore, Pittsburgh, Cleveland, Detroit, the Gary-Calumet area, and Chicago—alliances were being forged to restore pride among ethnic groups in their national origins, to fight an expressway that was being planned to cut through a neighborhood, and to make their voices felt on such issues as air and neighborhood pollution, inequitable taxes, garbage collection, and zoning.[39] The Calumet Community Congress was founded by 950 delegates from 142 church, civic, fraternal, and labor organizations in the Calumet industrial area of northern Indiana.

A new and hopeful dimension in these community organization efforts is that they are not negatively based and anti-Negro. ("If we don't organize them, George Wallace or some other demagogue will," a CCC worker in Gary has said. Wallace carried Glenn Park, a white ethnic enclave on the south side of Gary, in Indiana's 1964 Democratic Presidential primary.) Many of them are working with Negro organizations to defuse some of the racial tensions of the areas. In Detroit, where three out of five residents are either Negro or Polish, the Black-Polish Conference led by a Negro Congressman, John R. Conyers, and a Polish priest, Rev. Daniel P. Bogus, helped cool two tense situations—one during the mayoral campaign in which a Pole defeated a Negro, and another after a policeman was shot dead outside a black church.

A central figure in stimulating and maintaining contact with these community organizations has been Msgr. Geno C. Baroni, an Italian immigrant miner's son who marched in Selma and worked in the black ghetto in Washington, D.C. As director of program development for the U.S. Catholic Conference's Task Force on Urban Problems, he is, in effect, the Catholic Church's chief ethnic strategist. In a widely publicized conference held in Washington, D.C., in June, 1970, Baroni helped focus national attention on the problems of low-income white ethnics and later co-authored the 1970 Labor Day statement of the U.S. Catholic bishops. The latter called attention to the "continued neglect of the white ethnic working class," noted that bigotry exists among them but rejected the view that "these people are the primary exponents of racism in our society." It urged "white society . . . to spend less time looking for a scapegoat for this racial crisis and more time considering how to assist the people in those communities which are situated on the racial frontier." [40] Two months later, representatives of the USCC met with President Nixon and urged him to take steps to give white ethnics, many of them Catholics in northern cities, a sense of fuller participation in the American mainstream.

The emergence of a large group of angry and volatile Americans in recent years is an important political fact of life and its implications have not been lost on politicians. Ironically, while Middle Americans have formed, largely, the natural constituency of liberals and the Democratic party historically, it was conservatives and the GOP who first grasped the meaning of their revolt and took steps to capitalize on it. The battle plan for the victory of conservatism in 1968—the combined vote for Nixon and Wallace was 57 percent—was drawn up by a brilliant, twenty-eight-year-old political theorist and demographer, Kevin P. Phillips, who went to work for Richard Nixon's chief political adviser, John Mitchell, prior to the election. Of Irish-Catholic background, Phillips had grown up in the ethnically polyglot Bronx in New York which nourished an ethnoreligious view of American life and politics.

After the election, Phillips published *The Emerging Republican Majority*,[41] the most important analysis of American politics since Samuel Lubell's classic, *The Future of American Politics*. In it he analyzed certain changes that had taken place in the American electorate leading to what he termed "a new cycle of Republican hegemony" and laid out a regional religioethnic strategy to take advantage of these changes. While these ideas were described by political analysts as Nixon's "Southern strategy," they were, in fact, considerably more sophisticated. The Phillips-Nixon, Middle America approach was based on recognition of the declining importance of older cities and the development of a new urban-suburban complex made up of lower-middle-class and middle-class Americans, many of them Catholics. (Almost one out of every four people in this country is Catholic.) In effect, the new Republican majority was to eschew the old-line and more liberal WASP northeast section of the country, Negroes, Jews, and the new youth culture. It was to focus instead on newer areas of the country and constituencies—the sun-belt states of Florida, Texas, California, and Arizona to which older and more affluent Americans were moving, the South and Middle West and less glamorous but politically potent Middle America.

> The great political upheaval of the Nineteen-Sixties [Phillips wrote] is not that of Senator Eugene McCarthy's relatively small group of upper-middle-class and intellectual supporters, but a populist revolt of the American masses who have been elevated by prosperity to middle-class status and conservatism. *Their* revolt is against the caste, policies and taxation of the mandarins of Establishment liberalism.[42]

The practical expression of these views was the successful 1968 election and the considerably less successful 1970
campaign which featured the highly charged, alliterative
speeches of Vice-President Spiro Agnew. Both campaigns
saw GOP strategists focusing on Middle American fears
of crime, the use of violence in racial and other social
change, youth revolt on campuses, new permissiveness in
conduct and culture, and, of course, backing the boys in
Vietnam. During his first two years in office, President
Nixon introduced anticrime and antiobscenity legislation
in Congress, appointed a representative to the Vatican—
the first time since Franklin D. Roosevelt—and filed,
through the Justice Department, a "friend of the court"
brief before the U.S. Supreme Court on the constitution-
ality of certain forms of aid to parochial schools. (Phillips
had urged Nixon to release a proposal supporting aid to
parochial schools during the homestretch of the 1968 campaign.[43])

These moves could be dismissed as political expediency,
although they fitted neatly into the ideology of a conservative administration; another branch of that administration,
however, was attempting, also, to move it into more liberal
and substantive channels. Moynihan, who was Assistant
Secretary of Labor under President Kennedy and later
served President Johnson, entered the administration as
Nixon's urban affairs adviser and sought to implement
"new pluralist" and depolarization theories. The key effort
was the startling Family Assistance Program announced by
the President in the summer of 1969. Largely developed
and pressed by Moynihan, FAP sought to terminate the
widely criticized welfare programs that had developed
since the New Deal and substitute a federally supported
economic floor for all Americans, including the working
poor. The move came under sharp criticism of liberals

and, ultimately, from organized labor, because the floor was too low—most recently $2,300 for a penniless family of four—forcing mothers of small children to go to work, and for other reasons, and from conservatives who believed it would destroy incentive and was a step toward socialism. In addition, Assistant Secretary of Labor Jerome M. Rosow was working on a report to the President, "The Problem of the Blue-Collar Worker," which was leaked to the press in the spring and published in the summer of 1970. It called for better job conditions and opportunities, tax advantages, improved health, status, and education for lower-middle-income families.

During the first two years of the Nixon Administration, however, the Moynihan-Rosow proposals did not move forward. FAP was stymied by criticisms from liberals and conservatives and by the failure of the President to push aggressively for his plan. As the Rosow proposals began to be discussed inside the administration, there was evidence of timidity and lack of real financial support. Rosow admitted in an interview that no major new legislation or tax relief was in sight and the emphasis was to be placed on low cost reforms of present laws and new job standards for private industry.[44] "Many are suspicious that the Nixon administration is only making the appearance of a move, with no substance," Colman McCarthy wrote in *The Washington Post* on July 13, 1970. "In fact, the confidential report reinforces this suspicion by saying candidly that the ethnics are 'overripe for a political response.'"

The Nixon Administration had, in fact, failed to move aggressively and creatively on the Moynihan-Rosow proposals and other substantive programs. It substituted, instead, the rhetoric of the 1968 and 1970 campaigns. This and its insensitivity to the anger and frustration of black Americans reveal the essential weaknesses of the Middle

America political strategy of conservatism. Apart from the intrinsic merits of FAP and the Rosow proposals, however, they represent a fundamental movement, at least in concept, beyond the New Deal–Great Society–Kerner Commission strategies that liberals and social activists have been locked into. The latter, it is true, had been calling for coalitions of blacks and whites and the poor generally around common needs. Nevertheless, poverty and other federal programs were either geared to alleviating the problems of the black poor or *looked as if they were,* thereby turning off many whites. A conservative political administration had given birth to a broad-based strategy that seemed modeled after some of the ideas of Bayard Rustin and others of providing "something for everybody." The Harris survey reported shortly after announcement of FAP that most Americans favored the plan while at the same time opposing older welfare programs.[45]

Despite the fact that the Nixon–Middle America strategy was carefully aimed at capturing the natural constituency of the liberal-left by exploiting issues and identifying with the values and goals of working-class ethnic groups, the liberal-left in the late '60s seemed unable to mount an adequate response. Much of its energy was given over to getting out of Vietnam on terms that many Americans believed included acceptance of defeat, poverty programs that accomplished little for blacks but managed to antagonize whites, and attacks on police harshness at a time of rising crime and violence. One segment of the Democratic Party, under the banner of New Politics, was calling for a coalition of the Left built around the socially alienated in our society and relegating union labor and Middle America to the ranks of the bigots. To the degree that the liberal-left looked over its shoulder at its disappearing allies, it largely wrung its hands at growing political impotency and the "drift to the right."

Just prior to the 1970 off-year elections, a strategy devised for liberals appeared with publication of the book *The Real Majority*, by Richard M. Scammon and Ben J. Wattenberg. In it, they argued that America was a centrist society in which the great majority "are unyoung, unpoor and unblack . . . middle-aged, middle-class, middle-minded." [46] Politicos, they said, could not get too far away from the views and values of the center and retain potical viability. They noted, also, that Americans were no longer voting on the basis of traditional bread-and-butter issues. They were manifesting their concern now about the "Social Issue"—the youth culture, race, drugs, violence, crime, and campus disorder. Liberals and Democrats were urged to "finesse" this issue. If the electorate could be convinced that *they* were concerned about "law and order," the code word for the "Social Issue," they could be as pro black as they wanted and gain support for other necessary social changes. Scammon and Wattenberg constructed a scenario by which liberals could capture the center:

—Do *not* say, "Well, I don't agree with the Students for a Democratic Society when they invade a college president's office, but I can understand their deep sense of frustration."

—Do say, "When students break laws they will be treated as lawbreakers."

—Do *not* say, "Crime is a complicated sociological phenomenon and we'll never be able to solve the problem until we get at the root causes of poverty and racism."

—Do say, "I am going to make our neighborhoods safe again for decent citizens of every color. I am also in favor of job training, eradication of poverty, etc., etc."

. . . and so on. After each utterance . . . add . . . : and what have Richard Nixon and the Republicans done about it? Nothing! [47]

The Real Majority became the political text for many liberals and Democrats during the 1970 elections. Wattenberg joined former Vice-President Humphrey's staff during the summer, and the latter was soon making well-publicized speeches against violence and calling for punishing lawbreakers. Advertisements for Senator Philip Hart, of Michigan, now showed a policeman looking approvingly upon him. Senator Harrison Williams, of New Jersey, made a radio appeal to voters to help him in his fight against crime. Adlai Stevenson, III, of Illinois, made the prosecutor of the "Chicago Seven" cochairman of his campaign and wore a flag on his lapel.[48] By and large, the strategy worked. The Social Issue was "finessed." Democrats gained especially in the number of new governors elected and in statehouses across the nation.

But if *this* new politics works, it is also, as Michael Janeway has pointed out, "The Politics of Quackery." "Scammon and Wattenberg don't really 'trust the people,' as they righteously claim," he writes. "They distrust people's ability to find their way past fear and misconception." [49] Although they explicitly disclaim this, their approach reflects an attempt to manipulate Middle America for political ends rather than any fundamental respect or liking for working Americans and their special view of American life. Was there not a better case that could be made for the values, accomplishments, and aspirations of Middle Americans? There were few writers and intellectuals in the '60s who were willing to make such a case. One of the few was Eric Hoffer, the outspoken San Francisco longshoreman whose books, essays, and celebrated television interview with Eric Sevareid have attracted wide attention.

Hoffer celebrated the virtues of Middle America openly and unabashedly. "Whose country, then, is America?" he asked. "It is the country of the common—the common men and women, a good 70 percent of the population—who do most of the work, pay much of the taxes, crave neither power nor importance, and want to be left alone to live pleasurable humdrum lives." [50] Hoffer took pleasure in the achievements of America's astronauts (described by one intellectual as "thoroughly conventional and middle class and essentially dull people") and called attention to the great resourcefulness and natural decency of working people. Drawing on his own personal experience, he wrote:

> Once, during the Great Depression, a construction company that had to build a road in the San Bernardino Mountains sent down two trucks to the Los Angeles skid row, and anyone who could climb onto the trucks was hired. When the trucks were full the drivers put in the tailgates and drove off. They dumped us on the side of a hill in the San Bernardino Mountains, where we found bundles of supplies and equipment. The company had only one man on the spot. We began to sort ourselves out; there were so many electricians, mechanics, cooks, men who could handle bulldozers and jackhammers, and even foremen. We put up the tents and the cook shack, fixed latrines and a shower bath, cooked supper and the next morning went out to build the road. If we had to write a constitution, we probably would have had someone who knew all the whereases and wherefores. We were a shovelful of slime scooped off the pavement of skid row, yet we could have built America on the side of a hill in the San Bernardino Mountains. [51]

Hoffer has been at times wrongheaded and intemperate, but he has framed the issue: Are Middle America values and attitudes so negative and unredeeming? Has the attack on "Victorianism" and greater sexual freedom and openness of recent years been such a liberating and satisfying experience as contrasted with working-class reticence? Even though their national pride and patriotism has been expended in an unnecessary and increasingly unpopular war, are their sacrifices not worthy of at least respect? In the final analysis, are working-class or Middle Americans automatically racists and reactionaries? There is no evidence in the revolt of Middle America of any desire to turn the clock back on the social and economic reforms of the past two generations and, in fact, a willingness to extend these. Louis Harris and Associates published the following table[52] early in 1971 on how Americans view certain issues:

	Favor pct.	Oppose pct.	Not sure pct.
Spending more money on air and water pollution control	83	7	10
Get all troops out of Vietnam by end of 1971	61	20	19
Increase Federal programs to help poor	56	28	16
Help blacks move faster toward equality	52	31	17

Many working-class whites, of course, are intolerant of other viewpoints and need to be less rigid.

There is, however, less bigotry among the so-called "white ethnics" than other segments of the population. A national survey conducted for the Urban League by Louis Harris and Associates in March, 1970, reported that half of the native whites, compared to about two fifths of the Irish, Italian, and Poles, believe that the push for racial equality has been too fast. Likewise, two fifths of the native Americans, but only about one third of the white ethnics, disapprove of the Supreme Court's desegregation decision. About one fifth of the native whites favor separate schools for blacks and whites compared to a substantially smaller percentage of the others. Commenting on the study, Whitney Young said that it suggests "that some Americans may be projecting their own prejudices onto minorities of recent foreign origin." [53] Many low-income white ethnics identify with the problems of lower-income minority workers because they and their parents have had similar experiences and will support gains required by the latter if these do not come out of their own limited possibilities and future.

It is clear that the nation's major social priority has to remain remedying the damage created by several hundred years of systematic discrimination against and exploitation of the black man. Although tremendous and often overlooked progress has been made here—outside the South, for example, young husband-wife Negro families have 99 percent of the income of whites—the situation of the black family has deteriorated in recent years. In March, 1970, the Census Bureau reported that 40 percent of nonwhite children had one or both parents missing. The sharp rise in welfare recipients that threatens to bankrupt some cities is only one example of the desperate plight of so many blacks.

The issue has come increasingly to be how to deal with black rage and Middle American fears. "New pluralist" or depolarization strategies are aimed at accomplishing this. They call for maintaining and extending the commitment to black America while at the same time recognizing and dealing with the serious problems of working or white ethnic groups. It is still too early to judge but there is the possibility that the two movements can compliment and aid each other. There is no reason why the gains of the poor must be made at the expense of the near poor. Together, they can cause the creation of a "bigger pie" for all Americans. The development of black studies in the public schools, for example, has already opened the door for similar efforts with regard to Poles, Jews, Irish, and other ethnic groups.

Nevertheless, the "new pluralism" has been criticized by some segments of the liberal-left. In September, 1970, the American Jewish Committee and the United States Catholic Conference programs were attacked publicly by the National Committee of Black Churchmen as "ill-advised" and "perilous" courses of action. The NCBC charged in letters to both organizations that the struggles of "blacks and browns to attain economic, political and educational equity in America" have been given "secondary priority" in efforts initiated by both groups. "Surely you need not be reminded that the job of aiding the black and brown communities to reach even the modest levels . . . already existing among white working class people has barely gotten under way," the letters said. "Have you raised our hopes and expectations of assistance from you, only to dash them to pieces when the pressure and flak intensify upon you?"

In response, Roman Catholic Bishop Joseph L. Bernardin, general secretary of the USCC, admitted that the new concern "requires focusing attention on the problems and legitimate complaints of the ethnic working class." But, he added, this does not mean any "deemphasis on the problems of the black community," nor any change in the church's determination to serve the "urgent—and too-long neglected—needs" of blacks. Irving Levine responded that to build a future "black-white coalition for progress" requires dealing with the "legitimate and social and economic problems of lower-middle-class Americans" and reducing "negative passions" now polarizing whites

against blacks. He reminded the NCBC also that the re-
oriented approach came in response to requests by some
blacks that whites work harder in their own communities
to dispel opposition to black goals.[54]

"New pluralist" and depolarization strategies have been
an attempt on the part of some segments of the liberal-
left to establish fresh lines of communication with Middle
America. The latter can move in any direction politically
in the coming years. It has been ardently wooed by conservatives and, more recently, by the liberal-left, but it
owes its allegiance to neither and is rightfully suspicious
of both. It will support, doubtlessly, those who honestly
respect their values and goals, deal sensibly with their
interests or needs, and who, one suspects, appeal to their
better natures. In spite of the anger of working Americans
at the neglect and insensitivity of many liberals and intellectuals, there exists respect for the man of learning.
Penn Kemble believes also that the liberal-left has exaggerated the nature and depth of the conservative backlash in
the same way it proved insensitive to the forces that
brought it into existence. He suggests that a thoughtful
appeal to Middle America's democratic traditions and
radical impulses could convert it to "a new politics of
hope." [55]

There are signs of growing awareness of this. In a gesture that may symbolize the effort of some intellectuals
to develop a dialogue with working-class whites, John
Galbraith, the economist and former national head of
ADA, congratulated George Meany, president of the AFL-
CIO, early in 1971 and sought a meeting following the
latter's criticism of the economic policies of the Nixon
Administration. The Ford Foundation, which has directed
much of its effort in the urban arena for at least a decade
to attempts to alleviate the problems of the black poor, at

about the same time announced grants of almost a million dollars for projects involving white, working-class Americans. In a recent speech, Hubert H. Humphrey urged liberals to "let hard-hats know that they understand what is bugging them and that they too condemn crime, riots, violence and extreme social turbulence." [56]

The revisionist historian and hero of the New Left, William A. Williams, has called upon the New Left to "start dealing with large numbers of Americans, however misled or mistaken we may consider them, as human beings rather than as racists and stupids to be jammed up against the wall. For the self-righteous arrogance in the Movement is at least as dangerous to its future as The Establishment." [57] And Harold Cruse, a black militant theoretician often criticized for his extremism, has declared:

> If the Negro leadership is hampered by deficient conceptualizing of American group reality, then the Negro movement will defeat itself in the long run. It will defeat itself by encouraging other unassimilated ethnic groups to turn against the Negro minority, in a pro-Anglo-Saxon Protestant "racial" coalition. It will defeat itself by utilizing mechanical narrow-minded agitational tactics that will discourage other unassimilated ethnic groups from assuming a pro-Negro attitude in the furtherance of their own group cultural rights. The Congress of Racial Equality (CORE) has been most guilty of such tactics in the North, for example, where it indiscriminately carries demonstrations into ethnic neighborhoods without giving due consideration to local neighborhood sentiments. This approach, however, stems out of the dominant NAACP ideology which does not sanction the reality of neighborhood group sentiments.[58]

In the few short years that the concept of Middle America has emerged, it has caught on but it has not yet caught up. There is still a vacuum of concern and willingness to translate this into action within many segments of the liberal-left and cultural elite who help shape ideas and programs in our society. Just as poverty suddenly became an issue and the Kerner Commission reported in a seemingly startling new insight how endemic white racism is, there must be a greater recognition of the problems and possibilities of Middle America: The key to our viability as a society lies in the way in which the political-managerial, the communications, and the intellectual-ideological elites respond to this crucial group of Americans in the coming years.

The readings that follow are divided into six sections. The authors represent a wide variety of viewpoints. With some of these I agree in whole or in part, while others are some considerable distance from my own positions. The selections have been chosen, however, to illustrate the nature and implications of the emergence of Middle America and approaches to dealing with it.

NOTES

1. Robert C. Wood, "Small Town in a Great Society," The Bemis Lecture Series, Lincoln, Massachusetts (unpublished written manuscript, Dec. 8, 1967).

2. Gus Tyler, "The White Worker" (unpublished manuscript prepared for the Task Force on Group Life of the American Jewish Committee, May, 1970), p. 6.

3. Irving M. Levine and Judith M. Herman, "The Ethnic Factor in Blue Collar Life" (an unpublished paper in the National Project on Ethnic America of the American Jewish Committee).

4. Nathan Glazer and Daniel Patrick Moynihan, *Beyond the Melting Pot* (M.I.T. Press, 1970), p. lvi.

5. Earl Rabb, "Intergroup Relations and Tensions in the U.S.," *American Jewish Yearbook* (American Jewish Committee and Jewish Publication Society of America), p. 202.

6. Published in *The New York Times*, March 1, 1970. This conservative strain has been underestimated. A black professor complained in an article in *The New York Times Magazine*, "Colleges Are Skipping Over Competent Blacks to 'Authentic' Ghetto Types," Dec. 13, 1970, pp. 36–52. My favorite example, however, is an editorial from the *Philadelphia Tribune*, Dec. 22, 1970. "What is really needed in large urban school districts in Philadelphia and elsewhere in the United States," this black newspaper wrote, "is the good old-fashioned 'drill system' method in which a certain amount of discipline is present."

7. As quoted by Dennis H. Wrong in "The Case of the *New York Review*," *Commentary*, Nov., 1970, p. 53.

8. Richard Lemon, *The Troubled American* (Simon and Schuster, Inc., 1969, 1970), p. 191.

9. "The White Northerner," *Atlantic*, June, 1966, p. 55.

10. "Radical Chic: That Party at Lenny's," *New York Magazine*, June 8, 1970, pp. 26–56.

11. Daniel Patrick Moynihan, *Maximum Feasible Misunderstanding* (The Free Press, 1969), p. 179.

12. Glazer and Moynihan, *Beyond the Melting Pot*, p. lxiii.

13. Norman Wexler, *Joe*, a screenplay (Avon Books, 1970).

14. The reaction to the series has been good, but one letter writer complained: "I am the wife of a blue collar worker. You know, as I know, that bigots are not confined to a group or race or a religion. And you should know, as I know, that ridicule of a group, a race, or a religion will not change the ideas of a bigot—personal contact and reason perhaps will. I have appealed to CBS, etc., etc., in an effort to stop this senseless attempt to downgrade an entire group of people." *The Evening Bulletin* (Philadelphia), Jan. 28, 1971.

15. See, for example, the Foreword to Lenora E. Berson's *Case Study of a Riot*, by Alex Rosen, dean of the New York University Graduate School of Social Work (Institute of Human Relations Press, 1966), pp. 5–6.

16. Seymour M. Lipset, "Working-Class Authoritarianism," in *Political Man* (Doubleday & Company, Inc., 1960), pp. 97–130.

17. Edward Greer, "The 'Liberation' of Gary, Indiana," *Trans-Action*, Jan., 1971, p. 32.

18. Tyler, "The White Worker," p. 12.

19. Penn Kemble, "On Eric Hoffer," *Commentary*, Nov., 1969, p. 81.

20. *The New York Times*, Nov., 27, 1970.

21. Seymour M. Lipset and Earl Rabb, *The Politics of Unreason: Right-Wing Extremism in America 1790–1970* (Harper & Row, Publishers, Inc., 1970).

22. Rabb, "Intergroup Relations," p. 201.

23. Reference should be made here, also, to the pioneering work done by older scholars such as Marcus Hansen and Oscar Handlin. The thrust of their work, however, as Rudolph Vecoli points out in his essay, tended to show immigrants disappearing into the broader American society after much conflict and suffering, whereas the "new pluralists" emphasized those qualities of ethnicity that remain into the second, third, and even later generations.

24. Edward C. Banfield and James Q. Wilson, *City Politics* (Harvard University Press, 1968).

25. Gerald D. Suttles, *The Social Order of the Slum: Ethnicity and Territory in the Inner City* (The University of Chicago Press, 1968).

26. Harold J. Abramson, "Ethnic Pluralism in the Central City" (an unpublished paper presented to the Statewide Consultation on Connecticut's Ethnic and Working Class Americans, held at Albertus Magnus College, New Haven, Conn., April 17, 1970).

27. Gerald Lesser and Susan S. Stodolsky, "Learning Patterns in the Disadvantaged." *Harvard Educational Review*, Vol. XXXVII, No. 4 (Fall, 1967) pp. 546–593.

28. Morris Gross, *Learning Readiness in Two Jewish Groups: A Study in "Cultural Deprivation"* (an Occasional Paper published by the Center for Urban Education, N.U., 1967).

29. Gerhard Lenski, *The Religious Factor*, rev. ed. (Anchor Books, Doubleday & Company, Inc., 1963; originally published in 1961).

30. *The New York Times*, March 11, 1970.

31. Murray Friedman and Peter Binzen, "Politics and Parochiaid," *New Republic*, Jan. 23, 1971, pp. 12–15.

32. T. W. Adorno, E. Frenkel-Brunswik, D. J. Levinson, and R. N. Sandford, *The Authoritarian Personality* (Harper & Brothers, 1950).

33. Levine and Herman, "The Ethnic Factor," pp. 10–11.

34. See especially Greeley's articles, "Intellectuals as an Ethnic Group," *The New York Times,* July 12, 1970, pp. 22–34; and "Malice in Wonderland: Misconceptions of the Academic Elite," *Change,* Sept.–Oct., 1970, pp. 7–9.

35. Bayard Rustin, "Mobilizing a Progressive Majority," *The New Leader,* Jan. 25, 1971, p. 3.

36. *Newsweek,* Oct. 6, 1969, p. 29.

37. Peter Schrag, "The Forgotten American," *Harper's Magazine,* Aug., 1969, pp. 27–34; and Marshall Frady, "Gary, Indiana," *ibid.,* pp. 35–45.

38. Levine and Herman, "The Ethnic Factor," p. 26. Accompanying this has been, also, a revival of more traditional cultural patterns. This includes "country" and "western" music, religious book sales, and more nostalgic forms of entertainment.

39. "A Rising Cry: 'Ethnic Power,'" *Newsweek,* Dec. 21, 1970, pp. 32–36.

40. Msgr. Geno C. Baroni (ed.), *All Men Are Brothers,* Report on Urban Ethnic Affairs, Nov. 10, 1970 (Task Force on Urban Problems, United States Catholic Conference, 1312 Massachusetts Ave., N.W., Washington, D.C. 20005).

41. Kevin P. Phillips, *The Emerging Republican Majority* (Arlington House Publishers, 1969).

42. *Ibid.,* p. 470.

43. Gary Wills, *Nixon Agonistes* (Houghton Mifflin Company, 1970), p. 267.

44. *The Philadelphia Inquirer,* Jan. 7, 1971.

45. *The Philadelphia Inquirer,* Oct., 1969.

46. Richard M. Scammon and Ben J. Wattenberg, *The Real Majority* (Coward-McCann, Inc., 1970), p. 21.

47. *Ibid.,* p. 286.

48. Amy Malzberg and Geraldine Rosenfeld, "America Votes, 1970: The Center Holds" (a Research Report of the American Jewish Committee, Dec., 1970), pp. 4–5.

49. Michael Janeway, "The Politics of Quackery," *Atlantic,* Dec., 1970, p. 73.

50. Eric Hoffer, "Whose Country Is America?" *The New York Times Magazine,* Nov. 22, 1970, p. 121.

51. As quoted by Kemble, "On Eric Hoffer," p. 80.

52. *The Philadelphia Inquirer,* Sept. 27, 1970. A follow-up study on the Kerner Commission report stated that although most Americans blamed Negroes for inferior employment, education, and housing deficiencies, there was also support for the principles of nondiscrimination in housing and overwhelming opposition to discrimination in employment. The study of white beliefs about Negroes noted "a long-term shift away from traditional beliefs and toward greater sensitivity to the difficulties experienced by Negroes in America" (Supplemental Studies for the National Advisory Commission on Civil Disorders, July, 1968, U.S. Government Printing Office, Washington, D.C.).

53. News release, Aug. 19, 1970, and other related materials, Research Department, National Urban League, 425 13th St., N.W., Suite 529, Washington, D.C. 20004.

54. Religious News Service, Sept. 21, 1970, and George Cornell, "Blacks See Churches Veering to White Workers' Problems," *The Evening Bulletin,* Oct. 10, 1970.

55. Kemble, "On Eric Hoffer," p. 82.

56. "Having established credibility," Humphrey added, "we can more easily cope with a different violence: the social and psychological violence of the slum, which is the breeding ground of physical violence" ("Liberalism and 'Law and Order' —Must There Be a Conflict?", remarks before the American Bar Association, General Practices Section, Aug. 11, 1970).

57. William A. Williams, "An American Socialist Community?", *Liberation,* June, 1969.

58. Harold Cruse, *The Crisis of the Negro Intellectual* (William Morrow and Company, Inc., 1967).

PORTRAIT
OF THE
MIDDLE AMERICAN

I

WHO IS THE MIDDLE AMERICAN? "JOE KELLY HAS REACHED His Boiling Point" presents a picture of a New York hard-hat. "Kensington, U.S.A." examines the underlying forces that have given rise to Middle American anger and frustration, while in "The Problem of the Blue-Collar Worker," Assistant Secretary of Labor Jerome M. Rosow presents in broad outline his program to alleviate some of these tensions. What emerges from these articles is a portrait of a group of Americans with blind spots and racial antagonisms but persons, nevertheless, with many serious problems that our society has been ignoring for too long.

By Murray Friedman

Kensington, U.S.A.

SINCE 1964, the nation has been beset by Negro riots, with racial explosions in Detroit, Newark, and other cities this summer the most destructive of all. Americans have begun—however inadequately—to attempt to understand the causes and deal with the consequences through crash efforts to provide employment for the jobless, recreational opportunities to school dropouts, and other poverty programs.

But racial violence has not been limited to Negroes. In the same period, there have been a series of white racial explosions resulting from Negro move-ins in white neighborhoods or in response to Negro militancy. Over the long run, these can have as grave consequences as the more spectacular riots of the past summer. Rioting has taken place in Brooklyn, sections of Chicago, in Cicero, Illinois, in Folcroft near Philadelphia, in the Kensington section of Philadelphia, and most recently in Milwaukee. In Kensington, white rioting raged for five days and nights. Only with great difficulty were the police able to bring the disturbances under control.

White rioting has been obscured because the explosions

Reprinted from *La Salle*, a quarterly La Salle College magazine, Vol. 11, No. 4 (Fall, 1967). Used by permission.

in Watts, Detroit, and other cities have been more destructive in property damage and loss of life and the perpetrators are white urban ethnic groups who are generally ignored. These groups, however, like Negroes, are victims of certain deep-seated urban pathologies. Yet while there has been much analysis of Negro rioting—and more are on the way—there has been little or no attempt to understand the underlying factors involved in white racial explosions.

There are, of course, essential differences between recent white and Negro racial revolts. The white revolt is aimed at maintaining the *status quo*, while the Negro seeks to upset it. Both, however, have much in common. To dismiss Kensington's white rioters as a bunch of "misguided bigots" is as simpleminded as blaming "outside agitators" for Detroit. Kensington is a concrete example of what *Ebony* magazine recently called "The White Problem in America."

The problem lies deeper than the surface signs of bigotry. White Kensington looks, feels, thinks, and acts in many ways like a Negro ghetto. It is an older section of the city, cemented to the North Philadelphia Negro ghetto where a damaging riot occurred in the summer of 1964. Factory buildings are interspersed with red-brick, single-family homes. Many of the latter evidence a considerable degree of deterioration and there are a number of abandoned and boarded-up residences.

Neighborhood facilities, such as schools, playgrounds, and pools, are run-down and—often—simply not functioning. The Kensington Hospital has reported in a survey of community resources "deteriorating plant and inadequate facilities to carry out full programs on our own." The Kensington Christian Center notes in the same document: "Lack of adequate funds is the sole reason why we are so understaffed. Also, our building is very old and in need of extreme repair. . . . This area will have to be developed if we are to really assist our community."

In Kensington live 187,000 people—predominantly Catholic. Almost a third of the residents are persons of foreign-stock backgrounds—first-, second-, and older-generation Irish, Poles, English, Germans, Italians, Russians, and, surprisingly enough, a small number of Puerto Ricans and Negroes. The latter have come in as the Negro ghetto east of Second Street in North Philadelphia expands into Kensington. Rioting has usually developed here among whites fearful of inundation by Negroes when the latter move in several streets beyond the invisible boundary separating the two areas.

As in the Negro neighborhoods of North Philadelphia, most Kensingtonians are semiskilled or have no skills at all. The general median income for families ranges from between $300 to $1,600, below the city generally. In the Coral Street area, where the rioting against the Wright family took place, 800 of 5,000 families have incomes below the established poverty level of $3,000 annually.

Only a small number of Kensingtonians complete high school and go on to college. The Philadelphia School Board has reported that District Five, in which Kensington is located, and District Three, areas of concentration of poor whites in the city, scored lower than Negro districts in basic educational abilities, including reading and arithmetic.

The problems of Kensington and other areas that have experienced white rioting, however, cannot be laid completely at the door of poverty any more than the all-Negro riots. The homes, while inexpensive and aging, are often well kept up. Though a step or two above most Negroes on the economic ladder—many have moved into the lower middle class—Kensingtonians are beset by economic problems and status anxieties. The process of upward movement has been slow and hard fought. Frequently, the gains made are endangered by the possibility of loss of jobs, slowdown in the economy, or are drained off by inflation. One senses a feeling of displacement among the people living here, an ebbing of the joys and pleasures that once characterized working-class life.

These anxieties are increased as they watch—in their opinion—the lawlessness of Negro violence in Watts and Detroit being rewarded by special federal and city efforts to aid the Negro. The news media inform them daily of new civil rights legislation and Model City and other poverty programs such as VISTA and "Get Set," pouring into seemingly favored Negro areas of the city.

Sister Catherine Newhart, of the Lutheran Settlement in the heart of Kensington, tells of a board meeting at the Settlement when board members, returning to their automobiles after the meeting, found their tires deflated. Asked why she had done this, one girl caught running away responded: "I know what you were doing in there. You were planning to build a community center for the niggers in Haverford [another branch]." As a young lawyer from a poor section of Boston told Harvard psychologist Robert Coles: "The ministers and the students come on Saturdays to tutor the Negro kids and take them to the park. They drive right by this neighborhood without blinking an eye. . . . Who has ever cared about this neighborhood? White they may be, but they too feel as left out as any Harlem Negro."

The unmet and insensitive handling of the needs of older and poor sections of white, urban, ethnic America by community officials and planners are as much a national scandal as similar failures in Negro ghetto areas.

They are an important factor in the "white backlash" in Chicago, Boston, Philadelphia, and other cities. An examination of Philadelphia's capital building program for 1966 to 1971 shows there is little in the way of parks, playgrounds, pools, libraries, and health centers being planned for Kensington. The only improvements involve $112,000 for the swimming pool on Montgomery Avenue and Moyer Street—noted, incidentally, as presently unusable—and $450,250 for the St. Mary's Hospital urban-renewal area. The latter provides little direct benefit to Kensingtonians and will replace a small park. And while a new federally funded licensing and inspection effort is getting under way in Kensington, the Model City program planned for Philadelphia will cover only Negro ghetto areas.

The failures of city government officials and planners in attending to Kensington's needs are matched by certain internal weaknesses of residents which result in frustration and a high explosive level. These weaknesses grow, in part, out of a working-class, ethnic style of the people living there.

The native Kensingtonian possesses a fierce parochialism and neighborhood pride. "Kensington against the world," is the local motto. As recently as the Korean war, two young men told Larry Groth, deputy director of the Commission on Human Relations and a former resident of the area, they had never been out of Fishtown, a section of Kensington, until they were drafted into the army. Low economic achievement is due as much to certain group standards as lack of opportunity. The tradition has been for a young man to go into the factory or plant where his father works rather than to aspire to something better. Even if he did set his sights higher, he is likely to provoke the comment, "What's the matter? Think you're better than your old man?"

The white Kensingtons of America also have a way of handling difficult situations with physical violence. "If you get hit by an automobile," an irritated mother will tell her child, "I'll break your arm." In Chicago this past summer, white ethnic groups began to organize and arm themselves as a means of retaliating against Negro rioters. Alert action by the police in several cities prevented a full-scale confrontation between angry whites and rampaging Negro rioters.

[There is a significant psychological difference in the origins of recent white and Negro violence. The white Kensingtonian seeks to *maintain* his identity by keeping the Negro, a group just below him on the social scale, from overtaking him. By violence and appeals to "blackness," Kenneth Clark and others have pointed out, Negroes are attempting to *gain* an identity and overcome their passiveness as well as the deprivation of the past.]

First, second, and older generations of Irish, Poles, and other nationality groups who give Kensington its special flavor have been unable to develop adequate communal machinery for dealing with the social and personal problems they face. A resident will go to the local committeeman to fix a parking ticket or to seek help in getting a youngster out of trouble with the law, but Kensingtonians have rarely organized themselves to exert pressure on elected officials to obtain parks, playgrounds, adequate lighting, trash collection, and proper enforcement of the housing code. In this complex society, Kensingtonians, like ghetto Negroes, need a great deal of help from civic officials—which, ironically, they often refuse to accept—in dealing with their problems. They harbor an old-world or ethnic suspicion of authority, and hesitate to bring government into their lives.

It is important to understand why first- and second-generation ethnic and working-class whites have been so ineffective in developing leadership and machinery for dealing with their massive problems. William I. Thomas and Florian Znaniecki, in their classic study, *The Polish Peasant in Europe and America,* point out that those who migrated to this country were people who no longer were adequately controlled by tradition but had not yet learned how to organize their lives independent of tradition. They had come out of a world where things change very slowly and there was sufficient time to adjust to change. "Persons from peasant backgrounds," Thomas and Znaniecki reported, "are members of a politically and culturally passive class. They have no tradition of participation in the impersonal institutions of a society."

These group styles and cultural patterns continue to lock in the people who live in the Kensingtons of this country. Some observers also attribute their difficulties to what John J. Kane, the noted sociologist, refers to as a lower-class orientation found among some Catholics. Kane argues that there is among them an attitude toward education and work that anchors them to jobs that have less prestige and income. "It seems that Catholics creep forward rather than stride forward in American society," he writes, "and the position of American Catholics in the mid-twentieth century is better, but not so much better, than it was a century ago."

In all fairness to the Catholic Church in Kensington, priests from the local diocese took to the streets in an effort to quell the rioting. However, many residents are annoyed at the increasingly pro-civil rights position of the church. This is, to many of the people of Kensington, another source of irritation and frustration.

One is struck by one basic element found also in studies of explosions by Negroes in Watts and other parts of the country. Beyond their aggressive and seemingly self-confident behavior is an underlying feeling of powerlessness. Here are people with severe problems they are unable to deal with, that the community is overlooking, and who find it difficult to take their place in an increasingly middle-class American society. In short, while white Kensingtonians differ from ghetto Negroes in the kinds and causes of their difficulties and how they view the racial *status quo, both* groups are Americans in trouble.

If this analysis is correct, it provides a clue to shaping a strategy to help the Kensingtons of America. We must look up somewhat from our concentration on the problems of Negroes. Irving Levine, director of the American Jewish Committee's urban affairs department, has pointed out that liberals, until now, have been transfixed by the Negroes—to the *disadvantage* of the Negro. It is necessary to develop programs aimed at meeting the needs of working class and foreign-stock white groups in our society, as well as for Negroes. It is apparent that civil rights gains have been stalemated in many parts of the North and West because the groups who are resisting have been so vigorously left out.

A strategy that calls for working with people—many of them first- or second-generation and older nationality groups—in upbuilding their neighborhoods and communal institutions through rehabilitation of housing, obtaining better schools, parks, and swimming areas, a more sensitive handling of urban renewal as well as other community supports, is more likely to have success than simply dismissing white rioters as "a bunch of bigots." Such an approach is likely to develop more acceptable racial adjustments than abstract appeals to brotherhood or "proving" to them how neighborhoods need not decline in value when Negroes move in.

There is still another reason for attempting to deal more effectively with the problems of first-, second-, and older-generation, white nationality groups in our communities. They are far greater in number than most people realize. The 1960 census reports that there were 1.1 million in the Philadelphia metropolitan area as compared to 680,000 nonwhites. The figures for Chicago were 2 million to 900,000; Los Angeles, 1.7 million to 590,000; and New York, 4.7 million to 1.3 million. Many of these people, of course, have risen economically and moved out of the older sections of our cities. Those who have not made it, however, represent the same social and political dynamite as the forces that make for a Watts or Detroit.

We have seen evidence of this not only in white rioting against Negroes but in the defeat of Proposition 14 and the success of Ronald Reagan in California, the defeat of the civilian police review board in New York City, the attention former governor George C. Wallace has received in many parts of the country and the growth of groups like the John Birch Society. The lack of community analysis and programs dealing with the present social condition of older ethnic groups, Levine points out, has led to a broadening of the kind of sentiment on the part of these groups that starts with an anti-Negro posture but ends with political allegiance to a broader form of organized reaction. The Kensingtons of America are natural targets for ultraconservative movements.

Civil rights progress and social welfare gains, generally, have resulted during the past three and a half decades from a coalition of working-class ethnic groups with liberals, intellectuals, church groups, and Negroes. The cement that held together these diverse elements was the depression and economic gains scored by the New Deal and its political successors.

The race revolution has shattered this coalition. While it cannot be restored in its old form, there is a need to develop a new political alliance that will include the economically disadvantaged of all races and the forces pressing for inclusion of the Negro into all areas of American life. This will be impossible to bring about, however, until the community becomes more sensitive to the values, attitudes, and problems of white urban ethnic America. It is clear that additional energy, thought, and money must be found and expended on these passed-over groups while we step up the war to eliminate the causes of Negro rioting.

By Richard Rogin

Joe Kelly Has Reached
His Boiling Point

"When you were still up on Broadway you could hear the ruckus, the hollering. The peace demonstrators trying to outshout the construction workers. The construction workers hollering, 'U.S.A., all the way' and 'We're Number One.' And the peace demonstrators screaming up there that the war was unjust and everything else, right by the Treasury Building on Broad Street there.

"There was just a lot of hollering and screaming going back and forth until whoever the individual was—oh, he was no spring chicken, he was forty, forty-five years old—that spit on the flag. I was maybe four or five rows back in with the construction workers. I saw him make a gesture, you know, a forward motion. That was it. That was the spark that ignited the flame. It came out in the roar of the crowd. 'He spit on the flag! He spit on the flag!' And of course the construction worker got up there on top of the monument and he gave him a good whack and off came the guy's glasses and I guess he followed his glasses off the pedestal there.

"And then there just seemed to be a rush, a mob scene. The chant then was, 'Get the flags up on the steps where they belong. It's a government building.' And they can say what they want about the New York Police Department, they coulda had the National Guard there with fixed bay-

---

From *The New York Times*, June 28, 1970. © 1970 by The New York Times Company. Reprinted by permission.

onets and they would not have held the construction workers back then.

"When we first went up on the steps and the flags went
up there, the whole group started singing 'God Bless
America' and it damn near put a lump in your throat. It
was really something. I could never say I was sorry I was
there. You just had a very proud feeling. If I live to be a
hundred, I don't think I'll ever see anything quite like that
again."

JOE KELLY's big chin and right hand tremble as he is
caught in the deep, remembered passions of that noon-
time on Friday, May 8. He is thirty-one years old, a brawny
6 feet 4 inches, 210 pounds, blue eyes and receding red hair
under his yellow plastic construction helmet decorated
with U.S. flag decals and "FOR GOD AND COUNTRY."

It is now late afternoon, nearly two weeks later, and we
are sitting in a gray wooden construction shanty on the
sprawling World Trade Center site in lower Manhattan
where he works. Joe is a well-liked, skillful mechanic in an
intricate and demanding trade, elevator construction—
installing the elevators and the heavy complex machinery
to make the cars run.

On that violent day, soon after he came down for his
half-hour lunch break from the forty-second floor of the
soaring red steel skeleton of Tower A—another high, seemingly timeless, world which will rise 110 stories overlooking New York and the industrial hinterlands of New
Jersey, where men walk almost casually on springy planks
laid over open steel now seventy flights up—Joe Kelly
reached his "boiling point." He found he could not "sit
back" any longer, and he became a demonstrator for the
first time in his life. Though "not much of a shouter," and
a strong believer that violence solves nothing, he also
shouted and threw his first punch in more than ten years.

During that long menacing midday several hundred construction workers, accused by reporters of using metal tools as weapons, were joined by office workers on a rampage through lower Manhattan. They beat up and injured seventy antiwar protesters and bystanders, including four policemen. With cries of "Kill the Commie bastards," "Lindsay's a Red," and "Love it or leave it," they surged up to City Hall. There they forced the flag, which had been lowered to half-staff in mourning for the four dead Kent State students, to be raised again. Then, provoked by peace banners, they stormed through Pace College across the street. It was a day that left New York shaken.

His face taut with fury, Mayor John V. Lindsay went on television to call the workers' attacks "tough and organized," though the unions promptly denied any influence. But he lashed out even more strongly at the outnumbered police whom many witnesses had accused of inadequate preparations and of standing by tolerantly during the assaults on the peaceful rally. Only six arrests were reported. He charged the police with failing as "the barrier between [the public] and wanton violence."

Others called the workers bullies or Nazi brownshirts. "We have no control over what they want to call us," says Joe Kelly. "But I think that the large majority of people, going as high as 85 or 90 percent, are more than happy. Not so much for the violence but for the stand that we took. And now they're standing up. The construction worker is only an image that's being used. The hardhat is being used to represent all of the silent majority."

It was the wild start of two weeks of almost daily noon-hour, flag-waving, bellicose, damn-Lindsay (the most common signs called him a Communist or a faggot) and praise-Nixon countermarches through downtown New York, which Joe Kelly enthusiastically joined. Some of his fellow workers even happily lost an hour's pay for marching too long after lunch. Despite the fact that many of the men returned late following Friday's slugfest, none were docked. "I was going to dock one man who came back an hour and a half late," says Frank Pike, general elevator construction foreman, "but he said, 'I saw these kids spit on the flag. What could I do?' How could I dock the man?"

The union word had come down: "Demonstrate all you want but be careful, no violence." Others say that the union tried to stop the men from all informal demonstrations. In any event, there was no more major violence; thousands of helmeted police patrolled the streets.

The construction workers loaded their unfinished skyscrapers with huge U.S. flags and their hardhats became a national symbol of fervent support for the Nixon Administration and its Indochina war policy. President Nixon was even presented with a hardhat at a White House ceremony. The climax came on May 20 when an estimated one hundred thousand construction workers and longshoremen sang and chanted from City Hall to Battery Park in a massive display of jingoistic sentiment probably unparalleled during the uncertain years of the Vietnam conflict.

That day Joe Kelly was given the honor of carrying the gold-fringed American flag with the gold eagle, its wings outspread, on the top of the pole, leading a contingent of hundreds of his fellow workers from Local No. 1, International Union of Elevator Constructors. With his yellow helmet on, he marched, resolutely serious-faced, rarely showing a thin smile, ignoring the pretty secretaries leaning over the police barriers. He displayed the training he received when he was an M.P. with an Army honor guard stationed in Heidelberg, West Germany. Around him Broadway boomed with the chants: "We're Number One," "U.S.A., all the way," "Good-by Lindsay, we hate to see you go." The marchers sang "God Bless America" and "You're a Grand Old Flag." "Yankee Doodle" and "Over There" blared forth. The workers cheered and whistled through the applause from spectators and the shower of ticker tape and computer cards from high office windows.

They marched to the green lawns of Battery Park, with the breeze coming off the upper bay cooling a hot blue day. Joe Kelly's friends came up to him and shook his hand, saying: "Beautiful." "Like a champ, Joe." Joe clenched and unclenched the fingers of his right hand, which had held the flagpole for two hours. "I feel fine," he said. "This is terrific. It'll wake a few people up. This will happen not only down here but in the rest of New York and across the country now." The first thing to happen, though, was that Frank Pike docked himself and all the elevator constructors an hour's pay for parading instead of working. A few men never made it back to the job that afternoon.

Within the next few weeks in belligerent defense of Nixon's Southeast Asia policies, nearly twenty thousand construction workers paraded (and pummeled antiwar spectators) in St. Louis, and several hundred workers scuffled with students holding a peace rally at Arizona State University in Tempe.

Joe Kelly is proud, confident, and outspoken in the old American style. He is almost mystically proud of his flag, his country, the Establishment, and eager to end the Indochina war by striking more aggressively, though the deaths of young soldiers and innocent civilians sadden him. He is determined to be on guard against Communism and to crush it wherever it threatens his nation. Joe is convinced that a subversive conspiracy of teachers, influenced by foreign powers, is brainwashing the students to Communist beliefs. Distressed by the hippie life-style of so many youths, he is also furious at student radicals who burn and shut down schools which his taxes pay for and which most of his fellow workers cherish because they never had a chance to go to them. He is a stalwart charter member of Richard Nixon's silent majority, a devout Roman Catholic and fiercely loyal to his President, whose office he regards with almost holy respect.

"The Pope to the Catholic Church is the same as the President to the American people," he says. "He's the one who decides. He's infallible when he speaks of religion as far as the Catholic Church goes. I'm not saying Nixon is infallible. But he's Commander in Chief of the Armed Forces. He's in charge."

Vietnam: "I just hope that these people give Nixon the play to go in there in Cambodia and knock the living hell out of their supply lines. If this is what it takes to stop the loss of American lives, well, let's go the hell in there and get it over with."

My Lai massacre: "I don't believe anybody in the United States, nice and cozy, has a right to judge them [the accused] until everything comes out in the trial."

Kent State: "They [the National Guardsmen] must have felt their lives were threatened; that's why they shot."

Inflation: "I have faith in Nixon. I think he'll curb inflation, given the chance."

High taxes: "If this is what it takes to run this country, I don't mind paying them. You couldn't live anyplace else like you do here."

The flag: "I think of all the people that died for that flag. And somebody's gonna spit on it, it's like spitting on their grave. So they better not spit on it in front of me. You think you could get it better someplace else—well, then, don't hang around, go there."

Unemployment: "I don't know where they're getting these figures from [up to a five-year high for all jobs and 11.9 percent in construction] because here in New York you got a [construction] boom going on."

Joe Kelly has what used to be faithfully accepted as the old-fashioned, authentic American credentials: he is hard-working, conscientious, obedient and trusting in authority, an adherent of law and order, patriotic, sentimental, gentle and affectionate with his loved ones, angry and determined to right wrongs as he sees them, moderately compassionate, a believer in the virtues of his way of life.

To the antiwar protesters and others grieving and critical over America's present course in Indochina and what they perceive as unfeeling repressive policies at home, he probably appears as an anachronism. To them, he is Joe Kelly, yesterday's comic-book hero, a relic from the somehow simpler, self-righteous days of the old world wars when, with a grin and a wave and a song, Americans marched off to solve the world's problems. "The Jack Armstrong of Tower A," one of his fellow workers called him approvingly.

Joe Kelly and millions of Americans like him would not share the gloomy conclusion of John W. Gardner, a Republican and chairman of the National Urban Coalition, that the country is disintegrating. They see a country in momentary disarray, under stress, but they retain a sturdy optimism. They know but do not suffer the dark fear that a complex and subtle civil war is wasting the land with hate and with overt and invisible violence: white against black, conservatives against liberals, workers against students, old against young, fathers against sons. Even the old hawks of organized labor now face opposition within their own ranks over the Indochina war.

America heaves against the old grain. The kids are on the loose trying to shake off the crusty habits of the country the way a snake sheds its skin. The antis feel depressed by their own Government, if not worse, and sense mendacity everywhere.

The kids, Joe Kelly thinks, ought to feel lucky to be in America where they have the legitimate right to dissent and stage peaceful demonstrations. If they did the equivalent of burning draft cards or desecrating the flag in Russia or China, they would, he says, be shot down in the street.

"These kids," he says, "they can do as they feel like. I mean burn, loot, steal, do anything they feel like in the name of social reform. But can the average Joe Blow citizen go out and do this?" A crime is a crime, he says, even if it's for social reform, and he argues that there is a double standard of justice for students, especially in New York.

What about the kids' mockery of the Puritan ethic? "If they don't want to educate themselves or go out and work hard for a living and make a few dollars, spend a few dollars, and save a few dollars for a rainy day, that's their prerogative. But in general, again, this has been bred into them somewhere. This is not the American way."

Joe Kelly never thought the picture presented by his hardworking life would need any defense. There is his pretty blonde wife, Karen; two strawberry-blonde daughters, Robin Lynn, four, and Kerry Ann, one and a half, and now a newborn son, James Patrick. "I had two cheerleaders," he says, "now I got a ballplayer." There is also a collie named Missy and a newly bought brick-and-shingle, two-story, $40,000 house on an irregular 50 by 100 foot lot, tastefully furnished, with a modern kitchen ("All you can get for two arms"), and a freshly sodded lawn on one of those breezy Staten Island streets with the gulls overhead, children pedaling red tricycles, the hum of an electric mower, and a man hosing down a gleaming red Dodge Challenger, all the residents of the neighborhood blue-collar whites, doing well.

Joe Kelly and his neighbors, the steamfitter, the bus driver, the policeman, the TV color processor, have worked too hard to get to that street to give it all up. They have had too many peace protests, too many moratoriums, too many harsh laments and shouted obscenities against their country, too many rock-throwings and strikes and fires on campuses where they want their children to make it, too many bombings and too many Vietcong flags waving down the streets of their city, too many long-haired youths and naked boys and girls, too many drugs, too much un-Americanism, not to feel angry and resentful.

Joe Kelly sits on his plastic-covered orange couch in front of his new Motorola Quasar color TV console and seethes as he watches the six o'clock news day after day. What really galls him, he says, is what he considers small groups of radical students closing down schools. "In California," he says, "they burned a bank to the ground. You just watch and boil. Who do these university presidents, responsible people, think they have an obligation to? The students are burning something every day. They're taking over something in the chancellor's office every day."

And then that Friday morning, Joe Kelly mounted his turquoise Triumph 500-cc. motorcycle, rode down to the ferry slip, read *The Daily News* and had a coffee as the ferry crossed to Manhattan, then rode his motorcycle again to his job. When he walked into the shanty on the building site, he heard that a shoving incident the previous day between peace demonstrators and construction workers elsewhere in the downtown area had triggered the men from a number of skyscrapers to action. For the workers, "it was the straw that broke the camel's back," he recalls. Spontaneously, Joe says, perhaps a quarter of the World Trade Center's 212 elevator constructors decided to go down the seven blocks and "see what this peace demonstration was all about."

> "My partner, Tommy, he climbed up on top of the light stanchion down on Wall Street and planted the flag up there, right in front of the Treasury Building, to a great round of applause. The flags were up on the top steps. The construction workers and the Wall Street workers, they had the steps of the Treasury Building filled and the demonstrators were now down in the street.
>
> "And they started to chant in unison, '—, no, we won't go,' and they just kept it up. And all of a sudden, just the same as the movement had started up onto the steps, the movement started back down off the steps. This chant that they kept up, it just raised the anger to a degree that it just seemed that everybody would just want to get down there and disperse them. When I say, 'disperse,' I don't mean physically take these kids and manhandle them, but just to break them up, break up the group and break up this chant because it just seemed so un-American.
>
> "I guess the average construction worker is what you would call a flag-waver. You can call me a flag-waver any day of the week. I think that's something to be proud of, to be a flag-waver, to be proud of your country. And these kids just kept it up and kept it up.
>
> "As the movement started down off the steps, again there was a certain amount of them [protesters] that wanted to stand their ground, and they're dealing with men that work with iron and steel every day of the week

*and do manual labor every day of the week, and they just
made a mistake. They just never heard about that dis-
cretion business. I will say this: there was as many of these
antiwar demonstrators whacked by Wall Street and
Broadway office workers as there were by construction
workers. The feeling seemed to be that the white-collar-
and-tie man, he was actually getting in there and taking as
much play on this thing as the construction worker was.*

*"This was something. Listen. I'm thirty-one years old.
I'd never witnessed anything like this in my life before,
and it kinda caught me in awe that you had to stop and
see what was going on around you. It was almost un-
believable. This was the financial district of New York
City, probably the financial district of the world, and here
was this mass clash of opposite factions, right on Wall
Street and Broad, and you could hardly move, there were
so many people taking part in this aside from the five hundred construction workers. It was just something that you
had to stand back and blink your eyes and actually look a
second and third time, and you couldn't believe that this
was actually taking place in that particular area.*

*"There was one kid came after me, I don't know why.
He just came flying out of the crowd. I don't claim to be
a violent person. I couldn't possibly remember the last
time I ever struck anybody. It had to be at least ten years
ago, maybe twelve years ago. And for some reason this
guy picked out somebody and it just happened to be me.
He came running at me with arms flailing and I gave him
a whack and back he went. He went down, I know that,
and I just figured he wouldn't be back for more."*

Joe Kelly was brought up on Staten Island along with
his younger sister, Eileen, who is now a telephone company secretary. His mother had come to America on the
boat from County Cavan. His father, who was born in
New York, was a paymaster for Esso tankers coming into
the port of New York until he died of a heart attack in
1959 at the age of forty-five.

"My father," Joe Kelly recalls, "used to take me out to the ships on Saturdays to pay off. As a kid they used to let me steer, or let me think I was steering, and let me turn on the radar."

Joe went to elementary and high school at St. Peter's, a parochial school on Staten Island. "I wasn't any angel," he says, "I'm sure of that." He had little trouble passing his subjects and developed a special interest in American history. His major passion, though, was basketball. In high school he played forward on the varsity and was a right-handed pitcher for the baseball team. In the afternoons he delivered *The Staten Island Advance* and worked in a drugstore. He graduated from St. Peter's in 1956 with no specific ambition. He went off to St. Peter's College in Jersey City on a basketball scholarship and lasted a year, passing his courses but admittedly lacking interest in his studies.

With the feeling that he had "had enough school for a while," Joe became a seaman for Mobil Oil for three years. He served on coastal tankers between Texas and Maine and also aboard vessels in the Great Lakes and in New York harbor. Fearful of getting enmeshed in a life he didn't particularly relish, he quit suddenly and enrolled in a night business course at Staten Island's Wagner College. During the day he worked for Coca-Cola, visiting companies that were having trouble balancing their accounts; he hated this job, and left it after a year.

The elevator constructors had just come off a strike in 1960, work was piled up, and some of Joe's friends in the trade asked him if he wanted to come in. Joe says he "jumped at the opportunity" and he is now clearly a man who appreciates his work. His first job, before he was drafted into the Army in 1961, was with a crew automating the elevators at Bergdorf Goodman. When he came out of the service two years later, after enjoying the regimented military life, he went right back to elevators, where he has been ever since.

In 1965 he married a Staten Island girl, Karen Kelsey, who worked as an IBM operator for the Irving Trust Company at 1 Wall. Her father is an office manager for a freight-forwarding concern and, like her, a Republican. Then the children started to arrive and last summer, two days after Joe began what was to become a three-and-a-half-month strike, they moved into their own two-family house. The upstairs six-room apartment is rented to a plumber and his family at $200 a month.

His first big jobs after the Army were in what is called the modernization department of the Otis Elevator Company, for whom he still works—putting automatic elevators in the Municipal Building, in 15 Broad Street, in Con Edison at 14th Street, and in 61 Broadway. Then three or four years ago things began to slow up. "That was about the time," he recalls, "when every Friday the ax was falling and you never knew whether you were gonna have a job Friday afternoon or not." But Joe managed to hang on and he never lost a day because of a layoff. Now elevator constructors talk of a ten-year feast in New York.

Two and a half years ago he was switched to elevator installation and went to work on the General Motors Building. It was his first time on high open steel. "The first morning I will never forget," he says. "The building had just recently been topped out. This was somewhere around the first or second week of January. So when I arrived up on the top of the building, which was about the fifty-second floor, I looked out over the horizon and I saw one of these clocks that flashes the time and the temperature. It was ten minutes after eight and it was minus 2 degrees, and I thought I'd made the biggest mistake of my life."

But he endured the bitter winter cold—and the heights never bothered him. He worked on the TWA terminal at Kennedy Airport on an escalator job, picked up odd electrician's and rigger's jobs during last summer's strike, and late last fall finally became a mechanic after seven long years of apprenticeship as a helper. He started at the World Trade Center, considered the biggest elevator job in the world, just before Christmas.

Until the last two years or so, Joe Kelly had been making about $8,500. Now he is up to $6.86 an hour, and with double pay for the abundant overtime at the Trade Center, he expects to earn between $15,000 and $18,000 this year.

"This is the first year that I've ever made anything like this," he says. "It took ten years to get here but now I guess I've arrived." He also augments his salary and renting income by bartending three nights a week.

Elevator construction may be well paid, but it is a hard trade and can be dangerous. A good friend of Joe Kelly's, Mike Clancy, forty-two years old with five children, plunged twenty-five floors to his death several months ago at the World Trade Center.*

Workers must also beware of tools or material falling from higher stories. "Like if anybody drops anything," says Joe, "they immediately scream, 'Look out below,' and you got to get under something just as quick as you pos-

---

* In a moving display of the men's strong sense of solidarity, from the young long-haired mod types to grizzled veterans in overalls, more than $18,000 was collected for the Clancy family. Helpers gave $25, mechanics $50, and elevator constructors on other job sites pitched in, as did men in other construction trades. On matters close to the heart—a death on the job, their country in trouble—the men tend to react according to the group working pattern of their trade, en bloc and with great fervor.

sibly can so it will ricochet off of that instead of off of you."

Joe attends noon Mass on Sundays and he also coaches basketball and baseball teams in a boy's league in Blessed Sacrament parish. (After the Army, he spent three years as a weekend counselor at an orphanage on Staten Island.) His reading consists of *The Daily News*, the *Advance*, the sports section of *The New York Post* and *Popular Mechanics* magazine. The Kellys go out to the movies perhaps every six weeks and may stop in afterward for "a couple of drinks in a nice, quiet, respectable place." Once a week his wife leaves him at home when she goes to play bingo. There is usually a Christmas party for the men on the job, and Otis throws a picnic in the summer. Recently, the elevator constructors and their wives had a $20-a-couple dinner dance at the Commuter's Cafe on Cortlandt Street, across from the Trade Center site. Proceeds from a raffle went to Mike Clancy's family.

On television, Joe enjoys Johnny Cash and Jackie Gleason and sometimes Dean Martin. He likes to be in bed by 11 P.M. Before he was married, Joe played basketball four nights a week in a community-center league. With family responsibilities, his heavy work schedule, and his relative slowness of foot today, he has cut it out completely. "I go down once in a while to watch and eat my heart out," he says.

Joe gets his extravocational workouts now around the house, putting in sod, helping to grade the backyard for a large above-ground plastic swimming pool for the children, planting two blue spruces and yews and rhododendrons in the front.

The Kellys haven't been able to take any vacations, though Joe has had two weeks off yearly and will get three weeks under the new contract starting this summer (there was either a strike, or they were saving for the house, or the children were too small). Perhaps twice a summer they drive down to the New Jersey shore around Belmar in their 1967 English Ford station wagon and go swimming.

Why does he work so hard? "A lot of people ask me that," he says. "I wanted the house. Right? I wanted something nice for the wife and the kids, someplace where the kids could grow up and have their own backyard. They wouldn't have to be running out in the street. And now I have the house and I want it fixed up nice. And maybe when it is fixed up nice, I'll relax a bit." Meanwhile, he is at the "boiling point."

"My belief is, physical violence doesn't solve a damn thing. One party has to sway the other party to his belief and then the argument is settled. I honestly don't believe that there will be any more physical violence in New York City. I think that one Friday and it's over with. I don't like to see anybody get bounced. I saw some of those kids go down and I didn't think they were gonna get up. I certainly don't agree with them. I would much rather prefer grabbing them by the head of the hair and taking a scissors and cutting their hair off, something that was much less violent but you still would have gotten your message across.

"Up at City Hall it became obvious that they had better get that flag back up to the top of the mast. Within a few minutes the flag went back up and everybody seemed nice and happy and again they started singing 'God Bless America' and the national anthem and again it made you feel good. Not that I like seeing those four kids out in wherever it was, Kent, get killed. I don't like to see anybody get beat up, never mind lose their life.

"I don't think Mayor Lindsay has the right to put that flag at half-staff. That flag represents this country, so the leading representative of the country, who is President

*Nixon to me, is the only one that has the power or the
right to raise or lower a flag.*"

Joe Kelly says he never even asked what his father's
politics were, believing it to be a man's private affair. How
did he arrive as a militant member of the no-longer-silent
majority? What brought him to believe that Communism
was undermining America from within?

"Two people stand out in my mind," Joe says, "why
I'm taking part. Joe McCarthy often said, beware of this
school system; they're going to infiltrate, brainwash the
kids. And Khrushchev in 1960 banging on the UN table.
He said they wouldn't have to take over this country physically, they'd do it from within." Though he was only a
youngster during McCarthy's heyday, Kelly says: "It's
something I've read somewhere along the line." He feels
that the students are only dupes in the hands of subversive teachers who, Joe hints, are under the control of
foreign powers. In some way, the bad teachers have to
be weeded out, he says.

Joe Kelly first voted in 1960, when he chose John F.
Kennedy over Nixon for President because he was impressed with Kennedy's performance in the TV debates.
Though he still reveres President Kennedy, he wouldn't
vote that way again. By 1964 he had swung to the right
and voted for Goldwater over Johnson. In the 1965 and
1969 New York mayoral races, he voted the Conservative
party line for William F. Buckley, Jr., and John Marchi.
He cast his ballot for Nixon for President in 1968.

It was the Goldwater campaign that crystallized Joe's
feeling about the war in Vietnam. "I think that it all goes
back again, like history repeating itself, to Hitler," he
says. "When Hitler kept marching into these countries
and, instead of just fighting Hitler's country, you were

fighting all these countries after a while. You just can't let Communism take over everything around you because when they got everything around you, they're gonna come after you."

Three men who command his admiration now are John Wayne, Vice-President Agnew, and Chicago Mayor Richard Daley. In fact, Joe wishes New York could borrow Daley for six months to give the city a stiff dose of law and order. He has complete disdain for Mayor Lindsay. He believes Lindsay has turned New York into "welfare city" and is trying to be the champion of welfare recipients and the young antiwar generation in a bid for the Presidency. "Do what you want in Lindsay's city—" he says caustically, "burn the schools. He's got to raise the budget this year to pay for what they burned down."

Of the recent influx of minority workers into his once closely bound union, he says: "They're here to stay, entitled to. But if they're going to work with us, if we go up on the iron and risk our lives walking it, by God, they have to go along with us. There've been several instances in the city where they've refused because they didn't have to."

As for a black family living on his street, he is adamantly against it, feeling that panic-selling would drive down the value of his property. "I had to bust my backside for five years to get that down payment for that house," he says. "I am not interested in seeing all that go down the drain."

It is on this precious ground—his home and his family —that he takes a defiant, mildly worried stand. He would like his daughters to go to college or nursing school and his son to get as much schooling as possible, to become a doctor or a lawyer—"something where he can use his head to make a living, not his back like his old man does."

While his wife hopes and prays that her daughters will never wear their hair straight and long like the hippies and that her children's minds will be protected in parochial schools despite the danger of lay teachers, Joe Kelly tells a story about a neighbor's friend's son, a boy of sixteen.

"This boy," he says, "came home from school one day and he told his father he was a bum, that he was part of the Establishment. And this fellow was a World War II veteran, decorated several times and wounded twice. And he just turned around and he gave the kid a good whack and I guess he broke his jaw or broke his nose and the father was in a turmoil. This is his own flesh and blood talking to him.

"I cannot imagine having my kids come home and tell me I'm a bum because I believe in the Establishment—and there is nobody that believes in the Establishment more than I do. The more I see of this stuff, the closer I try to become to my kids. I believe that my way is correct, the Establishment way, law and order first, and this is what I'm gonna do my damndest to breed into them so that they don't get some other off-the-wall ideas."

Joe says that if his children ever called him a bum because he believes in the flag, they'd better leave his house. "I would do everything to control myself not to hit them. I mean, this is what I brought into the world. But it's awful hard. I certainly can see that man flying off the handle and whacking the kid. Oh, yeah, he certainly did regret it. But his big question is, Where did his kid get this trend of thinking?"

Joe Kelly doesn't believe that melees such as the memorable one at noon on May 8 are any solution. So his answer, he says reflectively, is to arm himself with education, engage in dialogue.

"When they throw a point at you," he says, "be able to talk to them on their theories on socialism, Communism. This is the best way—to talk them out of the stuff instead of just saying it's un-American or using your fists."

Ironically, Mayor Lindsay has said much the same thing: "Perhaps their [the construction workers'] demonstrations, in the end, will help us break through to a new dialogue in which we not only talk, but listen."

By Jerome M. Rosow

The Problem
of the Blue-Collar Worker

THE SOCIAL and economic status of blue-collar workers has become a subject of increasing concern in the last few years. Recent reports have identified the economic insecurity and alienation which whites in this group have felt. What such reports have failed to note is that there are some two million minority-group males who are skilled or semiskilled blue-collar workers who are full-time members of the work force and who share many of the same problems as whites in their income class. This nonwhite group also shares the same concern as white workers for law and order and other middle-class values. Many have moved from subemployment to low-income, entry-level jobs, but they now feel blocked from further opportunity.

In 1968, 34 percent of all minority-group families were in the $5,000 to $10,000 income category. Of course, on the average, most black families are still not anywhere nearly as well off as white families: The median income of all Negro families was $5,590, that of all white families $8,937. But the point is that both these groups have essentially working-class economic and social problems related

---

Reprinted with the permission of Jerome M. Rosow.

to wage, tax, and government benefit structure for the nonpoor—a fact not given adequate recognition by the media, which, to the extent that it emphasizes only the black ghetto, perpetuates a stereotype.

We should recognize:

1. The common *economic* problem which many blue-collar workers of both races have (mostly white, of course, in numbers); and

2. The common *social* problems concerned with housing, education, jobs, and personal safety which are related to income class but also are a function of the close proximity of the blue-collar workers to disadvantaged people.

The preceding two points are worth further consideration.

1. *The Economic Squeeze*

Forty percent of American families—including seventy million family members—have incomes between $5,000 and $10,000 a year and might be termed "lower-middle income." The head of the household is usually a vigorous, fully employed blue-collar worker with heavy family responsibilities, although many of this group are also in white-collar or service jobs. It is precisely when his children reach their teens and family budget costs are at their peak that two things happen to the bulk of such male breadwinners:

They reach a plateau in their capacity to earn by promotion or advancement;

Their expenses continue to rise, as the last family members are born, as they become homeowners, as car and home equipment pressures mount, as the children may become ready for college, or support is needed for aging parents.

The American wage and salary structure does not respond directly to this situation, since it is based on the ethic of "equal pay for equal work." It does not provide additions for either growing family size or age (except as it may reflect job seniority); payment is exclusively for work done—the same pay is given to everyone in the same job; and, unlike the situation in many other countries, the wage structure is not supplemented by public payments based on family size, although income-tax exemptions give some recognition:

Income needs for a growing family rise faster than are normally provided by advancement. Family budget costs for a two-child family are three times the needs of a single individual, according to BLS, while a typical semi-skilled steelworker's increase in job level results only in a wage rise of somewhat less than one and a half times.

The result is illustrated by the accompanying table, which portrays the case of a typical steelworker. The worker has some margin beyond his budget needs when he is young, but only if he saves and does not acquire a living standard commensurate with his pay. If he does not anticipate later family needs by adequate early savings— and usually he does not—he begins to be squeezed in his later thirties, and finds himself in deeper straits as his children reach their teens.

Many other industries have even fewer promotion opportunities than steel. A study of eleven major industries estimated that one third of all nonsupervisory jobs were dead-end. The lack of an adequate adult education system geared to workers hinders movement out of these

COMPARISON OF FAMILY BUDGET COSTS
AND STEELWORKERS' EARNINGS

(1967 Budget Costs and Wage Rates)

Age	Family Status	Family Budget Costs		Pay Grade	Estimated Annual Earnings	
		Dollars	Index		Dollars	Index
22	Single	$ 3,358	100	2	$5,747	100
23	Married, no children	4,538	135	2	5,747	100
28	One child under 6	5,627	168	7	6,629	115
38	Two children, older 6 to 15	9,076	270	12	7,510	131
41	Two children, older 9 to 18	10,347	308	15	8,039	140

Budget costs and wage rates as of 1967.

Annual earnings are based on hourly rates, with no further adjustments for effect of seniority on immunity from layoffs and opportunities for more overtime and no allowance for the value of fringes.

Grade 15 in the chart is approximately the midpoint of the U.S. steel job evaluation wage structure and is at beginning point of skilled craftsman wage scales.

Family budget costs are based on BLS Moderate Living Standard for a four-person family, spring, 1967, and include occupational expenses, gifts and contributions, life insurance, social security payments, and federal, state, and local income taxes, in addition to the goods and services for family consumption. For equivalence scale appropriate for total budget, see Table A-1, p. 14, BLS *Bulletin* 1570-2.

jobs. Relatively few firms have work-site education and few community colleges direct courses for upgrading purposes to blue-collar workers.

Upward job mobility is also hindered by age discrimination against older workers; by lack of detailed, free information about other jobs; and by the high costs of private employment agencies (which often have job openings that the Employment Service does not have).

The result for semiskilled blue-collar workers as a whole is that when general wage rate increases are added to increased individual earnings due to promotion, real income has somewhat less than doubled in the past two decades, which is still not enough to meet the cost of the same standard of living throughout the period. Males aged forty-five to fifty-four years in 1968 who had one to three years of high school—the educational level typical of blue-collar workers in that age group—had increased their incomes by only 84 percent between 1949 and 1968.

The worker who established his standard of living when he was single or first married thus finds that he can maintain it only by:

a. Having saved when he was younger (which he didn't do); or

b. Moonlighting on a second part-time job; or

c. Having his wife work even in spite of the obstacles to doing so; or

d. Continued pressure for wage increases.

If a younger worker has no opportunity for advancement, the entire annual productivity-related rise in wages, about 3 percent, is needed just to *keep up* with his increasing family needs. If such a worker wants to improve his standard of living, he must be able to move up the ladder. The pressure on wages promises to increase as those born in the post-World War II baby boom move into their late twenties and early thirties, and thus assume family responsibilities in the next five years. Workers in the twenty-five to thirty-four age group will represent 25 percent of the labor force in this decade.

This problem is intensified by inflation. Since 1965, money wages have advanced 20 percent, *but* real earnings measured in true purchasing power remained almost static. These men are on a treadmill, chasing the illusion of higher living standards. Thus their only hope seems to be continued pressure for higher wages. Their only spokesmen seem to be union leaders spearheading the demand for more money wages. They are overripe for a political response to the pressing needs they feel so keenly.

The *tax* structure offers little relief to this worker, since it gives only small recognition to family size considerations. Even the Tax Reform Act of 1969 does not provide adequate relief for these families:

A married couple with an $8,000 income who have two children will pay $263 less under the new law—which doesn't fully take effect until 1973—than under the old one. This fails to bridge the budget gap described above.

Deductions for family members are token in character, even under the new tax law, and provide more at higher income levels than at lower or moderate levels (the $750 deduction is a tax savings of $125 for the person in the 16 to 17 percent bracket and $300 for the person in the 40 percent bracket). Moreover, the size of the tax deduction has no relation to the age of the children, even though budget costs for older children are more than for younger ones.

There is no provision for tax relief as family education costs rise, either in terms of the $100 a year that it costs to send a child to school or the additional cost of going to college.

Regressive state and local taxes also hit heavily at this group. Average state and local taxes are almost $700, and have increased rapidly in recent years. Moreover, in at least some states income is redistributed from lower-income to higher-income groups to subsidize higher education for the children of the latter.

Government policies on child care designed to enable the wife to work also give little relief. At present, families with an income of $6,900 or above cannot deduct child-care expenses. This figure was set in the Internal Revenue Act of 1964 and is now unrealistically low. Adjusted to current prices, the ceiling would be about $8,200. Government child-care centers under Head Start and WIN are for the "poor," and so do not help this group. Their costs for child care (when not provided by other family members) may run from $25 to $40 a week. The Family Assistance Act of 1970 will aggravate this problem. Welfare mothers will receive subsidized child care to facilitate their move from welfare to work. Lower-income mothers who seek work and are outside the welfare system will incur the full cost or be unable to add to family income.

Finally, high transportation costs, wage discrimination, and lack of education and training also discourage many blue-collar wives from working or minimize their contribution to family income. Yet it is precisely working wives who make very meaningful contributions to the family income, and who have the potential to make even more: in the 40 percent of husband-wife families where wives do work, median income in 1968 was $10,700, compared to $8,200 where they didn't. Part-time employment has almost doubled since 1956 and provides a new opportunity for more women to combine work with family responsibility.

The problem of restricted economic opportunity for the blue-collar worker also spreads into the next generation. The children of this group in our society are not "making it" to the same degree that children in the middle and upper-middle classes are.

Despite the broadening base of college enrollments, we still find marked evidence that the lower-income groups have a much smaller proportion of their children continuing beyond high school. Only one fourth of the youth in college are from the half of the families with a below-median income. Worse yet, the great majority of high school dropouts are not from the disadvantaged ghetto population. Many white and black school dropouts are from this lower-middle-income group; in some of the urban areas the dropout rate for this group runs about 30 percent. Here we sense the stirrings of a new type of unfortunate cycle, as some of the children of these blue-collar workers are unable to achieve a reasonable entry into productive society. Twenty percent are unemployed in the fall following the year they drop out of school. Present efforts to reduce youth unemployment (e.g., Neighborhood Youth Corps) are geared to disadvantaged youth—not these people.

Other government aids—minimum wage, training, welfare payments—are not for this group because they have presumably "made it," and whatever the government may have done to keep employment and jobs up generally has faded or is overwhelmed.

Economic insecurity is compounded by the fact that

blue-collar workers are often the first to feel the effects of an increase in unemployment, feel most threatened by automation, and are also more dependent on sheer physical health for their livelihood than white-collar workers. Yet there is inadequate protection for temporary or permanent disability under state workmen's compensation laws.

There are other dimensions to the problem too: the shortage and high cost of housing; the high cost of medical and legal services, the lack of inexpensive entertainment and recreation facilities (e.g., few summer camps for the worker's children).

All these factors add up to an economic squeeze and insecurity for the workingman. We have no package of solutions to deal with this problem. However, in fashioning any attack, certain things should be recognized: (1) that government aid being given to the disadvantaged is sorely needed, and (2) that it would be impossible and undesirable to try to modify the American wage structure; and (3) that almost anything which could be done by the government would cost money.

2. *The Social Squeeze*

People working and living close to the margin of economic needs are under constant pressures. These pressures have an economic base but find other outlets, other frustrations of a social nature.

People in the blue-collar class are less mobile, less organized, and less capable of using legitimate means either to protect the *status quo* or secure changes in their favor. To a considerable extent, they feel like forgotten people —those for whom the government and the society have limited, if any, direct concern and little visible action.

Some of the problems which "bug" the blue-collar class include:

Fear of violent crimes. This is a growing fear of crime in the inner cities and this fear is spilling over to the outer ring of the metropolis—primarily areas where they live. Economic immobility blocks a flight from these conditions.

Class status. Many of these workers are immigrants or sons of immigrants; they feel unsure about their place in the mainstream of American society. Some live in mixed neighborhoods—feeling the pressure of constant succession by lower-status groups, especially minorities. As the minorities move up a bit, they squeeze these people. Minority inroads in housing, schools, and jobs create fears. They worry over merging of seniority lists, changing entrance requirements for jobs, and lower admissions standards for public schools.

Feeling of being forgotten. These people are most exposed to the poor and the welfare recipients. Often their wages are only a notch or so above the welfare payments of the liberal states. Yet they are excluded from social programs targeted at the disadvantaged—medical aid, housing, job training, Head Start programs, legal aid, and the like. As taxpayers, they support these programs with no visible relief—no visible share.

Educational level. Since most blue-collar workers have barely completed formal high school education, they have limited leverage to change occupations, and they have limited mobility to use their education as a lever to escape from their economic and social problems. Overt hostility between ethnic and racial groups is probably greater between less educated groups than between more educated groups. Thus, the blue-collar worker is more prone to transfer his economic and social frustrations to racial and ethnic prejudices, and of late to overt hostilities.

Low status of blue-collar work. The American working-man has lost relative class status with the growth of higher education. Changes in the nature of the labor force have dramatized the professional and technical experts to the relative detriment of the skilled worker. Skilled workers also have hostility toward those below them at semiskilled and unskilled levels, and the feeling is mutual. But all blue-collar workers, skilled or not, have been denigrated so badly—so harshly—that their jobs have become a last resort, instead of decent, respected careers. Manual and skilled occupations have become almost invisible in terms of the propaganda of today. Fathers hesitate—and even apologize—for their occupation, instead of holding it up as an aspiration for their sons. This attack has been so strong, so emotional, and so unfounded that the workers have suffered a loss of self-respect and the nation is suffering a loss of future manpower.

Low status also derives from the working conditions and nature of much unskilled and semiskilled work. Much of it is oppressively tedious, noisy, and mind-numbing, with little room for human contact. Research has found a significant relation between poor mental health and such types of work.

Let us examine the problem of the low status of blue-collar work further:

According to union leaders, the blue-collar worker increasingly feels that his work has no "status" in the eyes of society, the media, or even his own children. While the nation has, in recent years, sold the importance of science and technology to our younger people, it has neglected to communicate the importance of some ten million skilled blue-collar workers who are responsible for transforming the ideas of scientists and the plans of engineers into tangible goods and services. These workers make and maintain the models, tools, and machines without which industrial processes could not be carried out. They exercise considerable independent judgment and are responsible for extremely valuable equipment and products.

A good auto mechanic, for example, must know hydraulics, pneumatics, electricity, and some chemistry and other skills. Yet many youth learn that status accrues to the white-collar job (and so "prefer" it), even though a job in coveralls, such as mechanic, may pay better. The average mechanic working for a metropolitan auto dealer earns nearly $10,000, yet there is a short supply of them due to lack of interested youth. A recent survey showed that only one out of four male high school seniors wished to work as blue-collar workers, even though almost half of all jobs in the economy are blue-collar jobs.

Schools tend to reinforce this tendency, since most teachers know little about blue-collar work. So do the media; the only publicity given to workers is when they are out on strike and there they are often shown in a bad light.

Adding to the problem is that fact that the long-term narrowing of manual skill wage differentials (temporarily halted) has relatively worsened the position of semiskilled and skilled blue-collar workers compared to the unskilled. At the same time, high-skilled white-collar workers have been making substantial and publicized improvements in their economic position, with salary increases often far higher than wage increases. Furthermore, the educated workers with college and advanced degrees have been getting the biggest pay gains.

The result is chronic and inflationary shortages in many skilled blue-collar fields; a feeling of failure for the many youth who won't get white-collar jobs; exacerbation of racial friction when black youth refuse to take "dirty" blue-collar jobs offered them "by a white society," even when they may be good-paying; and a general resentment by blue-collar workers which is translated into wage demands.

Resentment is likely to worsen with any increase in unemployment, together with a continued push for opportunities for the disadvantaged, plus the addition of returning veterans to the labor force.

3. *Possible Directions for Action*

Our attention has been focused on an analysis of the economic and social situation faced by the blue-collar worker and not on private or public steps that might be taken to relieve the pressures he faces. Still, the analysis itself identifies several specific areas of concern:

Upgrading. What can be done to assist the worker in moving out of a dead-end job?

Income. Upgrading will provide more income, but this may need to be augmented by a job for the wife, and perhaps in other ways.

Expenses. The workingman's budget squeeze can be relieved through subsidized housing, transportation, recreation, and education and various kinds of tax relief.

Social issues. Such things as low status of blue-collar work, poor urban environment, and inadequate medical facilities contribute to a feeling of neglect and should be addressed.

Again, though we have not developed a specific action program, some ideas appear worthy of consideration by the Nixon Administration to reach out and come to grips with many of the basic needs:

a. Job Upgrading. The JOBS program is placing a new emphasis on upgrading for both disadvantaged and others but even more manpower services could be provided the blue-collar worker. Much authority exists but imaginative proposals are needed for such things as instruction in plants, community college courses designed to meet specific skill shortages, worker leave of absences, and loans for noninstruction expenses. The Employment Service could do more to help the blue-collar worker get ahead—through such steps as counseling and upgrading, soliciting jobs for experienced workers and opening its offices nights and Saturdays to serve the employed as well as the unemployed.

b. Child Care. The Nixon Family Assistance Plan will provide child care facilities for welfare mothers who go to work. Child care facilities might next be provided to slightly higher income groups on a partial fee basis. This would enable many more mothers to work and relieve the costs of child care for those who already work. Steady expansion of part-time employment opportunities can open new avenues for wives to work without neglecting their family role. Tax relief for child care is now limited to families earning less than $6,900 and this could be raised to $10,000, with deductions increased to $900 for the first child and $1,200 for two or more children. This change can be made with little revenue loss. The public pressure for action in this area is expected to mount.

c. Education for Adults. The Vocational Education Act of 1968 is already financing evening courses for about three million adults. However, this meets only a fraction of the need. Moreover, above and beyond vocational education, there is a need to allow workers to study for high school diplomas and for two-year community college degrees. For many blue-collar workers and their wives, the result should be new or better jobs and promotions. Increased education also frequently leads to less racial hostility.

d. Higher Education for the Worker's Children. The right to higher education implicit in the President's Higher Education Message for college loans and grants where families are earning less than $10,000 is a significant promise to the blue-collar workers. The President also proposed a $100 million program for training in critical occupations in community colleges. This should be the first step in a steady thrust toward increased federal support of these colleges which are of such importance to the blue-collar worker's children. These opportunities should be targeted to these people.

e. Tax Policy. The Tax Reform Act will give a tax reduction to families earning $5,000 to $10,000. However, this does not go very far in alleviating the squeeze on this group. Revenue sharing should be emphasized, since it will tend to help them by raising taxes through the progressive federal tax system rather than through the regressive local and state systems. In addition, a review should be made of possible further ways to relieve the tax burden on this group, including possibly increasing the amount of the tax exemption for older children, since budget costs for them are greater.

f. Higher Status for Blue-Collar Work. Efforts should be made to enhance the status of blue-collar work. Public relations work would help, as would more effective guidance and placement in blue-collar jobs by secondary schools (including more visits by workers to the schools). Other possibilities are national awards for outstanding craftsmen; portrayal of various skilled trades on postage stamps; a series of vocational guidance films for youth, on skilled trades; programs for schoolteachers to visit plants and offices; training for foremen and supervisors; federal standards for decent working conditions and/or establishing a job environment subcommittee of the Environmental Quality Council to investigate oppressive noise, heat, air pollution, and the like.

g. Recreation Facilities. Recreation and vacations, a major problem for the blue-collar worker and his family, might be made more available through vest-pocket parks, more development of public lands near metropolitan areas, and mortgage guarantees for low-income recreation facilities.

h. Transportation. Automobile expenses are a major item to the blue-collar worker. Moderate budget costs for the U.S. automobile owner are more than $900 yearly for replacement, insurance, and maintenance. More mass transit is part of the answer. If no-blame auto insurance would reduce costs as much as has been claimed, it might also be helpful.

i. Housing. Action has been taken to pump more mortgage money into the housing market, which should increase the houses available to low-income workers and reduce their cost. The most significant potential for reducing housing costs is probably in Operation Break-through and other efforts to increase productivity in construction. HUD and the Domestic Council are obvious focal points for policy direction.

j. Disability Protection. On the job and off the job accidents are still a major hazard for the working population.

New attempts should be made to develop modern temporary disability insurance and workmen's compensation systems.

k. The Federal Government as a Model Employer of Blue-Collar Workers. The Federal Government should continue its policy of wages comparable with private employment. But it could go beyond this on nonwage matters. It could become a model employer by careful attention to such things as upgrading possibilities, subsidized child care, part-time employment for women, and partially subsidized recreation and vacation facilities for low-income federal workers.

The White House working group could develop feasible ways by which to meet the needs of blue-collar workers in some or all of these areas.

THE SILENT REVOLT

II | OF

MIDDLE AMERICAN YOUTH

PERHAPS THE MOST FORGOTTEN OF ALL THE "FORGOTTEN Americans" are working-class youth. The process begins with run-down and largely ignored public and parochial schools which destroy human potentiality in Whitetown —actually Kensington—described by Peter Binzen in *Whitetown, U.S.A.* It is continued in the attitudes of hostility and contempt with which nonacademically oriented youth are frequently treated—the "greasers"—by some segments of the community. (As researchers from the University of California at Berkeley have shown, the celebrated generation gap is, in reality, a gap between those who go to college and those who do not.*) And it ends on the assembly line and in other dead-end jobs where a union gerontology described by Lewis Carliner, in "Labor: The Anti-Youth Establishment" as well as the employer limit their opportunities. The 1970 census reports, for example, that among employed men sixteen to nineteen, 56 percent are in blue-collar jobs.

Like upper-middle-class youth in high schools and on college campuses, working-class young people are experiencing, also, an identity crisis. Rarely, however, does this take the form of open revolt. "You Say You Want a

---

* Office of Public Information, University of California at Berkeley, September 15, 1970.

Revolution," a statement developed by a group of Pittsburgh high school students, captures the deep anger and resentment that exists among them. Most often, Middle American youth are inarticulate, which may be an outgrowth of an ethnic style, the sense of powerlessness they feel, or both. In 1968, for example, those under thirty accounted for only 17 percent of the vote in the national election, and even in those states which permitted eighteen- to twenty-year-olds to vote, only 33 percent did so.

Although the nation has focused its attention in recent years on the youth culture as symbolized in Woodstock and campus disorders, Middle American youth are more numerous, believe good citizenship consists primarily of obedience to law and pride in country, and feel it important to fight the spread of Communism. (Institute of Survey Research Newsletter, Summer, 1970.) The anger that is building in Middle American youth is potentially an explosive force.

By Peter Binzen

The Schools of Whitetown —Then and Now

B EYOND THE FACT that many Whitetowners are totally unsympathetic to Negro aims and efforts in education, there are three reasons why the school situation in Whitetown and Blacktown today is so explosive. First, education is vastly more important in this age of electronics, moonshots, instant communications, computerized everything, than at any previous time in history. When the immigrants were tipped out of school at eighth grade in 1910 or 1920, it didn't matter very much because America's relatively crude, unsophisticated economy had jobs for unskilled, undereducated workers. Less so today.

Second, the Negro thrust in education has come at the time of the first really substantial federal spending on schools. For about a century and a quarter after the schools were started, Washington treated public education as almost exclusively a state and local responsibility. Its only aid went for vocational training. Important federal assistance began with the National Defense Education Act of 1958 and was greatly expanded with the Elementary and Secondary Education Act of 1965. Through ESEA's Title

I alone, a billion dollars a year now goes to schools with concentrations of pupils from low-income families.

The third point is that the Federal Government, seeing greater educational needs and deficiencies in Negro areas, wants to put most of its emphasis—and money—there. To the extent that this is being done, it is being done at the expense of Whitetowners, whose educational shortcomings are often almost as serious as those of the Blacktowners.

"For the next generation or so," Harold Howe, II, then United States Education Commissioner, wrote in the *Harvard Educational Review* in the winter of 1968,

> I believe we must tip the educational scales in favor of our minority youngsters and commit a major share of our resources to providing superior educational programs for them.
>
> In a sense, this is inequality in reverse—an extra loading of the balance in favor of those who for generations have seen the weights on the other end.

As justification for this policy, Howe quoted President Johnson:

> You do not take a person who for years has been hobbled by chains and liberate him, bring him up to the starting line of a race and say, "You're free to compete with the others," and justly believe that you have been completely fair.

One of the difficulties with Howe's "extra loading of the balance" is that the scales, as the examination of nineteenth-century and early twentieth-century schools indicates, have never been heavily tipped in favor of working-class white children. Not historically and not now. In his mammoth, federally financed study in 1966, *The Equality of Educational Opportunity*, James S. Coleman, of Johns

Hopkins University, found no significant difference in the school facilities currently provided white and nonwhite children in this country. His surprising discovery is often overlooked.

"The [Coleman] study set out to document the fact that for children of minority groups school facilities are sharply unequal and that this inequality is related to student achievement," reported Harvard researchers Susan S. Stodolsky and Gerald Lesser in the *Harvard Educational Review* in the fall of 1967. "The data did not support either conclusion. What small differences in school facilities did exist had little or no discernible relationship to the level of student achievement." *

Coleman decided that schools' physical facilities weren't of major importance in determining school "output"—despite what everybody had thought. The job ahead, as he saw it, was to "overcome the difficulties in starting point of children from different social groups."

But the children of Whitetown haven't been getting much of a head start. Since Sputnik, says Mario Fantini, of the Ford Foundation, improvements in American education have merely "strengthened the *status quo,* enabling the system to serve better those it has always served best." And those it has always served best are the white middle class, now largely in the suburbs.

Certainly, one finds little to cheer about in the schools of Whitetown, U.S.A. Philadelphia's Kensington section is an example. Its schools are old, its classes large. Its drop-

---

* Daniel Patrick Moynihan, President Nixon's Special Assistant for Urban Affairs, thinks Washington sought to conceal this crucial fact from the press and public. Its fifty-two-page summary of the Coleman Report dealt mostly with school segregation and "withheld from all but the *cognoscenti,*" says Moynihan, "any suggestions that major and, in effect, heretical findings had appeared." His article appeared in *Harvard Educational Review*'s Winter, 1968, issue.

out rate is very high and its college-going rate is very low. Kensington has more cases of pediculosis—nits and lice—in pupils' hair than any other section of Philadelphia, and a greater proportion of underweight children and children with cavities.

Most significantly, the administrative district comprising Kensington and adjoining black North Philadelphia regularly ranks last among the city's eight districts on all measures of academic promise and achievement, from the Iowa Test of Basic Skills to the California Test of Mental Maturity. Some inner-city districts that are 90 percent or more Negro produce slightly higher test scores than does Kensington's district. Despite its glaringly obvious deficiencies, Kensington is excluded from such federal programs as Model Cities. Many of its schools fail to qualify for aid under ESEA. The neighborhoods, though poor, are not quite poor enough.

The Whitetowns of other cities evidence similar inequities. "Boston's poor whites," says Assistant Superintendent of Schools William L. Cannon, "face the same educational deficiencies as the 'soul brothers.'" He sees a "very high correlation" in the test scores of black and white pupils in low-income sections. Says George Thomas, assistant dean of Harvard's Graduate School of Education: "The poor whites in Boston are less well served than the poor blacks. Less money goes into their areas—partly because of federal directive. The whites are prouder and more quiescent, the blacks more concentrated. Only in rare cases have the whites learned a lesson from the hustling black community. There's more action in [black] Roxbury than in the white areas. In general, Roxbury is much more together."

Charlestown's Harvard School is testimony to what has been permitted to happen in that old section of working-class Caucasians. The school was built in 1871; its outside fire escapes are rusty and its wooden doors creak; it is a certified firetrap. (In an interview, its principal defended the school's continued use on grounds that "schools almost never burn on school time.")

The Harvard School is dimly illuminated. In one room, when I was there, a lone light bulb (it appeared to be 60 watts) dangled from an 8-foot cord that ran from the high ceiling to a point just above the teacher's desk. The building is a rabbit warren of little closets and rooms tucked planlessly here and there off corridors. You encounter the dusty auditorium by surprise on the third story. There is one toilet seat per floor. There is no play yard.

An elevated line linking Charlestown to downtown Boston, five minutes away, rattles nearby. The school sits back from a busy commercial street, and heavy trucks trundle past all day long. (The trucks run within six feet of the living room of a Charlestown resident who has an important job in the Boston city government. Like so many Whitetowners, he's proud of the old place and is damned if he will move.)

The principal of Harvard School is responsible also for two other Charlestown elementary schools, one built in 1866 and the other in 1893. All three schools are small, enrolling a total of only about eight hundred children, mostly of French-Canadian, Polish, and Italian descent. In the next few years they are to be replaced by a single new building. The point is, though, that the "morbid, desolate crumbling" school of "rank smells" and pervasive gloom that Jonathan Kozol, in *Death at an Early Age,* found destroying the hearts and minds of Negro children in Boston's Roxbury section, exists in white Charlestown too.

Some of the oldest schools in Cleveland serve its poly-

glot West Side. This is a section in advanced stages of decay. It lost four thousand people between 1960 and 1965,
now counts twenty-seven thousand, 96.9 percent of them
white. You still see Polish delicatessens, Ukrainian social
clubs, and Russian Orthodox churches there. In the last
fifteen years, however, many of these ethnic groups have
moved to suburbs like Parma (using freeways that slice
through their old neighborhoods to get back and forth).
In schooling, employment, and family income, the West
Side rates under Cleveland city averages.

Especially hard hit is the so-called Near West Side,
across a smoky, industrial valley from central Cleveland.
In this dingy, trash-strewn neighborhood many of Cleveland's estimated fifty thousand Appalachian whites live in
urban hillbilly squalor. Despite their poverty, these people,
like all Whitetowners, have pride. To them, the public-
welfare program is nothing more than a huge black boon-
doggle. Staying off relief, therefore, becomes a badge of
distinction. Stay off they do—and their schools suffer.

"We measure poverty by welfare cases," explains Mrs.
Rose Cira, research associate in the Cleveland Board of
Education's division of educational research. "Because they
lack welfare cases, the Near West Side schools often fail to
qualify for federally financed programs. They are not considered target schools. They don't get the concentration of
moneys and services that the [predominantly black] East
Side does. There is a discrepancy that we're constantly trying to eliminate."

Another reason why Appalachian whites don't sign up
for welfare is that they're often on the move—down to
West Virginia and Kentucky, and then back again. They
don't stay put long enough to qualify. The result is that
their schools have the highest pupil-transiency rates in the
entire city. When I visited the Kentucky Elementary

School on the Near West Side in June, 1968, its pupil turnover stood at 130 percent—and climbing. The school enrollment was nine hundred, but twelve hundred boys and girls had been admitted or transferred out since the previous September.

"No sooner do we get children working to an acceptable pace," complained Mrs. Mary B. Diggs, the principal, "than they're gone. Many of the families still own farms back in the hills or have relatives there. They go 'home' for the spring plowing and we don't see them for six weeks."

Principals and teachers report the Appalachian white youngsters now are falling behind Negro pupils not only in attendance but in effort and achievement. "Negro parents," said Miss Mary Gulmi, principal of the Tremont School, which dates from 1875, "are aware of the importance of education. They take advantage of the opportunities offered them. The poor whites are satisfied with truck-driver jobs paying $90 to $100 a week. They don't stress education, they don't push, they're not too concerned that their kids aren't doing well. We've made the Negroes conscious of the need for education but not the poor whites. One of these days they're going to be outstripped."

At the 115-year-old Hicks Elementary School, teachers said the 25 percent Negro enrollment was, on the whole, more interested, curious, and aware than the 50 percent Appalachian white enrollment. "The Southern whites are ignorant of the help available to them," said one teacher, "or else they refuse it. They want to go back to the hills. They don't talk to teachers as Negroes do—that is, as equals. There is less parental participation among the whites."

"Motivation of family is greater among Negroes," agreed Mrs. Marian B. Harty, a principal who has served in poor-white and poor-black schools. A veteran teacher saw a psychological difference: "When I first came here thirteen years ago," she said, "the Negro was hangdog. Now he'll fight, push; he's very aggressive. It's the Appalachian whites who are insecure. It's hard to motivate them. The best readers are the Negro children. Not that they're brighter; they've just got more drive."

Bill G. is a blue-eyed ten-year-old with dungarees and a faded striped shirt open at the collar. His blond hair is cut short. Bill's father is in the Army somewhere. His older brother is going to high school in West Viriginia. Bill lives with his mother, who is a waitress and has a drinking problem, and with his sister and Cecil. Cecil? "He's livin' with us now." Bill was born in West Virginia, was taken to Texas at the age of two, returned to West Virginia, then moved to Cleveland with his mother when he was in second grade. They frequently drive back to the old hometown, Webster Springs, West Virginia. The 350-mile trip takes seven hours.

When he first moved to Cleveland, Bill was "sceered" of his teachers, but now his schoolwork has improved. His long-range prospects are dim, however. Comparatively few Appalachian whites get through high school and fewer still go to college. At Cleveland's 2,200-student Lincoln High School more than 25 percent of the enrollment was Appalachian white, but only one Appalachian white student ranked in the top 10 percent of his graduating class in 1968.

As is so often the case in black slum schools, Near West Side school officials blame pupils like Bill and parents like his mother for the children's failure to achieve. "They don't like school rules; they don't see the reason for homework," Miss Gulmi said of the parents. "If you ask for a note explaining a child's absence, the parent will say, 'Well, we overslept.' They are kind of free spirits. Any ordinary demands that a school would make—they just don't like to do it."

Besides appearing lackadaisical and apathetic, the Appalachian whites also exhibit the ferocious prejudices and free-floating aggression that Dennis Clark finds in the ethnic Americans. Mrs. Annette J. Maddox, Hicks School principal, told of a twelve-year-old Kentuckian who, after two weeks at Hicks, announced bluntly: "I hate niggers. I hate all niggers. I ain't never met no niggers like niggers at this school. These niggers are the worst I ever met."

Mrs. Maddox warned the boy not to speak that way. "You have to go to school with 'niggers,' as you call them," she said. "There are colored teachers in this school and I am colored. You'll find the colored here as nice as those in Kentucky." The boy was adamant: "Ain't nobody gonna make me like no niggers." And at the end of the school year he refused to join in the promotion exercises because so many of his classmates were black.

It is this kind of poor-white boy who needs special help. But as federal aid is allocated in Cleveland, he's not getting it.

Detroit's Ruddiman Junior High School serves a predominantly Polish neighborhood in the northwestern part of the city near the militantly all-white suburb of Dearborn, where police teach housewives how to shoot guns. Many of Ruddiman's families would like to move to Dearborn but can't afford to. A large public-housing project gives the school its only Negro pupils—about 10 percent of the enrollment of almost eleven hundred.

Ruddiman dates from a one-room school built in 1861 that is still standing and is still used. Four additions have been tacked onto it and all are under one roof. The inevitable freeway carries motorists within 15 yards of Ruddiman's front entrance. For two thirds of Ruddiman's families, incomes range from $6,000 to $9,000 a year. The other third are in the $3,000 to $4,000 poverty range. Since the school neighborhood ranks just above Detroit's poverty level, Ruddiman doesn't get a dime under Title I of ESEA.

When I visited Ruddiman, its principal, Mrs. Dorothy P. Cooper, a peppery little woman with glasses, an upswept hairdo, and a sense of outrage, was scrounging around for half a dozen spotlights for the school's upcoming fine-arts festival. "If this were a Title I school," she said bitterly, "I could order these lights and have them in a week. But as it is, we'll just have to go without."

Even among Ruddiman whites with the highest family incomes cultural deprivation is acute, although not always obvious, according to the principal. Of the Polish parents, she said:

Many have enough money but lack the cultural background of selectivity. They are permissive, indulgent, well-meaning but poorly advised. They let their children make course decisions, and it's the children themselves in many cases, not their parents, who elect not to take college preparation.

Social life is limited. Many of our children have never been downtown [six miles away]. Shopping centers are their social gathering places. When they take a summer vacation trip they come back talking about how many miles they covered, how many states they passed through, not what they saw. This is the way people out here think. They visit Disneyland but not the Grand Canyon.

Mrs. Cooper's indictment extends across the board of American society generally. Her point was, however, that although most Ruddiman children aren't poverty-stricken, they still need special programs to lift their sights and their values. The school offers none. There is much racial prejudice in the neighborhood (and one suspects it might exist within the school faculty and administration), but there are no special intergroup education efforts aimed at improving the racial climate at Ruddiman.

Ruddiman is a typical Whitetown case: its constituency is poor but not poor enough. Its problems, while genuine, are hidden. Its people are, in the main, uncomplaining. "They don't ask for anything," said Mrs. Cooper, who seemed both admiring and vexed. "They have pride. This is the one thing these people have. They plug along as best they can. They don't expect help and they don't get any."

At Detroit's school administration building, Assistant Superintendent Louis D. Monacel recognized the problem. Dr. Monacel directs state-federal projects for the Detroit schools. "We're not programming federally for these [white] people," he said. "The criteria are tightly woven to the ghetto."

What this means, he suggested, is that the sons and daughters of white factory workers are probably getting shortchanged. "We assume too much," he said. "We assume that we don't have to counsel them, push them, make sure they take advantage of every opportunity. But without that counseling they drift out of school. I've kind of ignored these people and assumed they were doing fine. They aren't. We've got to take some of the responsibility."

Monacel contrasted the expectations of a young, bright, ambitious black student today with those of a white trade-unionist. "If the Negro has anything, he can make it," said Monacel.

Colleges and universities all over America are running for Negroes. They've got to have them. In a way, this is shabby. Where were the colleges ten years ago? But it's also good because Negroes who want to and have ability can get into the best universities.

Meanwhile, the white unionist feels the ground being cut from beneath him, or thinks he does. The one thing he has is job security and the new rules are changing that too. Detroit is a union town and Detroit schools deliberately close apprentice training classes if they're not racially integrated. It is only right and just that we do this. But think how it affects the white unionist.

Detroit, with about three hundred thousand pupils, is the nation's fourth largest school district. Its superintendent is a thoughtful, pipe-smoking, career educator named Norman Drachler. Dr. Drachler worries about the schools' lack of support in white ethnic neighborhoods.

"In the so-called Polish corridors," he said, "we lose millage and we lose it consistently." He meant that these areas vote against school-tax increases. "They're concerned that every dollar goes to the Negro," Dr. Drachler continued. "They're concerned about law and order, about vandalism. In these areas I don't hear questions about the relevancy of the curriculum, as I hear in the Negro communities. Maybe it's a key that we don't have a single representative of ethnic groups on our [elected] school board. Not a Pole or an Italian. There was a thrust and they didn't make it."

Dr. Drachler believes the estrangement is temporary. In his opinion, the white ethnic groups "more and more identify with the white Protestant culture that prevails in our textbooks and in our schools.

"I don't think they want to be different," he said. "They want to assimilate and become Americanized. But they are very suspicious of our so-called Negro alliances. And they are bewildered, as all of us are, by the strange change of pace in our society."

The Adlai E. Stevenson School in Chicago's Scottsdale section serves a different kind of Whitetown. Here the people have, in effect, fled to the suburbs, even though their postwar community in southwest Chicago is just inside the city limits. All the houses are new, most are in good repair, and most are single-family, owner-occupied dwellings. The first houses built in the 1950's sold for $13,000, but recent ones of brick with basements and two-car garages bring $25,000 plus.

Only 4 percent of Scottsdale's population is foreign-born. Virtually every European nationality group is represented: Poles, Irish, English, Norwegians, Swedes, Germans, Czechs, Austrians, Hungarians, Russians, Italians, Canadians, Dutch, Lithuanians. There are a few Chinese but no Negroes or Puerto Ricans in Scottsdale. There never have been and, if the present population has its way, there never will be. About 50 percent of the men are blue-collar workers. Many police and firemen live there. Scottsdale is two thirds Roman Catholic and heavily Republican. There are no "first families" and there is no real "establishment." What unites many of the people is the fact of their mutual "displacement" from their former homes in racially mixed neighborhoods downtown and their determination that "this shall not happen again."

There's nothing very attractive about Scottsdale's setting on the once forbidding prairie, but its people enjoy many advantages. Serving Scottsdale and surrounding communities are three public elementary schools, a large parochial school, a public high school with junior college attached, seven churches and a synagogue, two shopping centers, two hospitals, two movie houses, a public library, a bowling alley, and four parks.

Stevenson School (named, by the way, for the Chicagoan who was Vice-President in the second administration of Grover Cleveland, not for his grandson, the late Ambassador to the United Nations) opened in 1955 with 685 pupils. It has since been enlarged and its enrollment in kindergarten through eighth grade has doubled. The neat, trim two-story school has twenty-eight regular classrooms, five mobile classrooms, three full-time kindergarten rooms, a library, a cafeteria, a combination gymnasium-auditorium, and a home economics room. The school playground is large and well equipped.

The building is not without defects. It heats unevenly. The gym is inadequate and both the teachers' room and parking lot are too small. Maintenance and repairs are behind schedule. When I visited the school in May, 1968, a surprising number of windows were broken, the result of troublemaking by rowdy neighborhood youths, I was told. Compared to other schools in Chicago, though, Stevenson's problems are minimal. And that's just the point: Scottsdale wants to keep it that way. What it fears is change, racial change, change "forced down our throats" through school bussing or other integration devices.

Stevenson School's principal, Eleanor R. Coghlan, is a Scottsdaler in spirit, although she lives some miles away. She said Stevenson pupils consistently score above national norms on standardized tests—and she produced records to prove it. "Stevenson compares very favorably with the highest-income schools on the North Shore," she said. "We know how much higher we stand than the inner-city schools. And we know it's not just a matter of teachers or supplies. You find some marvelously dedicated teachers in inner-city schools. And those schools are loaded with help. They've got people walking around with nothing to do."

Mrs. Coghlan, a spruce, well-organized widow, said that, as a representative of the Chicago school system, she couldn't condone Scottsdale's openly segregationist views. "But I can understand," she said. "I have empathy. I am as aware as anyone of a need for a different climate. I take in-service courses on this very subject. But this community is certainly not ready. If they bussed in colored children, we'd have riots. They know this at the Board of Education."

Earlier, I had talked to Dr. John Byrne, district superintendent in Chicago's predominantly white Uptown section. "Rightly or wrongly," Dr. Byrne had said, "there is a feeling that we're carrying the ball for the Negro people." He argued that the anti-Negro prejudices of Scottsdalers and others in Chicago's "White Crescent" were socioeconomic in origin rather than racist. "These people live in small neat bungalows," he said. "They manicure their lawns and put pink flamingos out front. They buy this baloney about property values declining [when Negroes move in]. They see themselves losing their hard-earned investment. Middle-European people especially are land- and property-conscious. So this makes it hurt all the more."

Despite Chicago's efforts to raise the quality of Negro education, Dr. Byrne thought the school board was actually spending less in the ghetto than in white areas. His explanation was that in the black sections many of the teachers were new and at the bottom of the salary scale, while veteran teachers filled white schools. In other words, it's cheaper to run a school with novices than old-timers. City-wide, only 72 percent of Chicago's teachers in 1968 were "assigned"—that is, fully certified and with tenure. In some white schools, however, 95 percent or more of the teachers were assigned.

When I told Mrs. Coghlan what this district superintendent had said about spending in black and white schools, without identifying him by name, she blew up.

"What was that?" she demanded. "Who was it? I'll bet he's a new superintendent and I'll bet he's colored. I'll bet those two things."

She was half right—Dr. Byrne was newly appointed. But her angry reaction showed how high feelings run in school systems seeking social change. What she said next was also typical talk for Whitetown school administrators: "The Negro element is very vocal. No one is looking at this side at all. We are the forgotten men. We don't get one cent from the government. We get the bare minimum. We aren't given a thing."

It was a fact, however, that Stevenson School's staff consisted almost exclusively of veteran teachers. Indeed, the principal herself counted sixty teachers in other Chicago schools who were then on a waiting list for transfer to Stevenson. Some had been waiting for seven years. And virtually all wanted to transfer out of black schools. When and if they transferred out, their places would, in all likelihood, be taken by new teachers. Dr. Byrne seemed to have a point.

In Los Angeles, you will search in vain for an old ethnic neighborhood. There are no ancient Charlestowns or hard-bitten Kensingtons or other eastern-style Whitetowns of any description. Despite the sprawl and the smog, everything's up-to-date in this incredible 710.6-square-mile school district—almost two thirds the size of Rhode Island. Every year more than a thousand new classrooms are built and a forty-year-old school is considered obsolete. (In Cleveland, by contrast, more than half the schools are over fifty years old.) To an easterner, even the L.A. slums look good. "We have," said a school official, "the world's richest poverty areas."

Appearances are misleading. To find space for 27,500 additional pupils each year, Los Angeles has had to cut school costs to the bone. In building after building you find a principal, a secretary, and a fixed number of classroom teachers, but no other staff or extra help of any kind. That's all the exploding school system can afford. Most of its federal aid under ESEA's Title I provides "saturation" help for 60,000 poor Negro and Spanish-American children. Working-class white areas are generally excluded from these special programs. An example is the Valley East Elementary District, which includes the less affluent parts of Hollywood and North Hollywood. In 1968, Valley East enrolled 40,711 pupils—86 percent of them white—in fifty-four schools: a good-sized city school system, all by itself. Yet serving these 40,711 children was one art supervisor but no art teachers, one physical-education supervisor but no physical-education teachers, one music supervisor and thirteen music teachers. There were libraries in the schools but no certified librarians. Federal funds supported a project for gifted pupils in Valley East and one to teach English to Mexican-American children who made up 11 percent of the enrollment. They also helped maintain the librarian-less libraries. But that was it.

"We're a fringe district," said Mrs. Helene C. Lewis, administrative assistant to the district superintendent. "We need help but don't get it. These are forgotten people. [Shades of Scottsdale's Eleanor Coghlan.] They need that little push. We keep telling them downtown that these kids are almost as badly off as those in the ghetto. But nothing happens."

Just a block from Hollywood and Vine—crossroads of the celluloid world—is one of the schools that Mrs. Lewis was talking about. The Selma School sits on a back street seldom seen by tourists. Seventy-five percent of its pupils are white. Many of their parents were drawn to Hollywood by the bright lights. Almost invariably, dreams of stardom turn into nightmares of marriage tangles, drinking, often narcotics. Failing to strike it rich, these rootless people move on. So kids come and go at Selma School. It's like a revolving door. Of all schools in the entire Los Angeles district in 1967–1968, Selma had the highest rate of pupil transiency. It also ranked near the bottom in reading.

The principal, Miss Sarah Macaluso, saw a correlation. "When the transiency rate is so high," she said, "you can't blame reading disabilities on the teachers. We don't have the children long enough to teach them anything."

At the 74 percent white Grant School on Santa Monica Boulevard, in Hollywood, newly appointed principal Edith Dury said she was "floored" to find so much poverty and so many divorced and separated parents. In 1966–1967, Grant had the city's third highest pupil-transiency rate. "We have many families on public assistance," Mrs. Dury said. "We have many emotional problems—both children and parents. A mother was in this morning. She neglects her child shamelessly, yet she's flying to Germany for a vacation with some man. That's the kind of value system and morality you find here."

By skimping on such schools, Los Angeles educators are, in effect, perpetuating such ways of life. Nor is Valley East unusual. Twenty-five miles south of Hollywood, in the city's Harbor Area Elementary District, I talked to Superintendent Jack R. McClellan. He served in Watts before taking over the predominantly white Harbor Area in February, 1968.

"The low-income Caucasian community is not demonstrating," he said. "It's not demanding space in newspapers or on TV. These people are doing their best to meet their problems within their income. But they are saying to me, to principals, to teachers, 'We want what the others are getting.'"

Dr. McClellan thought they had a point. He was surprised that a drive to get money for working-class white schools had not been organized. "Apparently there is no leadership," he said. "The churches haven't picked it up."

One of the schools I visited in the Harbor Area was the Carson Street School, just off the Harbor and San Diego freeways in Torrance. Carson Street School is in a tough white neighborhood. Knifings, shootings, car thefts, and narcotics addiction are common. About one eighth of its families are on welfare and the bulk of these are one-parent families. Maybe half the parents were high school dropouts; very few have had any college experience. Carson Street enrolled almost fifteen hundred pupils, two thirds of them white, most of the others Mexican-American. *

To run this forty-nine-classroom operation, the principal, a New Englander named Minnie Queenen Wallace, could call on, besides regular teachers, one vice-principal, one music teacher, a corrective physical-education teacher, one day a week; a counselor one day a week; and a speech teacher three days every two weeks. That was the extent of supportive services for a big school bursting with problems. Because of overcrowding, Carson Street was on a "divided day," some children attending classes from 9 A.M. to 2 P.M. and others from 10 to 3.

Mrs. Wallace seemed proud of the fact that her parents

---

* California requires all school districts to conduct racial and ethnic surveys every year with pupils placed in categories designated by the State Department of Education. In Los Angeles the 1968 breakdown was "other whites" (the designation for all Caucasians except those with Spanish surnames), 54.1 percent; Negroes, 21.4 percent; Spanish-surname students, 20.3 percent; Chinese-Japanese-Korean, 3.5 percent; American Indians, 0.1 percent; "other nonwhite," mostly Samoans, 0.5 percent. Such racial distinctions, though invidious, are required under the civil rights legislation. These studies help Washington determine whether or not school districts are segregated in fact if not in law.

rarely registered complaints. "These people aren't asking for anything," she said. "The others have their hand out all the time." It was clear to whom she was referring.

At noon the day of my visit, the principal and new officers of the school Parent-Teacher Association had an end-of-year lunch at a nearby Howard Johnson's. There were nine mothers, all of them white and most from the Southwest. I heard no gripes about the school. The women were too busy talking about firearms. Eight of the nine said they had guns in their houses; the only unarmed officer of the P.T.A. was the lone college-trained one. The outgoing president said her husband was teaching her how to shoot both a .30-caliber rifle and a .22. "I think this is good," she said. Whitetown all the way.

In every big city, you find Whitetowners working in public schools as teachers and principals. They may have moved to the suburbs, but they remain Whitetowners in spirit. Their sympathies are with the working-class whites. And for them the conspiracy theory is genuine—and frightening.

An example is San Francisco's John P. Ward. He's principal of the Douglas Elementary School, just over the hill from Haight-Ashbury. In 1968, when I was there, Haight-Ashbury was a national symbol of youth in rebellion. On June afternoons, its sidewalks were thronged with freak-outs, cop-outs, loafers, lovers, exhibitionists, dilettantes, mystics, musicians, nihilists, Marxists, hippies, Yippies, pseudophilosophers, phonies. Everything that Haight-Ashbury stood for John P. Ward detests. He's convinced that because the Douglas School is 71.3 percent white, it is being discriminated against. He's convinced that because he's white, he's being discriminated against.

Ward, a new principal, runs a ten-teacher school for three hundred pupils, many from broken homes and living on welfare. Six of his teachers were new the previous September. A seventh is a long-term substitute replacing a teacher on sabbatical leave. Ward's only office help is a secretary who works six hours a day. He has, as he puts it, "two fifths of a speech teacher" (meaning one teacher two days a week) and two fifths of an instrumental-music teacher. Ward's guidance file is bulging. He must handle all discipline, all counseling, all special problems, plus the avalanche of paperwork and statistics-gathering required of principals these days.

All this seems to leave him little time for staff development or curricular innovation. So these jobs go undone. Douglas Elementary, in San Francisco's Eureka Valley, receives no ESEA help or federal aid of any kind. Ward's chief advantages are that the school is small and the building, which opened in 1954, is in good shape. But Douglas pupils, in the middle rank in reading, fall in the bottom 10 percent nationally. Compared with children across the country, all but the very best readers at Douglas are subpar.

As a result, Ward is a bitter man. "I spend too much of my time on social-welfare work," he said. "I spend more time on social welfare than I do on education. Society is deliberately dumping these problems in our laps. If that's the way the game is to be played, I need help. All of this is detracting from my educational role. It's taking its toll."

Ward considers Harold Howe's plan of tipping the educational scales in favor of minority-group pupils "absolutely discriminatory." "It's discrimination in reverse—discrimination against the productive elements of society. I've been getting complaints from parents, but they're fearful of being called racially prejudiced. They're scared to death of it."

What really outrages John P. Ward, though, is the overall racial atmosphere in San Francisco. He sees the press, the politicians, the business establishment, and the school system bowing to pressure from minority-group militants and actually conspiring to hurt the white working class. He specifically includes white principals among those being hurt. Ward, seventeen years in the system and an assistant principal for almost nine years, formerly headed the San Francisco Principals Association.

Of himself and his fellow Caucasian principals, he said: "We're living a life of hell. It's getting to the point where the work isn't worth it. You can be doing the finest job in the world and you're driven to your knees by false accusations. We're fed up with the injustice of it."

Ward went on to complain about something that is irking white principals and middle-echelon school administrators in big-city school systems across the country: that, in their efforts to promote black administrators, city school boards sometimes appear to be discriminating against whites.

"Someone somewhere has to stand up with the moral courage for what is right," said this San Franciscan.

> If the Negro has the stuff, he's going to make it. But only if he gets there on his own ability, will he gain respect. Superficial attempts to advance him won't solve anything.
> The Board of Education should say exactly this: "If you want to get ahead, buddy, you have to prove your worth and prove your responsibility." But as it is they're going to scuttle us [white school administrators] by forcing us to knuckle under. This is a compromise of principle. So what's going to happen? Top-flight people are going to the suburbs. They won't come here and subject themselves to the indignities and abuse.

Of course, Ward overlooked the fact that race, religion, and national ancestry have always been crucial factors in selection of school personnel. Historically, capable Negro schoolmen have been held back because of their color, and white incompetents have advanced because of *their* color. Ethnicity and religion also can be important. To get a top school job in Boston you must be Roman Catholic and you should be Irish. In most other cities white Protestants have dominated the school superintendencies. In San Francisco itself an open though unofficial quota system has operated to guarantee that the three major religious faiths are represented on the city school board. Such was the case in New York City too. Its board traditionally consisted of three Jews, three Protestants, and three Catholics until Negroes and Puerto Ricans were given representation in an enlarged board during John V. Lindsay's mayoralty.

Ward said he knew all this but believed that Catholics and Jews earned their right to good jobs in the San Francisco school system without resort to violence or Black Panther tactics. Maybe so. But the point is that group conflict and ethnic lobbying are a way of life in American schools and other institutions.

San Francisco pours most of its federal funds into minority-group schools. In 1967–1968, only 27 out of 105 elementary schools received a share of the city's $3.25 million ESEA Title I grant. Of the twenty-seven, 17 were predominantly Negro, 3 predominantly Chinese, 3 predominantly "Spanish surname," and 4 mixed—that is, no single racial or nationality group accounted for 50 percent or more of the enrollment. With its 1968–1969 ESEA funds cut, San Francisco reduced the number of aided schools from twenty-seven to nine. Of the nine, 6 were predominantly Negro and 3 Spanish surname. The reduction caused protests.

"We got calls from everybody," said Victor Rossi, coordinator for compensatory education. "They all said they needed help. I had to tell them that although they're eligible, they couldn't have it because of the shortage of funds."

The other side of the coin is that in San Francisco, as in other cities, you find white schools that need help but don't know it or won't admit it. The Ulloa School is one. It serves San Francisco's Sunset section near the Bay. Lower-middle- and middle-class families live there in stucco row houses, which, because of the city's skyrocketing real-estate values, cost upward of $25,000. Ulloa is 76 percent white; its only Negro pupils are bussed in. On Stanford-Binet reading tests, Ulloa's midpoint ranks in the bottom 15 percent nationally.

"When the test scores were published, to cover our embarrassment, we said our poor showing was due to the bussed-in children," said Mrs. Leona Lee, 1968 president of the Ulloa P.T.A. "But it wasn't. Their scores were published separately. We face the same problems as other areas and we need compensatory education just as badly as they do, but our people won't admit it. We've been fooling ourselves too long."

Ulloa parents spurn extra help because they consider themselves superior to Negroes. And this false pride, this prejudice, is not restricted to whites in the Sunset section. "Chinatown," said Mrs. Lee, who grew up there, "is one of the most prejudiced areas of San Francisco. Chinatown looks down on the Negro people. I can remember how my father used to say, 'Don't associate with this or that Negro.' "

Of course, this kind of thinking cuts both ways. A month later, I heard Robert B. Core, community coordinator for Opportunities Industrialization Center in New York and a Negro, report to a conference on ethnic America: "My parents in Pittsburgh told me not to kiss little Italian girls because they taste like garlic. Well, I checked —and it's not true."

After my visits to the Whitetowns of American big cities, I paid a call on Harold Howe, II, in his Washington office. It was a hot day in August, 1968. The United States Education Commissioner's tie was loose and his half-smoked cigar was unlighted. His feet were up on a coffee table, where they remained as we talked.*

About the school concerns of Whitetown, U.S.A., Howe professed to be stumped. "It's a hell of a perplexing thing," he said, "using federal dollars to bring about social change. This process is bound to cause abrasions. We're living in a very abrasive time and I see no likelihood of a letup."

Howe said there was no question but that the working white American identified by Robert Wood needed help. "But if you have to make a hard choice in deciding who will get federal education aid," he added, "you're forced back to the zero-to-three-thousand-dollars-level group."

Under Title I of ESEA, the biggest and most comprehensive federal school-assistance program ever devised, about nine million students in 16,400 school districts have been served. Howe's office had no racial breakdown. He thought that, including all programs in suburban and rural as well as urban areas, more white than nonwhite children were aided but that the proportion of black children served was much higher.

"In any program," Howe said, "you have the problem of the cutting point. It's pretty clear to us that if you disperse funds among a very large number of youngsters, much of the money will just be frittered away without doing much good. We have pressed for concentration. Without much success, I might add. The natural tendency is to give everybody a little, and that's what the school districts have done."

Commissioner Howe favored reducing sharply the num-

---

* Howe resigned as Education Commissioner on Dec. 31, 1968.

ber of children served so that more money could be spent
—a critical mass, he called it—on fewer pupils. In 1968–
1969, the districts averaged $110 per pupil in Title I pro-
grams. Howe wanted this raised to maybe $250 per pupil,
with no increase in Washington's outlay. "We want to
move from our present position of serving nine million
children under Title I to a point where we will be serving
only six or seven million," he said. "We will deny help to
some youngsters but more will get solutions to their problems. The trouble is that at present Title I's billion dollars
are spread too thin."

In Howe's view, working-class whites were "really hurting, particularly in terms of expectation. What they tend
to do," he said, repeating a point I had heard in several
cities, "is deny themselves necessities in order to respond
to what they see in magazines and on television. There's
an element of tragedy about this."

Black people, said Howe, have historically been denied
mobility in American society. The doors now are opening,
but Howe did not fear "overcompensation." He considered
it inevitable and probably necessary that city school systems should favor black administrators over white ones
of comparable training and experience. "Since central-city
school systems are full of black children," he said, "there is
some sort of vague rationality in having black administrations. If in doing that you awaken feelings of resentment
among those who haven't been able to use the mobility
always available to whites, I guess what you have to say
is, 'That's too bad.'

"That's where the element of tragedy comes in. I don't
know what you can do about it."

Reflecting later on what Howe had said and what I had
seen and heard in the big-city school systems, I concluded
that the failures of urban education—and suburban and

rural education, too—can't be blamed on money alone. Perhaps they can't be blamed on money at all. Lack of money didn't cause the basic problem today and a surfeit of funds won't solve it. It's much more complex and more difficult to deal with. Historically, the job of the schools has been to transmit the American culture as a coherent and credible system of values and ideas from generation to generation. As long as the national life-style, with all its imperfections, proved generally acceptable to most Americans the schools seemed to do an adequate transmission job.

But what we appear to be witnessing now is a mass rejection of this culture by Americans of all ages. The schools, and especially the colleges, are thus caught in a bind. They can no longer be mere transmission belts because the things they've been transmitting are now widely discredited as shoddy and second-rate. They must therefore seek to improve the culture by reforming the society. Hence their role as social-change agents. But in seeking to perform this function, the schools have managed to alienate everybody. Those favoring social change are convinced the schools, as currently constituted, are doomed to failure if, in fact, they ever really make the effort. These critics point to self-serving educational bureaucrats of narrow vision and social and racial biases—I saw many who fit this general description—as Exhibit A. Such limited people, they say, simply could not effect social change even if they wanted to. And there's some doubt that they want to.

Yet the schools are also distrusted by those opposed to change. They see school reformers seeking, however clumsily, to effect change. And they don't like it. These are the Whitetowners. They are ubiquitous and their number is legion.

Anonymous

You Say You Want a Revolution

WE WEAR Continental pants, silk gauchos, and leather jackets. We drive '57 Chevies while listening to Booker T. & the M.G.'s, Elvis, Bo Diddley, Creedance Clearwater Revival, and the Temptations. We dig dances and gangster movies, f---ing chicks, and fighting other dudes—and a quart of Thunderbird or a case of Iron City is an okay high. And we grease our hair back with Vitalis and Brylcream.

And you people out there who say you want a revolution and a better world—you call us street hunkies, slicks, and greasers. And you usually also figure we're stupid.

Well, it's true our education usually ends with high school, but we're not stupid. We've been on the street a long time. When you talk about police brutality, we could tell you a few things. And don't come telling us about the fist; we know what the fist means, and we know how to use it.

You guys can go out and protest about poverty or something, then go home to a hot meal in a warm house —let me tell you plenty of street hunkies know what poor

Reprinted from *I'm All Right*, a publication produced by high school students in Pittsburgh, Pa., February, 1970.

really means, and we've fought like hell all our lives to get ourselves together and stay strong. Some of us were *born* on the f---ing street.

We know this city needs change, we know the cops don't protect *our* people, and the education system doesn't seem to help *our* people, the good jobs don't seem to go to *our* people—but there's plenty of our people dying in Nam defending this way of life, or coming back home to sh---y jobs. We know there's something wrong and it's time for some change—but don't ask us to join up with you if all you want is the muscle.

Just remember, it's hard to be poor, and it's hard to get yourself together when all the time everyone is putting you down as white trash. Just remember that.

And maybe you ought to try to dig our way of life a little. We've got our own culture—and you ought to try to dig it. Or at least respect it. Sh--, you'd have a f---ing revolution right there.—A street hunkie who *knows*.

By Lewis Carliner

Labor:
The Anti-Youth Establishment

ARTHUR HINKLE, twenty-eight-year-old white factory worker, and Bradford Jones, twenty-three-year-old black factory worker, are two rank-and-file soldiers in a guerrilla war now being waged in the labor movement. At the moment the war is still sputtering; it hasn't fully broken out. Except for occasional flare-ups not always recognized as incidents in the war—the Wallace vote in some areas, the rejection of newly negotiated union agreements by the rank and file, the revolutionary unity movement among auto workers in Detroit—the shape of the conflict is only beginning to become visible.

Hinkle and Jones, it needs to be said immediately, are both fighting the old men—in the plant, in the union, in the community, and in the society. But because the best indications are that they don't yet know that this is what they are battling, they are not fighting side by side. Indeed, sometimes they are fighting each other.

Young American workers like Hinkle and Jones are older than other people we define as young in the United States and much older than young workers overseas,

Reprinted from *New Generation,* a quarterly journal of the National Committee on Employment of Youth, Spring, 1970. Used by permission.

where sixteen-year-olds and sometimes fifteen-year-olds go into factories to work as apprentices. In the United States, young factory workers are generally defined as between twenty-three and thirty-five. This makes the youngest factory worker older than the oldest student, except for graduate students.

This age difference accounts for part of the lack of understanding between young workers and students, although both have their backs up against the going Establishment. Class differences, resulting in widely opposite cultural and political attitudes, are another major factor. But even though they don't realize it, young workers, students, and black youth all have the same basic grievances. What escapes them, and affects them all, unequally but powerfully, is that the economic differences between young and old are generally more marked than differences between worker and boss, or black and white. The disparity in the situation between young and old is heavily weighted to the advantage of people over thirty-five. Bureaucratic dynamisms have operated to give the older men control over the agencies in the society which in ordinary circumstances conduct protest activities: unions, political parties, institutionalized reformist agencies. The slogan "Never trust anyone over thirty," which when it was first raised seemed to be a joke, is actually based on an empirical understanding of the treatment accorded by those over thirty to those under.

The under-thirty-five grievances are simple and inescapable, once they are looked at squarely. Young workers, like students, have less money and power than older people, although they often share the same responsibilities. The cries of students for participatory democracy and of blacks for self-determination have been heard across the country, but until recently there had been only mumbles of discontent from young workers. As would be expected, students and black people are far more articulate about what bugs them than are young workers.

But there are other reasons for lack of understanding about the problems of young workers.

Union newspapers, which represent the views of the union administration, deliberately do not air the grievances of young workers, nor do management publications. Young workers themselves have no organizations, as other dissident groups do, and no means for expressing their views except the traditional methods that workers have always invoked—repudiating their leaders and resorting to wildcat strikes.

There is currently a general belief that there has been a substantial increase in exuberantly violent wildcat strikes led and insisted upon by young workers. The strike at American Motors two years ago is often cited as an example of the kind of strike that is almost, but not quite, an epidemic.

But there is better evidence of disaffection in the rejection of contract terms by the rank and file after they have been negotiated by union officers and staff. Nationally, the number of strike-settlement rejections has been rising steadily since 1964, the earliest year for which data is available.

"A common cause of these rejections," according to the director of the Federal Mediation and Conciliation Service, "is the advent of a young work force. Many young workers who have grown up in a period of relative affluence have never experienced either a real depression or the early history of union struggles. Moreover, they are not very interested in attempts to acquaint them with these hard facts of earlier years. Many have never experienced a strike of any duration. When these facts are coupled with what may be loosely described as the current disillusionment of youth in other areas of activity, negative ratification votes are not surprising."

The implication in this assessment is that young workers are talking back to their elders and betters because they have not experienced the hardships that older union members suffered in earlier struggles. It reflects an attitude that is the object of resentment of young students, workers, and blacks throughout the country. The fact is that young people are a minority with the usual minority grievances: they are discriminated against in the matter of rewards and privileges, denied representation in the government of their society and its commercial and educational institutions, and required to be unwilling audiences to traditional declarations by the people in power that the protesters are too young, too inexperienced, too ignorant, too unprepared, and in general too damned insolent to merit serious consideration.

Against the claim that young workers strike and reject contracts because they have never met a payroll or walked a picket line in the winter of 1938, there is clear evidence in the current work situation and economic data that young workers have serious causes for complaint.

Within the union structure itself, neither the locals nor the national and international unions even begin to give young people the representation on governing boards that they are entitled to on the basis of their numbers.

The seniority system and the instinct of people to hang on to their jobs in a bureaucracy account for the fact that the labor movement has become what might be called a gerontocracy. The movement which rejects the view that seniority qualifies superannuated Dixiecrats for chairmanships in the key congressional committees has not turned its attention to its own trade-union arteriosclerosis.

On the job, young workers, especially in their earliest days in the plant, understandably resent the seniority system and frequently claim that the local union leadership and plant management are in league against them in matters of the distribution of overtime, promotions, and desirable transfers, and are deaf to such grievances connected with low seniority as having to work the second and third shift. Granted that the history of the trade-union movement is a powerful argument for the strongest possible seniority protection, other security provisions and full employment might still make it possible to give young people clearly defined opportunities to bypass seniority restraints in order to utilize a particular talent.

One characteristic of today's young workers that mocks the older workers' claim to know more and be wiser is the disparity in education between younger and older employees. At present, the majority of new employees are high school graduates and many have college training; in general they have better formal educations than those who deny them representation in the union.

Data compiled by both the unions and the Bureau of Labor Statistics reveal the importance of demographic facts to unions and the condition of workers, young and old. Each year some three million people enter the labor force and of these a third of the men and about a fifth of the women are employed in factories. In 1960 there were slightly more than thirteen million people in the labor force under twenty-five and by 1970 this figure will have increased to almost twenty million. Workers over forty-five will increase about 18.5 percent in the same period, while workers in the thirty-five to forty-four age group will decline. Thus labor leaders will soon have to deal with a constituency that is relatively old and relatively young, with the young in the majority.

The testimony everywhere in the society—especially in the political sphere, where grievances are the raw materials—is that young workers are being subjected to an intense propaganda attack against pensions and social security. In the plant they are told, very often by foremen, but by co-workers as well, that they are being taxed out of wage increases to provide pensions for the older workers.

Outside the plant, management-sponsored organizations and right-wing political groups bombard them with literature that insists that the social security program is a fraud perpetuated against young workers, that if an amount equivalent to what they pay into social security were deposited in a savings bank it would pay them far more than they will ever receive in social security benefits, that the social security fund is bankrupt, and that they are being taxed to pay pensions to the aged today because of this bankruptcy. All these allegations are demonstrably untrue but nevertheless increases in social security taxes have enraged young workers, especially since their own economic situation is not understood by the labor movement, the government, or even by the young worker himself.

Apart from the poor, no group in the society is under greater economic pressure than young workers. When they are told by their older co-workers in the plant that things have never been so good, wages higher, conditions better, vacations more satisfactory, and that all this is the result of the older workers' sacrifices, their reply is often, "So what? Things aren't all that good now." The truth is that for the younger worker things are *not* very good.

He spends on the average more than he earns and goes into debt each year. At the beginning of the '60s he was going into debt on an average of $100 a year, and he is probably going more deeply into debt now. He sees taxes for pensions and social security as money he could use to pay his bills and keep even.

Wealth and financial well-being among American workers are closely related to the age of the worker and of his wife and children. In part this is because workers under thirty-five are usually married to women whose full-time occupation is raising children. During this period they are under the heaviest economic burden most Americans ever have to bear—buying a home, often paying off the borrowed down payment on the house, buying a car, furniture, appliances, paying for their children.

When their children reach the teens, the situation changes. Often their wives return to work and the family income almost doubles; the house is substantially paid for; the installment accounts are paid off; bills are under control. Suddenly, instead of pressure, there is relative affluence.

The changing situation of the young worker growing old is revealed in Federal Reserve System statistics.

Families headed by persons under thirty-five had total assets valued at $6,304 in 1963, representing equity in a car, house, investments, insurance, and so forth. Scaled down by age, it is obvious that the assets of a family with a twenty-five-year-old head who has one baby and another on the way come to very nearly nothing. Families with heads in the thirty-five-to-forty-four age group are better off, with total average assets of $16,008, of which some $3,541 is invested, and with liquid assets of almost $5,000. Things are even better, financially, for the fifty-five-to-sixty-four-year-old group, whose resources averaged $32,527 in 1963 and who had, among other assets, some $12,212 in investments and $6,401 in liquid assets.

The young worker has a two-edged grievance: he is under an impossible financial burden, and part of his burden is due to the fact that he must help provide for the far more well-to-do older worker. Moreover, in recent years this situation has been compounded by inflation, which on the whole has benefited American workers. But in the case of the younger worker it means that he must pay $3,000 to $5,000 more for a house than he would have had to pay two years ago. In addition, his mortgage exacts a usurious 7½ or 8 percent interest in comparison with the 4 to 6 percent the older workers are paying off. No wonder it seems to him that the entire society is a seniority swindle designed to victimize him.

Young workers in Sweden, Great Britain, Japan, and a number of other countries are not tied in a bind that compels them to resent the pensions paid older workers. They receive housing assistance, grants on marriage, family allowances, and a variety of services to help them surmount the mountainous costs of raising a young family.

Unions and political parties responsive to the needs of young constituents should have long ago devised a program to meet these problems. Yet even the student loans offered today become a further burden to the young father who has to repay them. Perhaps there should be very long-term loans for young families, with minimal payments in the first fifteen years and higher payments in the last twenty-five years when inflation and the improved economic position of being an older worker would operate to reduce the required payments to a nominal charge.

Possibly social security could be tied to family-assistance programs for young people, down payments on a house, interest subventions, grants to buy furniture and appliances, and allowances for each child, so that the social security tax and pension deduction would be combined with benefits to the young as well as the old. Better still, loans to young workers could be paid back through a 1 percent surtax on income beginning at age thirty-five.

The unions should explore collective-bargaining ventures aimed at relieving the pressures on young people. But most important, the society and the labor movement should move to admit the young into the government of the community. Otherwise the Anti-Youth Establishment may be confronted from another direction in the society by the cry of "Up against the wall, you old gerontocrats."

III | MIDDLE AMERICA VS. THE LIBERAL CULTURE

CLASS CONFLICT HAS REEMERGED AS A SIGNIFICANT FORCE in American life in recent years but it has surfaced both as a cultural as well as an economic phenomenon. On one end of the scale is traditionalist, ethnic, Middle America and at the other, the liberal, upper-class culture. At stake is whose values, life-style, and even politics will prevail. In a manner that has tended to exacerbate the issue, Vice-President Agnew has seen this clearly and attempted to mine it politically. But he only recognized what was there. He did not create the issue.

Until now, it has not been much of a contest. Certainly in recent years, American culture has been most heavily influenced by its liberal upper classes who have been either indifferent or hostile to Middle America. In "Respectable Bigotry," Michael Lerner describes the various ways in which the cultural elite "put down" working and ethnic Americans. Rudolph J. Vecoli analyzes the failure of historians and other social scientists to examine ethnicity and, in fact, the de-ethnization of earlier minority-group scholars who broke through into academia.

As a result of the triumph of the liberal culture, there have been few spokesmen of any real standing willing to speak out for the values and goals of Middle Americans or, for that matter, the legitimacy of many of the current American institutions. Illustrative of a more sympathetic view of these are selections included here of Daniel Patrick Moynihan's memorandum to Richard Nixon as he assumed office in 1969 and from a journal kept by Eric Hoffer in 1958 and 1959. A measure of the difficulty in breaking through the cultural curtain that has separated liberals from Middle Americans is the admission of Eric Sevareid, who has done so much to bring Hoffer's views to public attention, that he had shied away from Hoffer's books for many years because Eisenhower had publicly praised one of them (Calvin Tomkins, *Eric Hoffer: An American Odyssey* [Perennial Library, Harper & Row, Publishers, Inc., 1970]).

Milton Himmelfarb's "Jewish Class Conflict?" and Haskell L. Lazere's analysis of the Jewish Defense League, "Haganah U.S.A.?" analyze the frustration of lower-middle-class Jews and the anger many feel toward "the Jewish Establishment." The Jewish Defense League, of course, offers no solutions to the problems these Jews face and often manages to achieve just the reverse of what it set out to do. It is an expression, however, of the tensions of those Jews who live and work on the urban frontier.

By Michael Lerner

Respectable Bigotry

WHEN WHITE YALE STUDENTS denounce the racist university or racist American society, one has little
doubt about what they refer to. One also has little doubt
about the political leanings of the speaker. He is a good
left-liberal or radical, upper-class or schooled in the assumptions of upper-class liberalism.

Liberal-to-radical students use these phrases and feel
purged of the bigotry and racism of people such as Chicago's Mayor Daley. No one could be farther from bigotry,
they seem to believe, than they.

But it isn't so. An extraordinary amount of bigotry on
the part of elite, liberal students goes unexamined at Yale
and elsewhere. Directed at the lower middle class, it feeds
on the unexamined biases of class perspective, the personality predilections of elite radicals and academic disciplines
that support their views.

There are certainly exceptions in the liberal-radical uni-

Reprinted from *The American Scholar,* Vol. 38, No. 4 (Autumn, 1969).
Copyright © 1969 by the United Chapters of Phi Beta Kappa. Used
by permission of the publishers.

NOTE: *The terms "radical," "semiradical," "left-liberal," and "liberal-to-
radical" are used in reference to "elite," "upper class," and "upper-
middle-class" students to refer to a broad but splintered and diverse
group of people.* (M.L.)

versity society—people intellectually or actively aware of
and opposed to the unexamined prejudice. But their anom-
alousness and lack of success in making an ostensibly intro-
spective community face its own disease is striking.

In general, the bigotry of a lower-middle-class policeman toward a ghetto black or of a lower-middle-class
mayor toward a rioter is not viewed in the same perspective as the bigotry of an upper-middle-class peace matron
toward a lower-middle-class mayor; or of an upper-class
university student toward an Italian, a Pole, or a National
Guardsman from Cicero, Illinois—that is, if the latter two
cases are called bigotry at all. The violence of the ghetto
is patronized as it is "understood" and forgiven; the violence of a Cicero racist convinced that Martin Luther King
threatens his lawn and house and powerboat is detested
without being understood. Yet the two bigotries are very
similar. For one thing, each is directed toward the class
directly below the resident bigot, the class that reflects
the dark side of the bigot's life. Just as the upper class
recognizes in lower-class lace-curtain morality the veiled
up-tightness of upper-middle-class life, so the lower-middle-class bigot sees reflected in the lower class the violence,
sexuality, and poverty that threaten him. The radical may
object that he dislikes the lower middle class purely because of its racism and its politics. But that is not sufficient
explanation: Polish jokes are devoid of political content.

Empirical studies do not show it, but it is my hunch that
shortly after Negro jokes became impossible in elite circles,
the Polish jokes emerged. They enjoy a continuing success
in universities even today. It also happens that while Frank
Zappa and the Mothers of Invention or Janis Joplin may
vie for top position in the hip radical affections, the cellar
of their affections—the object of their ample, healthy,
appropriate, unneurotic capacities for hatred—is securely

in the hands of that happy team of Mayor Daley and the Chicago police. Hip radicals in New Haven are often amused by the Italian Anti-Defamation League bumper sticker: "A.I.D.—Americans of Italian Descent." Poles, Italians, Mayor Daley, and the police are safe objects for amusement, derision, or hatred. They are all safely lower-middle-class.

Part of the vaunted moral development of college activists is their capacity for empathy—their ability to put themselves in the position of the Disadvantaged Other and to see the world from his circumstances. This theoretically leads them to empathize with ghetto blacks and therefore to distrust the authorities who oppress them. Unnoticed goes the fact that the "authorities" who get hated are the lower-middle-class police, the visible representatives of the more abstract and ambivalently regarded "power structure." Other favored targets for confrontation are the National Guard and the military, both bastions of the lower middle class. It is true that Dow Chemical representatives are attacked and that professors and university administrators are sometimes held captive. It is also true that the police, the National Guard, and the Army are the agents of societal racism, student and ghetto repression, and the war in Vietnam. But all these things should not blind us to the fact that the people toward whom bigotry, as well as political dislike, is directed by upper-class radicals are all too frequently lower-middle-class.

Radicals gloat over the faulty syntax of the lower middle class with the same predictability that they patronize the ghetto language as "authentic." They delight in Mayor Daley's malapropisms ("Chicago will move on to higher and higher platitudes of achievement") and in the lace-curtain cynicism of his denunciations: "They use language from the bordello, language that would shock any decent person." Why do they patronize one authenticity and mock another?

These upper-class attitudes are not a narrow phenomenon. *Time, Life,* and *Newsweek* print ghetto phrases in reverent spidery italics—surrounded by space to emphasize the authentic simplicity—beneath soulful pictures of the cleansing but terrible, terrible poverty of ghetto blacks or rural poor. They reprint Daley verbatim as the fool.

One of the strongest supports for this upper-class, "respectable" bigotry lies in the academic field of psychology. In much of what practitioners choose to investigate and interpret, cognitive capacity, moral development, and psychodynamic organization of lower-middle-class individuals are described as inferior to radical activities. Lower-middle-class people are more "authoritarian," more likely to have "closed" minds, more likely to rely on "law-and-order morality" rather than the more advanced "moral-principle orientation," and more likely to use "massive" ego-defenses such as repression instead of the more refined defenses like intellectualization and isolation. Lower-middle-class people are more likely to get stuck in a stage of "concrete cognitive operations" associated with low capacity for intellectual differentiation instead of advancing into "formal cognitive operations" with its high capacity for abstract thinking.

When George Wallace said his opponent was the kind of man who couldn't park a bicycle straight, he undoubtedly confirmed for a host of academic observers how concrete and primitive his concept of successful intellectual operations was.

Students in elite universities are described by psychologists as possessing many of the virtues that lower-middle-class authoritarians lack. These scholars frequently find that, among the elite students, radical activists have even greater moral and intellectual virtues than classmates from lower-class or more traditional families. If you examine the incidence of these virtues, they appear, not surprisingly, to cluster. It seems that psychologists are measuring something that has connected cognitive, moral, and ego-defensive manifestations. This something is related to class.

The academic yardsticks measure virtues that, as they are defined, appear most frequently in the children of elite psychologists and their classmates: in the children of the upper middle and upper class.

These virtues do seem to be the consequence of further (although not necessarily higher) development than the virtues of the lower middle class; that is, one must go through the developmentally prior lower-middle-class virtues to reach the elite virtues. Repression, obedience to law and prompt acceptance of authority are more "primitive" ways of dealing with reality than intellectualization, reflection on principles before obeying a law, and skepticism toward authority. One psychologist has urged that upper-class virtues are better in a Platonic sense than lower-middle-class virtues. It is revealing that he does not recall that Plato would undoubtedly have restricted the practice of upper-class virtues to the upper class in his city, arguing that in the interest of harmony other virtues must be required of the lower classes.

Should we believe that the psychologists have discovered an empirical basis for distinguishing between more and less developed men? Should we believe that the developed men are superior? We can start with two broad possibilities. Either "further development" is the artifact of class blindness, and upper-class development is merely different from lower-class development; or upper-class development is subsequent to lower-class development. I think the weight of the argument suggests the latter.

If we opt for this possibility, we must then ask whether

the further development is an achievement or a degeneration. Since this depends on our societal values, further choice is required: we can either compare directly the values of the further developed individual with the formal societal values or we can ask whether the survival of the formal societal values is enhanced by increasing the number of people whose personal values are similar to the formal values of the society.

This question forces us to be more specific about what we mean by the superiority of elite virtues in comparison with the virtues of the lower middle class. Recent analysts, lacking Plato's grasp of behavioral data and his rigorous empiricism, have been unrealistically idealistic in considering the consequences of changing a class distribution of virtues. That elite virtues are superior, Plato saw, does not mean that the society would be better or would even survive if all possessed them.

It may be that the lower-middle-class virtues provide operant support for a society that allows the upper class the luxury of elite virtues, much as Greek democracy was built on slave labor. I stress "operant support for American society" rather than "formal support of democracy" because the lower middle class is frequently denounced for disregarding formal democratic values such as regard for due process and for such freedoms as conscience, press, expression and movement.

Those who acclaim the elite radical virtues as superior to the virtues of the lower middle class would appear, if one admits that lower-class virtues provide operant support for American society, to have three alternatives. They can accept the distribution as necessary and good, in which case they espouse a troublesome elitism that cannot be reconciled with their radical views. Or they can argue that everyone should possess these virtues, in which case they are true radicals and should ask themselves whether they have considered in an unbiased light the implications of this position. Or they can do what I think most people do, which is largely to restrict—without admitting or even being conscious of the restriction—the practice of these superior virtues to the upper class.

The self-serving argument for upper-class hegemony then seems to be that the upper class is more intelligent, more moral, and more finely tuned in its ego-defenses than the lower class and that this makes it more fit to govern and to preserve such democratic values as equal access. But in the name of the preservation of these values, elite virtues must be denied to the lower class because their use would be disruptive. To preserve the society that guarantees access to power to those who are virtuous, we must deny the possession of virtue to the lower class and thus deny the access we are theoretically preserving.

Leaving aside the hard choices that a believer in the superiority of radical virtues must make, we can ask in broader perspective what alternative stances one may take if it is true that an upper-class background leads to further moral and intellectual development. They appear to be—

1. In the existing world a "further developed" man may govern worse rather than better. A principled orientation can be disastrous in world politics, as the principled architects of the cold war have shown. An ability to empathize may lead to concessions in negotiation that will be misread by the Other Side as blanket willingness to retreat when faced with force. Capacity to see issues in all their complexity may lead to Hamlet-like paralysis when any action would be preferable to none.

2. The further development of the upper class might make it best qualified to rule, as its *de facto* supremacy proves. In a roughly democratic framework there is a

chance for the few lower-class individuals who achieve upper-class virtues to rise to the top; that most leaders will be upper class by birth is necessary and even desirable to preserve social stability and to reduce the anxieties that result from situations of volatile status change.

3. Upper-class individuals are further developed than lower-class individuals, and it is an indictment of our resource-rich society that more people are not brought into these higher stages of development. Analyses claiming that this would destabilize society are too contingent to win credence; the destabilization, moreover, might result in a better society instead of a worse one.

4. This "further development" is development along a path that may lead to the overspecialization and extinction of the human race. It accepts the dubious values of a capitalist Calvinism and conceals assumptions about what constitutes higher development that are disastrous both for the individual and the species (and are rejected by the hippie culture). This building up of surplus repression in ever higher capacities for intellectualization destroys capacities for feeling, for activity, for love. Elephantiasis of intellect and atrophy of emotion are mirrored in American society, where our intellectual industry, technology, produces the antiballistic missile and the death-dealing gadgetry of Vietnam while our feelings are too atrophied to insist that the logic of our priorities is insane. There is the atrophy of individual sensation inherent in eating Wonder Bread, watching Johnny Carson, and smelling Right Guard.

These are a few of the attitude-policy alternatives that acceptance of the psychologists' findings could lead us to. The third and fourth arguments, which would appeal to liberals and radicals to varying degrees, have in common a disregard for the contributions of the lower-middle-class virtues to what is good as well as what is bad in American society. Let us now ask whether this disregard is based on close analysis of what American society would look like if we all possessed the "superior" elite values, or whether it is the result of an upper-class blindness toward what this might mean.

Operant supports of American society, conservatives and radicals agree, are very different from the formal democratic virtues that guarantee the procedures of a democratic policy. In the course of a brilliant denunciation of some mandarinic American political scientists, Noam Chomsky quotes Tocqueville: "I know of no country in which there is so little independence and freedom of mind as in America." Chomsky adds: "Free institutions certainly exist, but a tradition of passivity and conformism restricts their use—a cynic might say this is why they continue to exist."

Although radicals often condemn American society by juxtaposing the "traditional American virtues" of respect for democratic procedure with current breaches of those procedures, it seems probable that historically American justice was at least as pockmarked as it is today and that the lower-middle-class virtues are the real "traditional" supports that Tocqueville observed when he came to see how American democracy functioned.

These virtues—law-and-order morality, acceptance of authority, cognitive processes that present issues in broad terms, ego-defenses that prefer the violence of hockey to the savagery of the seminar table—undoubtedly play a part in whatever orderliness there is in daily American life. They help people accept and carry out decisions that affect them adversely. They help make football a high-salience issue and foreign affairs a low-salience issue, leaving the President, who should be in a better position to decide, a good deal of freedom from mass pressures. In a number of ways, one could argue, they account for what is good as well as bad in American life. Conversely, elite virtues may account for more of the bad aspects of American life than is usually assumed.

Some upper-class radicals, we suggested above, are able to assume that elite virtues are preferable to lower-middle-class virtues across the board because they unconsciously restrict their idea of who should practice these virtues and to what end. Radical students and ghetto blacks, within limits, are the groups from whom these people expect a moral-principle orientation rather than law-and-order morality. Blacks and students are expected to practice skepticism toward authority. If, on the other hand, the colonels, the police, teamsters, longshoremen, or garbage collectors practice prolonged skepticism toward constituted authority or act in accordance with their principles rather than in accordance with law-and-order morality, then the elite semiradicals have a vague sense that something must be done.

The upper class has reached a plateau of security from which its liberal-radical wing believes that it can mock the politics of the policeman and the butcher and slight their aspirations while still living genteelly in the space between them. I recall a personal example of how these assumptions sometimes work:

A few months ago some black children from the ghetto that is separated from Yale by the old people and students on my street made one of their biannual pilgrimages to Lake Place to break off all the aerials and windshield wipers on the cars. I was much more enraged the next morning about my car than I was about the distant and understandable riots that are filtered to me through *The New York Times*. I called the police largely, I suspect, because I wanted to be comforted by a typical policeman's observations on what-you-can-expect-from-*those*-kids. In my protected eastern existence I had never passed through an overtly racist stage. But sometimes I suspect I get satisfaction from the racism of others: they can say what I cannot even think, and since their racism is so vulgar, I get to feel superior to them in the bargain.

The policeman, a likely young Italian, arrived. After surveying the damage, he said: "Mr. Lerner, I know how you feel; but you've got to take into account the kind of environment in which those children were raised. I mean, if you or I lived in the places they have to live in or went through the same experiences, you can imagine . . ." I listened stunned. Here the man from whom I expected law-and-order morality was dishing out the moral-principled upper-class capacity to imagine oneself in the situation of the other. Like that of the unconsciously hypocritical radicals, my world depended on that kind of behavior being reserved for cocktail parties and seminars at which one comments from a discreet distance on the understandability of the behavior of ghetto blacks.

The hatreds do not go one way: ghetto blacks hate policemen, and policemen hate upper-class radicals. One hates one class up as well as one class down, although the hatred downward is more violent and the hatred upward mixed with aspiration. The natural alliance is between people a class apart who hate people in the middle for different reasons. This suggests why elite intellectuals, for all their analyzed self-awareness, show immediate "understanding" for the ghetto black's hatred of the policeman yet find police violence directed at a partially upper-class political demonstration a sure sign of incipient fascism.

Examine, on the other hand, the quality of the class-apart empathy radical whites have for ghetto blacks. The radicals are upper-middle-class youths with life histories of intellectual overcontrol. They have reached a point in their lives where, as Erik Erikson suggests, they can experiment with a little controlled regression-in-the-service-of-the-ego.

The response of a permissive upper-class parent, as reflected in *The New York Times,* is, "Society may have a great deal to learn from the hippies." Translated into jargon this might read: "Upper-class psychological controls may be too strict for changing psychosexual-social-historical realities. The young people experimenting with controlled regression may be showing the way in politics, drugs, and sex to a new synthesis."

From the point of view of the young people *doing* the experimenting, the value is diminished if anyone stresses the "controlled" or even experimental nature of their quest. The regression or the liberation from overcontrol is what matters. To them the lowest class shows—by fact or projective romanticization or both—a life-style characterized by open use of the violence, sexuality, and drugs that the experimenters find appealing.

The authenticity that the experimenters sense in the ghetto derives from the fact that lower-class violence and sexuality are not a consequence of tentative and strained regression in the service of the ego but represent a normal and stable class pattern deriving from social conditions, tension levels, and prevalent primitive ego-defense organizations.

When elite intellectuals urge that authentic black life-styles not be contaminated by bourgeois values, they are asking that blacks not lose temporarily the values whites lost temporarily in the process of becoming elite. In other words, the old path is from lower-class undercontrol to lower-middle-class overcontrol to the upper-class luxury of reducing controls again. Upper-class whites like to think blacks can move from undercontrol to the partial control pattern that *they* find most socially pleasing without the middle step. They do not realize partial control is usually a step taken from the strength of a background of increasingly sophisticated and differentiated overcontrol.

This self-centeredness is reflected in the programs organized for the education of blacks by upper-class whites and by blacks who have assumed university values. These programs usually stress a freedom and lack of controls that is appropriate to the fantasies of their organizers but scarcely appropriate to those who have only had ghetto experience. It is no wonder that programs organized by lower-class blacks without the funding and guidance of whites—such as the Black Muslim program for narcotics addicts, and Black Muslim educational programs in general—stress that ghetto people must learn the capacity for tight control that has characterized Mayor Daley and every other individual and group that has competed successfully in American society.

Since lower-middle-class police are repelled by the uncontrolledness of the lower class from which their families have escaped, they are understandably infuriated by the regression to violence, drugs, and sexuality in the class that expects their deference. The radical students and hippies are rejecting the values to which the lower middle class aspires and by which it is able to repress the behavior that the students are flaunting at it. When a Yippie girl pulls up her skirt in front of a lower-middle-class policeman and tells him that his trouble is that he has not had what she is baring in front of his face, one cannot expect an academically oriented response. And since every cocktail-party psychologist would expect the police to be authoritarian, low in capacity for differentiation, and scarcely able to maintain through primitive repression the violence in himself, why is the reaction to the police riot in Chicago so unbelievably un-understanding? Why do we expect that hippies and radicals and ghetto blacks can experiment with nonrestraint while the police must be models of restraint? Why can so few empathize with the frustrations of lower-middle-class life that have led to Chicago, to George Wallace, and ultimately to the Presidency of Richard Nixon? It is because of the really astounding bigotry and narrowness of a class that prides itself on ridding itself of racism and having a broad perspective. There is little broad perspective in the words of the *Times* columnist who wrote in shocked tones, "Those were *our* children on the streets of Chicago." That *Times* columnist and the hip radicals did not understand a nation that approved of the police action in Chicago because its children were in the streets of Chicago too. Its children were the police.

Racism and bigotry toward black people is frighteningly apparent at Yale. But at least the sore has been lanced and lies open. We can be aware of the ugly strains of societal racism still inside ourselves and our institutions, and we can struggle against them.

The hidden, liberal-radical bigotry toward the lower middle class is stinking and covered. When a right-wing Italian announced for mayor in New York, a brilliant professor in New Haven said, "If Italians aren't actually an inferior race, they do the best imitation of one I've seen." Everyone at the dinner table laughed. He could not have said that about black people if the subject had been Rap Brown.

The consequences of this bigotory are tragic. It would be less serious if it were not the product of an intellectually self-righteous class that is trying to provide functioning, *electable* alternatives to Richard Nixon and George Wallace. Those dissimilar men had the common intelligence and capacity for empathy—or shrewdness—to appeal to a genuinely forgotten and highly abused segment of the American population. It may be that only when radical intellectuals begin to show again, as they did in the 1930's, empathy for the hardships of lower-middle-class life and begin to integrate the aspirations of that class into their antiwar, antiracism framework, will it be possible to break up the Nixon alliance. Not until the upper middle class learns to deal with its own hidden bigotry will it be in a position to help destroy lower-middle-class bigotry as well.

By Rudolph J. Vecoli

Ethnicity:
A Neglected Dimension
of American History

TWENTIETH-CENTURY sociological literature is replete with notices of the imminent demise of ethnicity in America. In 1945, W. Lloyd Warner declared: "The future of American ethnic groups seems to be limited; it is likely that they will be quickly absorbed." A decade later, Will Herberg confirmed that ethnicity, if not dead, was rapidly dying. These epitaphs to ethnicity, like Mark Twain's obituary, have turned out to be premature. Recent events have shattered the assumption that the melting pot has worked its cultural alchemy. Ethnicity, by which I mean group consciousness based on a sense of common origin, has demonstrated renewed vitality in the second half of the twentieth century.

Clearly this resurgence of ethnic consciousness, this "new tribalism," springs from deep-seated social and psychic needs. The "Black Revolution" appears to have served as a catalyst, energizing other groups to both defensive and emulative responses. Just as in Canada, where the French nationalist movement has spurred Slavs and others

Reprinted from *The State of American History,* edited by Herbert J. Bass. Copyright © 1970 by Quadrangle Books, Inc. Used by permission of Quadrangle Books, Inc. The notes documenting this article in its original publication have been deleted here with the permission of the author.

to assert themselves, so black militancy has elicited responding ethnic nationalisms. "Black Power" brings forth echoes of "Irish Power," "Polish Power," and so forth. Inspired by the example of black Americans, white ethnics tend to see themselves engaged in an analogous struggle for liberation from the stigma and burden of inferiority.

Only the true believer can any longer sustain his vision of America as a "homogeneous society of undifferentiated men" where race, religion, or national origin do not matter. The inability to transmute twenty million blacks into the "historic American type" raised questions about how well the country's digestive system had worked in the past. Once the conspiracy of silence was broken, it became quickly apparent that it had worked only imperfectly if at all. Nathan Glazer and Daniel Patrick Moynihan were the first to say so: "The point about the melting pot is that it did not happen." As behavioral scientists have renewed their explorations of ethnic America, they have found the historical literature on the subject to be thin indeed. Charging that historians have failed to do their job, social scientists grumble that they have to do their own historical research on ethnic groups.

Sad to say, historians *have* neglected the dimension of ethnicity in the American past. We have been made dramatically aware of our deficiency in this respect by the sudden and widespread demand for minority history courses. The most pressing demand, of course, is for Afro-American history. History departments which would have scoffed at the notion a few years ago are now recruiting *black* Afro-American historians. Unfortunately, much of the contemporary concern with minority-group history is politically inspired rather than derived from an honest conviction of its inherent value as a field of study.

Clearly the historical profession has a responsibility to

maintain the integrity of scholarly standards, to prevent the perversion of history into special pleading, and to seek the advancement of knowledge beyond the pragmatic needs of the moment. Our ability to meet our professional responsibility, however, is crippled by our knowledge that we are morally compromised. Who, if not the historian, is responsible for the fact that lily-white and racist history has been imbibed by generations of students? Our sense of guilt has stimulated more breast-beating than hard thinking.

I suggest that a searching examination of the reasons for our failure would be more fruitful. Why has the history of the United States *not* been written in terms of the enormous diversity of race, culture, and religion that has characterized the American people from the seventeenth century until today? My answer will be phrased in terms of the historiography of European immigration; others better able than I can address themselves to the neglect of the history of Afro-Americans and other racial groups. What I have to say on this score is not meant as castigation of our professional forebears; rather, it is largely an exercise of self-criticism.

A joint committee of the American Historical Association and the Organization of American Historians recently issued a statement on "The Writing and Teaching of American History in Textbooks," which declared that the diversity of the American people "must be faithfully portrayed." By and large, the portrayal of this diversity has been an ideal to which we have paid lip service rather than a task to which we have addressed ourselves. A casual perusal of college and high school textbooks reveals that the factor of ethnic pluralism is not effectively presented. Aside from clichés about "a nation of immigrants" and "the melting pot," textbooks convey the impression of bland homogeneity. An unspoken assumption of American historiography has been that the important things have been said and done only by English-speaking whites. Negroes have not been the only "invisible men" in American history. Immigrants, Indians, and Hispanos have also usually appeared in the history books as faceless masses.

Nor are college students any more likely to be exposed to the "facts of life" about ethnicity. A survey of course offerings in one hundred colleges and universities revealed that thirty-eight offered courses touching some aspect of ethnic history; of these, twenty were general social and cultural history courses, nineteen Afro-American history courses, four American Indian history courses, and four immigration history courses. More than 60 percent of the institutions did not offer any course dealing directly with the history of group life in America. One cannot derive much comfort from the fact that sociology departments customarily offer courses in "American Minorities" or "Racial and Ethnic Relations." A recent review of such courses concluded that few of them provided a systematic analysis of group interaction, either historical or contemporary. Rather, they tended to concentrate on prejudice and discrimination, and to substitute moral indignation for a critical assessment of the subject.

But, I am assured, the field of immigration history appears to be flourishing today. After all, one can think at a moment's notice of ten or twenty excellent monographs which have appeared in recent years. I am not about to belittle the significant accomplishments of the historians of immigration, of which tribe I proudly claim membership, but my reading of the current state of health of this specialty is less sanguine. Despite the significant work of some very able historians, the study of immigration has been and remains an underdeveloped field of historical inquiry.

A generous estimate of the current number of American

historians who have a major interest in immigration history would be two hundred, or perhaps 2 percent of those now teaching American history at collegiate institutions. An analysis of doctoral dissertations in immigration history further suggests that this theme has been peripheral to the concerns of most American historians. Between 1893 (the year a student of Frederick Jackson Turner's completed the first dissertation on an immigration topic) and 1965, a total of 127 Ph.D. dissertations related to American immigration have been written. Of these, 9 percent were completed by 1925; another 35 percent between 1926 and 1945; and 56 percent between 1946 and 1965. That more than half of these dissertations have been written since 1946 might at first suggest that immigration study is booming, but the apparent upsurge merely reflects the general increase in the output of dissertations. Actually the percentage of history dissertations devoted to immigration-related topics has fluctuated around 1.5 percent of the total for three quarters of a century.

A topical analysis of the dissertations further reveals those large gaps in the literature of which immigration historians are only too aware. The great majority of the dissertations deal with the time period 1790 to 1920. Only four dissertations concentrate on the post-1920 era. This reflects the curious assumption that the history of immigration ends with the enactment of the restrictive legislation of the twenties. Most of the dissertations focus upon a particular immigrant group. The Jews, Irish, and Germans have received the most attention, with the Scandinavians, Italians, and Chinese lagging some distance behind. For dozens of other groups there is only a smattering of studies. As one might expect, the published literature reflects these lacunae.

Yet even if we had a library of competent studies of

each of the immigrant groups, this would not add up to a history of ethnicity in America. To paraphrase Clemenceau, ethnicity is too important to be left to the immigration historians. If, as has been claimed, ethnicity is one of the strongest influences in America today, how much more true this must have been in the past. It is difficult to conceive of any institution which has not been profoundly affected by the ethnic factor. Still, we have had histories of American cities, labor movements, religious denominations, politics, and schools in which the immigrants and their children appear merely as residents, workers, parishioners, voters, and pupils. The fact that they also were, as the case might be, Polish Catholics, Welsh Methodists, Eastern Rite Ukrainians, Greek Orthodox, Swedish Lutherans, or one of a multitude of other ethnic identities is not treated as being significant. That the history of a society whose distinctive attribute has been its racial, cultural, linguistic, and religious pluralism should have been written for the most part from an Anglo-American monistic perspective is indeed a paradox.

Two "explanations" are often advanced for the dearth of ethnic historical studies. One is the alleged language barrier. American students, it is said, lack the linguistic skills to undertake research on such exotic groups as Romanians and Croatians. John K. Fairbank gave the proper response to this objection: "The problem here is not: What languages do we read? The problem is: What is our intellectual and historical horizon?" When the profession places a correct evaluation upon ethnic studies, students will acquire the necessary linguistic facility.

The second objection has to do with the alleged lack of significant bodies of historical records for ethnic groups. Even historians who should know better speak of the "inarticulate nationalities." Such notions derive from the stereotype of the immigrants as uniformly illiterate peasants. Far from being inarticulate, the ethnic groups generated a vast amount of documentation. In 1910 more than a thousand newspapers and periodicals were being published in the United States in other than the English language. Immigration probably raised the volume of communication among the "common people" to its highest level in history. Consider the hundreds of millions of letters that have crossed the ocean both ways. Unfortunately, American libraries and archives have generally not troubled themselves with the collection of non-English-language materials. Only in recent years have systematic and successful efforts been made to gather the records of immigrant groups. Rich, untapped collections await the student of ethnic America.

I believe there are two basic reasons why American historians have neglected the dimension of ethnicity. One has to do with the prevailing ideology of the academic profession; the other with its sociology.

A prime article of the American creed has been a profound confidence in the power of the New World to transform human nature. Even the "wretched refuse" of Europe was to be transmuted by the irresistible combination of the natural environment and republican institutions. The classic statement of the doctrine of Americanization was pronounced by the Frenchman Hector St. John Crèvecoeur:

> He is an American, who, leaving behind him all his ancient prejudices and manners, receives new ones from the new mode of life he has embraced, the new government he obeys, and the new rank he holds. Here individuals of all nations are melted into a new race of men, whose labours and posterity will one day cause great changes in the world.

The belief in a "new race of men" created in the crucible of democracy became axiomatic to the conception of an American nationality. How else were Americans to emerge from the confusion of tongues, faiths, and races? But as Crèvecoeur pointed out, the immigrant must be stripped of "all his ancient prejudices and manners" in order to become a "new man." Rapid and total assimilation thus came to be regarded as natural, inevitable, and desirable.

A review of immigration scholarship reveals how pervasive and powerful the grip of the assimilationist ideology has been. It was the generation of progressive historians that first addressed itself to the study of immigration as a significant factor in American history. Imbued with the reform spirit of their time, they viewed American history as a process of struggle and growth toward a democratic order. Since, in such a society, differences of race, religion, and nationality were to be inconsequential, the progressive view demanded that the eradication of these "foreign" attributes be the theme of immigration history.

Frederick Jackson Turner and Charles A. Beard were the giants who towered over this generation of historians. Both were environmental determinists who stressed the primacy of economic forces, although, of course, with a difference. Turner was perhaps the first to call attention to the need for the study of immigration. When Turner delivered his frontier thesis, in language reminiscent of Crèvecoeur, he described the impact of the wilderness upon the European: "In the crucible of the frontier the immigrants were Americanized, liberated, and fused into a mixed race, English in neither nationality or characteristics." For Turner, the frontier was "the line of the most rapid and effective Americanization."

The historians who established immigration history as a field of study after World War I were almost to a man

Turnerians. Their basic concepts were those of the frontier and the section, and their theme was that of the adaptation of Old World cultures to New World environments. Like Turner, they were Midwesterners, but unlike him they were sons of German and Scandinavian immigrants. The works of Theodore Blegen on the Norwegians, George Stephenson on the Swedes, and Carl Wittke on the Germans are enduring accomplishments of this generation of immigration historians. But an aura of nostalgia lingers over their books; the "culture in immigrant chests" seemed destined to be buried with the first generation. "Americanization," Wittke observed, "moved irresistibly onward."

Marcus Lee Hansen, while of similar background, was able to transcend some of the limitations which characterized the work of his contemporaries. Rather than focusing on a particular nationality, Hansen took all of European emigration as his province and related it to the full sweep of American history. A student of Turner, Hansen expanded the impact of the frontier to European society. He urged the study of the "immigrant communities in America that formed the human connecting link between the Old World and the New." Despite such original insights, Hansen was fundamentally a Turnerian. In 1938 he told the Augustana Historical Society that "it is the ultimate fate of any national group to be amalgamated into the composite American race."

While many aspects of Turner's frontier hypothesis have been criticized in recent years, his proposition that the American environment profoundly transformed the immigrant has gone practically unchallenged. If the standard text on the westward movement now acknowledges the persistence of European traits as "equally" important with free land in shaping the nation, it also reiterates the Americanizing influence of the frontier and contains only a handful of references to specific ethnic groups. Certain recent elaborations of the Turner thesis, by David M. Potter, George W. Pierson, and Daniel Boorstin, are agreed upon an environmental explanation of national character. Intent upon establishing the homogeneity of the American people, they share a common neglect of sources of diversity such as immigration.

It remained for Merle Curti, a student of Turner, to translate the frontier thesis from an ideological pronouncement into a verifiable historical statement. In his pioneering work, *The Making of an American Community*, Curti utilized quantitative as well as qualitative data to determine whether the frontier indeed made for democracy and Americanization. Curti concluded that at least in Trempeleau County conditions did promote an equalization of opportunity and condition between the native- and the foreign-born. I think it significant, however, that no effort as such was made to measure the persistence of ethnicity.

That Turnerian determinism is far from being exhausted was demonstrated by the appearance in 1968 of a book entitled *The Immigrant Upraised*. A history of Italians in the trans-Mississippi West, it depicts them as aspiring yeoman-farmers drawn by the magnet of virgin land. Contrasting their condition to that of degraded sweatshop workers and organ-grinders in the eastern cities, the author asserts that the Western Italians achieved ready acceptance, rapid assimilation, and "success in the sun." In his foreword to the volume, Ray Allen Billington hails it as preparing the way for a completely new interpretation of immigration history.

If the faith of the Turnerians in the liberating effects of the Western environment was unshakable, they were less optimistic about the future of the immigrant masses in the industrial cities. It is significant that no one of them, not even Hansen, effectively addressed himself to this phase of immigration history. Turner, himself, was distinctly uncomfortable in discussing the Irish and other immigrants in the eastern cities. He doubted whether the melting pot could work under such circumstances and whether the denizens of the ethnic ghettos could be transformed into "the historic American type."

For Charles Beard the triumph of industrial capitalism was the main theme of *The Rise of American Civilization*. But Beard did not concern himself with the issues of assimilation or ethnicity. Viewed as "economic men," the immigrants simply played out their appointed roles in the scenarios of class conflict. As Lee Benson has pointed out, Beard did not even consider the variable of ethnic affiliation as a possible determinant of political behavior. For the followers of the Beardian-Marxist interpretation of American history, economic class was the only meaningful social category. Such a crude economic determinism was not conducive to an appreciation of the subtle play of ethnic influences.

It remained for a sociologist to develop a theory of assimilation which would comprehend the immigrant in an urban setting. Robert Ezra Park was perhaps the most influential student of racial and ethnic relations in twentieth-century America. A close observer of immigrant life, Park was early persuaded that the country could digest "every sort of normal human difference, except the purely external ones, like the color of the skin." Impressed by the ease and rapidity with which the immigrants acquired the language and customs, Park declared in 1913: "In America it has become proverbial that a Pole, Lithuanian, or Norwegian cannot be distinguished, in the second generation, from an American born of native parents." In 1926,

Park summed up his thinking about the process of acculturation:

> The race relations cycle which takes the form . . . of
> contacts, competition, accommodation, and eventual assimilation, is apparently progressive and irreversible. Customs regulations, immigration restrictions, and racial barriers may slacken the tempo of the movement; may
> perhaps halt it altogether for a time; but cannot change
> its direction; cannot, at any rate, reverse it.

Thus for Park and his followers assimilation was foreordained and unilinear.

Rather than posing an obstacle to assimilation, the city was Park's melting pot par excellence. For Park the impact of the city was quite similar to that of Turner's frontier; it broke the "cake of custom" and emancipated the individual. If this experience was painful and traumatic, Park left no doubt that he thought this price for individual freedom was worth paying. Within his theoretical scheme of urban ecology, Park associated spatial movements with cultural change. The process of assimilation was conceptualized in terms of physical mobility through successive zones of settlement. The movement of the immigrants outward from the ghetto culminated in their final absorption into the larger society. Where Turner had faltered, Park succeeded in expanding the assimilationist ideology to encompass the immigrants of urban industrial America.

Scholarship on racial and ethnic groups was also profoundly influenced by the rise of cultural anthropology —and particularly by the work of Franz Boas. The rejection of "scientific racism" and the establishment of the primacy of culture as the determinant of human behavior were obviously of fundamental importance to the study of ethnicity. But when anthropologists turned to the study of ethnic groups in modern America, their much-vaunted "cultural relativism" failed to immunize them against the assimilationist faith. Margaret Mead, herself a student of Boas, depicted the generational changes between immigrants and their children as involving a complete break and acculturation to the "American Way of Life" on the part of the second generation.

Fresh from field work among the Australian aborigines, W. Lloyd Warner descended upon Yankee City in the early 1930's. Among the subjects he investigated was ethnicity. His findings were reported in *The Social Systems of American Ethnic Groups*. Although it contains detailed descriptions of ethnic subcultures, the data are arranged within a Parkian theoretical framework. The various immigrant groups are depicted as moving along a continuum from peasant village culture to modern urban culture. Residential, occupational, and social-class indices are used to measure their movement up the escalator of social mobility toward total assimilation. Anthropologists thus proved to be just as susceptible to the ethnocentric appeal of the assimilation creed as other social scientists.

American historians, of course, were influenced by the significant work being done in the social sciences. In 1932 a committee of the American Historical Association on the planning of research urged historians to avail themselves of the new insights being developed in anthropology, psychology, and sociology. The report of the Eastern Conference on American History cited as one neglected area of research the history of race relations and of race acculturation. Not until 1939, however, were social scientific concepts explicitly brought to bear on the historical study of ethnic groups. At the American Historical Association meeting that year, Caroline F. Ware presented a paper on "Cultural Groups in the United States." She noted the neglect by American historians of ethnic groups that deviated from the dominant literate culture. Observing that the interaction of the immigrants with the modern city was creating a new industrial culture, she concluded: "In the still unexplored history of the nondominant cultural groups of the industrial cities lies the story of an emerging industrial culture that represents the dynamic cultural frontier of modern America." Unfortunately, Ware's manifesto was heeded by too few. Three decades later the industrial culture of modern America remains largely "unexplored history."

A significant breakthrough came with the publication in 1941 of Oscar Handlin's *Boston's Immigrants: A Study in Acculturation.* Informed by the insights of anthropology and sociology, the book expertly delineated the impact of immigration upon the culture, economy, ecology, and social structure of Boston. With the exception of the Irish, the newcomers assimilated readily. But the group consciousness and cohesion of the Irish were intensified by the bitter conflicts between them and the "others." From contacts of dissimilar cultures emerged an ethnic pluralism which left Boston a divided city. Here then was no tale of rapid, easy assimilation.

For several decades, Handlin has been the primary exponent, exemplar, and teacher of the history of American ethnicity. In essays and books, he has chronicled and championed cultural pluralism in American life. While acknowledging the ugliness of group hostility and prejudice, Handlin has contended that in a chaotic world, ethnic identity provides a much-needed source of stability and order.

Handlin, however, is best known for *The Uprooted,* and this work has had the greatest influence on the thinking of historians and social scientists. The theme of *The Up-*

rooted is the utter devastation of culture by environment. The immigrant is deracinated because none of his traditional forms of thought and behavior can be transplanted. Its grim environmental determinism places *The Uprooted* squarely in the tradition of Turner and Park. For all of them, the physical voyage from the Old World to the New was also a sociological journey from the traditional to the modern, from the sacred to the secular, from *Gemeinschaft* to *Gesellschaft*. Paradoxically, Handlin, who more than any other historian has advanced the study of ethnicity, in his most influential work reinforced the assimilationist ideology.

Ethnicity in American historiography has remained something of a family scandal, to be kept a dark secret or explained away. Even those historians who have dealt with the theme in a competent fashion have felt obliged to apologize for its existence. Ethnic studies thus have long suffered from the blight of the assimilationist ideology. Because of their expectations that assimilation was to be swift and irresistible, historians and social scientists have looked for change rather than continuity, acculturation rather than cultural maintenance. Since ethnicity was thought to be evanescent, it was not considered worth studying.

The sociology of the academic profession may provide yet another clue to the neglect of ethnicity. Although the shift from the patrician to the professional historian had a democratizing effect on historical study, the first generation of Ph.D.'s still tended to be drawn from middle-class Protestants of old stock. It is not surprising that interest in immigration history during this period was minimal, or that a nativist bias pervaded much that was written.

The sons of northern and western European immigrants began to enter the profession in the twenties and thirties.

Some of them devoted themselves to writing the history of their particular ethnic groups, but scholarly work on the "new immigration" was practically nonexistent. Few offspring of southern and eastern European parentage were as yet able to avail themselves of the academic profession as a ladder of upward mobility. One reason, as E. Digby Baltzell has noted, was that until the 1940's the major universities continued to be the preserve of old-stock Protestants. It has not been very long since certain history departments as a matter of policy did not hire Catholics or Jews, to say nothing of Negroes.

Since World War II, with the boom in higher education, the walls of ethnic exclusion around the groves of academe have come tumbling down. As a result there has been a significant influx of second- and third-generation Americans, many of them of Catholic and Jewish origin, into the historical profession. Yet there has been no out-pouring of ethnic studies by these sons and grandsons of immigrants. Why is this so?

Higher education in America has been one of the most effective agencies of acculturation (or, to use Joshua Fishman's term, "de-ethnization"). Its primary function, as Baltzell has observed, has been to assimilate talented youth from all segments of society to the Anglo-American core culture. College students of ethnic background therefore are prime candidates to become marginal men. For those who choose academic careers, the university may represent an escape from ethnicity. Milton Gordon has suggested that these "marginally ethnic intellectuals" constitute a distinct "transethnic" subsociety. Be that as it may, the second- and third-generation scholars do assimilate the academic ethos; they dedicate themselves to the life of the mind and the rule of reason. As emancipated intellectuals they reject the narrow parochialisms and tribal loyalties of their youth. The responses of certain academic men of Italian descent to an invitation to participate in a study of the Italian-American ethnic group illustrate this state of mind:

> I am too concerned with trying to erase all national boundaries—and nationalisms—to be enthusiastic about activities delineating any national groups.
> I do not believe there is room for an Italian minority. I suggest that Italians or persons of Italian origin have no recourse but to merge into the majority.

Here we have the interesting phenomenon of the intellectual who not only rejects ethnic membership for himself but denies the validity of ethnicity for all others as well.

The de-ethnization of scholars is related to the larger process whereby the most able individuals of ethnic origin have been systematically assimilated into the Establishment. This "brain drain" inevitably has had a major impact on the life of ethnic groups. Presumably it has deprived them of potential leadership and contributed to their cultural impoverishment. The estrangement of many intellectuals from their ethnic roots may have something to do with their alienation from popular culture, while the widespread anti-intellectualism among ethnic Americans may reflect their resentment of those aloof professors whom they regard as traitors and Uncle Toms. Many ethnic groups sponsor historical societies which attempt to record in a more or less scholarly fashion the role and contribution of their particular element to American history. These efforts have not been generally viewed in a kindly fashion by professional historians. But it has been the "standoffish" attitude of historians of ethnic origin which has been most resented. The Polish American Historical Association *Bulletin* recently complained about professional historians of Polish background who remained distant from the organization: "Why are they not members? Are they academic snobs who are so ambitious that they do not want identification with 'an ethnic group'?" Such academic snobbery, if such it is, is regrettable. For the cultivation of ethnic history might serve as one of the much-needed bridges between the university ghetto and the ethnic ghetto.

In addition, the academic milieu has generally not encouraged the pursuit of ethnic interests. How many graduate students have shied away from research topics for fear they would be suspected of ethnic chauvinism? And historians of ethnic origin have on occasion been reminded of their marginal status. A few years ago, the president of the American Historical Association commented: "Many of the younger practitioners of our craft, and those who are still apprentices, are products of lower-middle-class or foreign origins, and their emotions not infrequently get in the way of historical reconstruction. They find themselves in a very real sense outsiders on *our past* and feel themselves shut out." Filio-piety, as anyone who has read any American history knows, has not been peculiar to ethnic historians, yet they have been particularly suspect.

For a variety of reasons, therefore, the recruitment of scholars of ethnic background has not, by and large, had the fruitful consequences for historical study that one might have anticipated. Those who deliberately dissociate themselves from their group ties often reject at the conscious level any suggestion of lingering ethnic loyalty. But it has been suggested that their repressed ethnicity manifests itself in a sublimated fashion. Although we claim to be free of primordial ties based on race, religion, or nation, yet we have tended to identify with "the underdogs and disinherited in modern society." In our history as well as our politics, we have often championed the causes of "captive groups." A consideration of the ethnic backgrounds of white historians of black America lends substance to the notion of sublimation of ethnicity. Can it be, as Melvin M. Tumin has suggested, that we have "used our hard-won freedom from the enmeshment of our own primary groups with all their irrationalities only to be adopted into the equally disenabling and restricting network of other primary group loyalties? Can it be that we cannot bear to be without primary group loyalties, causes, and missions?"

Whatever the answer to that particular question, it is not my intention to promote the study of ethnicity as a "cause" or "mission." I do not conceive of historical scholarship as a form of advocacy or therapy, nor am I suggesting that historians of ethnic origin should necessarily devote themselves to the study of their groups. I think the doctrine that only the individual of a particular ethnic or racial background can "understand" the history of "his people" is pernicious. Often the "outsider" can bring to the subject certain perspectives which are denied to the "insider." The historian of ethnicity, whatever his origin, must, if he would remain true to his calling, eschew the role of advocate, no matter how noble the cause, in order to pursue the truth wherever it may lead him.

There are signs that the long winter of neglect of ethnicity is coming to an end. Perhaps the surest indication of spring is that publishers are scurrying about seeking to sign up authors for ethnic and minority history series. More solid assurances have come from the increasing number of books and articles by historians and others which deal competently with the ethnic factor. There is evidence that the heightened pluralism of society is being mirrored in a new scholarly interest in the sources of diversity. American historians are beginning to free themselves from their compulsive obsession with assimilation.

At this particular juncture of our national history, we have an urgent need for a clear-eyed scholarship of ethnicity. What the historian can best contribute is a realistic perspective on the dynamics of ethnic group life and interaction. In place of a homogenized American history, he must portray the complex variety of racial, religious, and cultural groups living together in conflict and concord. Our current concern with Afro-American history should not be allowed to obscure the larger whole of which it is a part. Certainly the racial polarization of which the National Advisory Commission on Civil Disorders warned— "two societies, one black, one white"—should not be projected into the past. Such an interpretation of American history would be a serious distortion of reality, ignoring as it would the class as well as ethnic factors which have been and remain important sources of differences among whites. The historian of ethnicity has the responsibility of insisting upon a pluralistic rather than a dichotomized view of the past.

An appreciation of our own diversity should not only enable us to deal more intelligently with group conflict at home; it should also permit us to relate more realistically to the rest of the world. Professor Fairbank has recently suggested that our survival may hinge upon our ability "to get a truer and multivalued, because multicultural, perspective on the world crisis." The arrogant assumption of the unquestionable superiority of the "American way of life" which underlies the assimilationist ideology is, I submit, an insuperable obstacle to such a world view. A recent statement by Senator Richard Russell, of Georgia, for example, expressed the ethnocentric doctrine of 100 percent Americanism in its starkest form. Commenting on the possibility of nuclear war, the Senator said: "If we have to start over again with another Adam and Eve, I want them to be Americans; and I want them on this continent and not in Europe." A candid recognition that the melting pot did not work, that we remain a congeries of peoples, that there are *many* American ways of life rather than *one*, might help us to discard our notion of ourselves as a "chosen people" and to affirm our common humanity with the rest of mankind.

By Daniel Patrick Moynihan

A Memorandum
to the President-Elect
January 3, 1969

BEFORE THE STORM BREAKS, as it were, on the 20th, I
would like to send in a few extended comments on
some of the longer-range issues that face you, but will
tend, I should imagine, to get lost in the daily succession
of crises.

I would like to speak first of the theme "Forward Together."

This appeal was much in evidence in your very fine
acceptance speech at Miami, and during the campaign
the logic of events, and your own sure sense of them,
brought it forward ever more insistently.

In the end it was the theme of the campaign and, in
the aftermath of victory, it stands as the most explicit
mandate you have from the American people. I would
hope it might be the theme of your Administration as
well.

It has fallen to you to assume the governance of a
deeply divided country. And to do so with a divided government. Other Presidents—Franklin Roosevelt, for example—have taken office in moments of crisis, but the

Text of a memorandum dated January 3, 1969, to the President-elect from
his chief adviser on urban affairs. Reprinted with the permission of
Daniel Patrick Moynihan. From *The New York Times*, March 11, 1970.

crises were so widely perceived as in a sense to unite the country and to create a great outpouring of support for the President as the man who would have to deal with the common danger.

Neither Lincoln nor Wilson, the two predecessors whose situations most resembled yours, in terms of the popular vote and the state of then current political questions, had any such fortune. No one would now doubt that they proved to be two of our greatest leaders, nor yet that their Administrations achieved great things. But, alas, at what cost to themselves.

Common Element Sought

A divided nation makes terrible demands on the President. It would seem important to try to anticipate some of them, at least, and to ponder whether there is not some common element in each that might give a measure of coherence and unity to the President's own responses and, by a process of diffusion, to provide a guide for the Administration as a whole.

I believe there is such a common element. In one form or another all of the major domestic problems facing you derive from the erosion of the authority of the institutions of American society. This is a mysterious process of which the most that can be said is that once it starts it tends not to stop.

It can be stopped: The English, for example, managed to halt and even reverse the process in the period, roughly, 1820 to 1840. But more commonly, those in power neglect the problem at first and misunderstand it later; concessions come too late and are too little; the failure of concessions leads to equally unavailing attempts at repression; and so events spiral downward toward instability.

The process is little understood. (Neither is the opposite and almost completely ignored phenomenon: Some societies—Mexico in the 1920's—seem almost suddenly to become stabilized after periods of prolonged and seemingly hopeless chaos.)

All we know is that the sense of institutions being legitimate—especially the institutions of government—is the glue that holds societies together. When it weakens, things come unstuck.

Contrast in People

The North Vietnamese see this clearly enough. Hence the effort through the subtleties of seating arrangements to establish the N.L.F. as an independent regime, and the Saigon Government as a puppet one.

In contrast, Americans, until presently at least, have not been nearly so concerned with such matters. American society has been so stable for so long that the prospect of instability has had no very great meaning for us. (As I count, there are but nine nations that both existed as independent nations in 1914 and have not had their form of government changed by invasion or revolution since.)

Moreover, we retain a tradition of revolutionary rhetoric that gives an advantage to those who challenge authority rather than those who uphold it. Too little heed is given the experience of the twentieth century in which it has been the authority of democratic institutions that has been challenged by totalitarians of the left and the right.

Even the term "authority" has acquired for many a sinister cast, largely, one suspects, from its association with the term "authoritarian." Yet it remains the case that relationships based on authority are consensual ones: That is to say, they are based on common agreement to behave in certain ways.

It is said that freedom lives in the interstices of authority. When the structure collapses, freedom disappears, and society is governed by relationships based on power.

Increasing numbers of Americans seem of late to have sensed this, and to have become actively concerned about the drift of events. Your election was in a sense the first major consequence of that mounting concern. Your Administration represents the first significant opportunity to change the direction in which events move.

Your task, then, is clear: To restore the authority of American institutions. Not, certainly, under that name, but with a clear sense that what is at issue is the continued acceptance by the great mass of the people of the legitimacy and efficacy of the present arrangements of American society, and of our processes for changing those arrangements.

For that purpose, the theme "Forward Together" responds not only to the deepest need of the moment, but also, increasingly, to a clearly perceived need, as the facts of disunity more and more impress themselves on the nation's consciousness.

What has been pulling us apart? One wishes one knew. Yet there are a number of near- and long-term developments that can be discerned and surely contribute significantly to what is going on.

Of the near-term events, the two most conspicuous are the Negro revolution and the war in Vietnam. Although seemingly unrelated, they have much in common as to origins, and even more as to the process by which they have brought on mounting levels of disunity.

The French philosopher George Bernanos once wrote: "There are no more corrupting lies than problems poorly stated." I, at least, feel that this goes to the heart of much of the present turmoil of race relations and foreign policy. In a word, those in power have allowed domestic dislocations that accompany successful social changes to be interpreted as irrefutable evidence that the society refuses to change; they have permitted foreign policy failures arising from mistaken judgments to be taken as incontrovertible proof that the society has gone mad as well.

The fact is that with respect to Negro Americans we have seen incredible progress since, roughly, the Brown v. Board of Education decision of 1956 and President Eisenhower's subsequent decision to send federal troops to Little Rock, thus commencing the second Reconstruction.

Nowhere in history is there to be encountered an effort to bring a suppressed people into the mainstream of society comparable to the public and private initiatives on behalf of Negro Americans in recent years.

Blacks Saw It First

As I would like to discuss in a later memorandum, the results have been dramatic. Yet it was only after that effort had begun, and had been under way for some time, that it became possible to see the true horror of the situation white America had forced on black America and the deep disabilities that came about in consequence.

The first to see this, of course, were the blacks themselves. The result on the part of many was a revulsion against white society that has only just begun to run its course. Large numbers of middle-class, educated blacks, especially young ones, have come to see American society as hateful and illegitimate, lacking any true claim on their allegiance. Well they might.

The problem is not that one group in the population is beginning to react to centuries of barbarism by another group. The problem is that this cultural reaction among black militants is accompanied by the existence of a large, disorganized urban lower class which, like such groups everywhere, is unstable and essentially violent.

This fact of lower-class violence has nothing to do with race. It is purely a matter of social class. But since Watts, the media of public opinion—the press, television, the Presidency itself—have combined to insist that race is the issue.

As a result, middle-class blacks caught up in a cultural revolution have been able, in effect, to back up their demands. This has led to a predictable white counterreaction. And so on. In the process, we have almost deliberately obscured the extraordinary progress, and commitment to progress, which the nation as a whole has made, which white America has not abandoned, and which increasingly black America is learning to make use of.

To the contrary, it has been the failures of policy that have seemed ever more prominent. The essence of the Negro problem in America at this time is that despite great national commitments, and great progress, a large mass of the black population remains poor, disorganized, and discriminated against.

These facts are increasingly interpreted as proof that the national commitment is flawed, if not indeed fraudulent, that the society is irredeemably "racist," etc.

This interpretation is made by middle-class blacks and whites who, outwardly at least, society would seem to have treated very well, but the continued existence of black poverty makes their argument hard to assail. Moreover, increasingly that argument is directed not to particulars, but to fundamental questions as to the legitimacy of American society.

War Also a "Disaster"

Vietnam has been a domestic disaster of the same proportion, and for much the same reason. As best I can discern, the war was begun with the very highest of motives at the behest of men such as McNamara, Bundy, and Rusk in a fairly consistent pursuit of the postwar American policy of opposing Communist expansion and simultaneously encouraging political democracy and economic development in the nations on the Communist perimeter and elsewhere.

At the risk of seeming cynical, I would argue that the war in Vietnam has become a disastrous mistake because we have lost it. I quite accept Henry Kissinger's splendid formulation that a conventional army loses if it does not win, the opposite being the case for a guerrilla force. We have not been able to win.

Had the large-scale fighting by American forces been over by mid-1967 (which is my impression of what Bundy anticipated in mid-1965), had the children of the middle class accordingly continued to enjoy draft exemption, had there been no inflation, no surtax, no Tet offensive, then I very much fear there would be abroad at this point at most a modicum of moral outrage.

But this is not what happened. The war has not gone well, and increasingly in an almost primitive reaction—to which modern societies are as much exposed as any Stone Age clan—it has been judged that this is because the gods are against it.

In modern parlance this means that the evil military industrial complex has embarked on a racist colonialist adventure. (I have heard the head of SNCC state that we were in Vietnam "for the rice supplies.")

But the essential point is that we have been losing a

war, and this more than any single thing erodes the authority of a government, however stable, just, well-intentioned, or whatever.

"Mob" Topples President

I would imagine that the desire not to be the first President to "lose" a war has been much in President Johnson's mind over the past years, and explains some of his conduct. But the fact is that he could not win, and the all-important accompanying fact is that the semiviolent domestic protest that arose in consequence forced him to resign.

In a sense he was the first American President to be toppled by a mob. No matter that it was a mob of college professors, millionaires, flower children, and Radcliffe girls.

It was a mob that by early 1968 had effectively physically separated the Presidency from the people. (You may recall that seeking to attend the funeral of Cardinal Spellman, Johnson slipped in the back door of St. Patrick's Cathedral like a medieval felon seeking sanctuary.)

As with the case of the most militant blacks, success for the antiwar protesters has seemed only to confirm their detestation of society as it now exists. Increasingly they declare the society to be illegitimate, while men such as William Sloan Coffin, Jr., the chaplain at Yale, openly espouse violence as the necessary route of moral regeneration.

The successful extremism of the black militants and the antiwar protesters—by and large they have had their way—has now clearly begun to arouse fears and thoughts of extreme actions by other groups. George Wallace, a fourth-rate regional demagogue, won 13 percent of the national vote and at one point in the campaign probably had the sympathy of a quarter of the electorate, largely in the working class.

Among Jews—I draw your attention to this—there is a rising concern, in some quarters approaching alarm, over black anti-Semitism. They foresee Negro political power driving them from civil service jobs, as in the New York City school system. They see anti-Semitism becoming an "accepted" political posture. With special dread, they see a not distant future when the political leaders of the country might have to weigh the competing claims of ten million black voters who had become passionately pro-Arab as against one or two million.

In the meantime, we must await the reaction of the Armed Forces, and the veterans of Vietnam to whatever settlement you get there. No officer corps ever lost a war, and this one surely would have no difficulty finding symbols of those at home who betrayed it. All in all there are good reasons to expect a busy eight years in the White House.

Rejection of Values

There is a longer-term development contributing to the present chaos which bears mentioning. Since about 1840 the cultural elite in America have pretty generally rejected the values and activities of the larger society.

It has been said of America that the culture will not approve that which the policy strives to provide. For a brief period, associated with the depression, World War II, and the cold war there was something of a truce in this protracted struggle. That, I fear, is now over. The leading cultural figures are going—have gone—into opposition once again. This time they take with them a vastly more numerous following of educated, middle-class persons, especially young ones, who share their feelings and who do not "need the straight" world.

It is their pleasure to cause trouble, to be against. And they are hell-bent for a good time. President Johnson took all this personally, but I have the impression that you will make no such mistake!

It is, of course, easier to describe these situations than to suggest what is to be done about them. However, a certain number of general postures do seem to follow from the theme "Bring Us Together." I would list five:

First, the single most important task is to maintain the rate of economic expansion. If a serious economic recession were to come along to compound the controversies of race, Vietnam, and cultural alienation, the nation could indeed approach instability.

It would be my judgment that the great prosperity of the 1960's is the primary reason we have been able to weather this much internal dissension. The lot of Negroes has steadily improved, and so has that of most everyone else. Black demands for a greater share have thus been less threatening.

The war has been costly, but largely has been paid for through annual fiscal increments and recent deficits. Consumption has been affected not at all. If this situation were to reverse itself, your ability to meet black needs, the tolerance of the rest of the society for your efforts, the general willingness to see military efforts proceed, would all be grievously diminished.

Second, it would seem most important to de-escalate the rhetoric of crisis about the internal state of the society in general, and in particular about those problems—e.g., crime, *de facto* segregation, low educational achievement —which government has relatively little power to influ-

ence in the present state of knowledge and available resources.

This does not mean reducing efforts. Not at all. But
it does mean trying to create some equivalence between
what government can do about certain problems and
how much attention it draws to them. For this purpose,
the theme you struck in presenting your Cabinet on television seems perfect: Yours is an Administration of men
with wide-ranging interests and competence whose first
concern is the effective delivery of government services.

There is a risk here of being accused of caring less
than your predecessors, but even that will do no great
harm if you can simultaneously demonstrate that you
do more. It is out of such perceptions that the authority
of government is enhanced.

Stress on Minorities

It would seem likely that a powerful approach to this
issue will be to stress the needs and aspirations of groups
such as Mexican-Americans, Puerto Ricans, American Indians, and others, which have also been excluded and
exploited by the larger society. This, of course, is something you would want to do in any event.

Third, the Negro lower class must be dissolved. This
is the work of a generation, but it is time it began to be
understood as a clear national goal. By lower class I mean
the low-income, marginally employed, poorly educated,
disorganized slum dwellers who have piled up in our
central cities over the past quarter century. I would estimate they make up almost one half the total Negro population.

They are not going to become capitalists, or even middle-class functionaries. But it is fully reasonable to con-

ceive of them being transformed into a stable working-class population: truck drivers, mail carriers, assembly-line workers—people with dignity, purpose, and in the United States a very good standard of living indeed. Common justice, and common sense, demands that this be done.

It is the existence of this lower class, with its high rates of crime, dependency, and general disorderliness, that causes nearby whites (that is to say working-class whites, the liberals are all in the suburbs) to fear Negroes and to seek by various ways to avoid and constrain them.

It is this group that black extremists use to threaten white society with the prospect of mass arson and pillage. It is also this group that terrorizes and plunders the stable elements of the Negro community—trapped by white prejudice in the slums, and forced to live cheek by jowl with a murderous slum population. Take the urban lower class out of the picture and the Negro cultural revolution becomes an exciting and constructive development.

Fourth, it would seem devoutly to be wished that you not become personally identified with the war in Vietnam. You have available to you far more competent advice than mine in this area, and I am sure you will wish to proceed in terms of the foreign policy interests of the nation in broader terms, but I do urge that every effort be made to avoid the ugly physical harassment and savage personal attacks that brought President Johnson's Administration to an end.

The dignity of the Presidency as the symbolic head of state as well as of functioning leader of the government must be restored. Alas, it is in the power of the middle-class mob to prevent this. I would far rather see it concentrate, as *faute de mieux* it now seems to be doing, on attacking liberal college presidents as "racist pigs."

I fear the blunt truth is that ending the draft would be the single most important step you could take in this direction. The children of the upper middle class will not be conscripted.

In any event, the present system does cast a pall of anxiety and uncertainty over the lives of that quarter of the young male population which does in fact require four to eight to ten years of college work to prepare for careers which almost all agree are socially desirable, even necessary.

Fifth, it would seem important to stress those things Americans share in common, rather than those things which distinguish them one from the other; thus the war on poverty defined a large portion of the population as somehow living apart from the rest.

I would seek programs that stress problems and circumstances that all share, and especially problems which working people share with the poor. Too frequently of late the liberal upper middle class has proposed to solve problems of those at the bottom at the expense, or seeming expense, of those in between.

Obviously the theme "Forward Together" is essential here, and there are other symbols at hand of which I would think the approaching 200th anniversary of the founding of the Republic is perhaps the most powerful.

In the final months of your second term you will preside over the anniversary ceremonies of July 4, 1976. It would seem an incomparable opportunity to begin now to define the goals you would hope to see achieved by that time, trying to make them truly national goals to which all may subscribe, and from which as many as possible will benefit.

It is hoped that our 200th anniversary will see the nation somewhat more united than were those thirteen colonies!

By Eric Hoffer

Excerpts from a Journal:
June, 1958, to May, 1959

September 4, 1958

I have said it again and again: the only thing that will cure the Negro's chronic ills is that the Negro community perform something that will win it the admiration of the world. Yet it is difficult to see what this something might be. A Negro revolt in Mississippi; a desperate battle to the last man, a Negro Alamo. Or an excellent Negro school for song and dance. Or an excellent trade school. Or a model organization for mutual help. It is the slow, hard way, and the indications are that the Negro will not take it. He would rather derive pride from an identification with the achievements of colored races elsewhere. Yet I doubt whether even a triumphant Ghana could ever be to the Negro in America what Israel has been to the Jews.

The crucial question is whether the Negro will ever give up his alibi of discrimination. You do not give up the imperishable advantage of an alibi for the short-lived exhilaration of achievement. There is trouble ahead. For the less justified the Negro's alibi the more passionately

will he cling to it, and the louder will he voice his grievances.

Were I a genuine American I would believe in the
possibility of the automatic absorption of twenty million
Negroes into the body of American life; that almost overnight, without special effort or an intermediate phase, the
Negro in America can become a human being first and
only secondly a Negro.

December 13, 1958

Four hours on the *Santa Anita*. Finished the job. In the
afternoon I spent several hours with Lili and the boy
shopping. The boy is a delight. Any day now he will be
talking fluently.

The quality of a social order may be gauged by several
criteria: by how effectively it realizes its human resources;
by how well it maintains its social plant; and, above all,
by the quality of its people—how self-respecting, benevo-
lent, self-reliant, energetic, etc.

The elimination of the profit motive in Communist
countries has not made people less greedy and selfish. The
increased dependence of the many on the will and whim
of the few has not made people more gentle, forbearing,
and carefree. From all that I read, it seems that the attitude of every-man-for-himself is more pronounced in a
communist than in a capitalist society. The compact unity
imposed from above has weakened the impulse toward
mutual help and voluntary cooperation. Moreover, where
failure may have fatal consequences, vying will not proceed in an atmosphere of good fellowship.

And yet, on the whole, there is less loneliness in a communist than in a capitalist society. People do not feel
abandoned and forgotten in a regimented society. This.

perhaps keeps people from cutting loose from the communist fatherland. The afterthought is that there is no loneliness in prison.

Again and again I come across the assertion that a society cannot grow and thrive without a culturally superior stratum which generates the impulses toward excellence and greatness. The axiomatic assumption is that, left to themselves, the common people will wallow in sloth or explode in anarchy. The happenings in this country refute this assertion. In the rest of the world at present there is evidence on every hand that the vigor and health of a society are determined by the quality of the common people rather than that of the cultural elite. It may even be true that the cultural elite performs best when society begins to decay. It was so in classical Greece, and it seems to be so in contemporary Britain. The sickness of Britain is not that its cultural elite does not write, compose, invent brilliantly, but that the majority of the population are without the taste for strenuous effort. To produce a piece of machinery Britain needs twice as many men on the job as Sweden, and four times as many as the United States.

December 14, 1958

Eight hours on the Norwegian ship *Tancred* at Pier 28. A very pleasant day. Jack Lurie and the Montenegrin Negus were with me. I did a lot of talking. It is remarkable how urbane and gentle our idealists are in their treatment of brazen phonies like Nkrumah, Sukarno, Sékou Touré, and others. If an American soldier or businessman had displayed a fraction of such megalomania, he would have been made the laughingstock of the world. But our intellectual establishment takes seriously the sheerest frauds in Asia and Africa. Nkrumah has a more than life-size statue of himself in front of his house (it cost about $200,000), and has his face on stamps and coins. Sékou Touré brags that he is going to institute forced labor, and revive the cutting off of an arm for theft, and you cannot hear even a murmur of outrage anywhere.

Now and then I wonder where my obsession with the intellectuals is going to lead me. If I could put together a small volume on the subject, I would get it out of my system. But it does not seem I shall ever write such a book. I shall keep pecking at it the rest of my life, and sicken in the process.

December 17, 1958

The weakening of my memory frightens me. Unless I note a thing down it slips my mind completely. The effort to remember what I forgot results in actual pain.

I have been off two days and didn't do a thing. Still, I am beginning to feel better. The stomach functions, and I have slept well. Why not go on like this and see what happens?

Most of our self-appointed experts on foreign affairs are convinced that Americans are not intelligent enough to formulate a foreign policy. Both domestic and foreign intellectuals seem to have a vital need for the assumption that the people who built and run this country are stupid. They are not bothered by the mystery of how stupid Americans tamed and mastered a savage continent and made it a cornucopia of plenty. Nor are they bothered by the evidence from every part of the world that where intellectuals are in power everything, including the weather, ceases to perform as it should. The crops don't grow, or if they grow, are not harvested. Nothing works smoothly and automatically.

December 29, 1958

Didn't get dispatched—too many ahead of me. Nor is it likely that I shall work tomorrow. The waterfront looks empty.

To ibn-Khaldun, past and present were as alike as drops of water. It is perhaps true that everywhere up to the end of the eighteenth century individual life had an immemorial, static quality—despite the inventions and reforms. Even in this country people around 1800 lived the way people lived in 3000 B.C. What we know as the spirit of an age is a new thing. Throughout most of history there was an ageless spirit rather than the spirit of an age. In addition to the static quality of everyday life there had been the unchanging nature of the ruling class. History up to about 1800 was made largely by aristocracies. My hunch is that the spirit of an age is determined by the type of humanity that makes things happen.

The difference between the eighteenth, nineteenth, and twentieth centuries is only partly due to differences in technology. What counts most is the human type that dominates each of them—the eighteenth, aristocrats; the nineteenth, the middle class; and the twentieth, intellectuals. Had the machine age been initiated by aristocrats or intellectuals, the nineteenth century would have had a different flavor and temper. The uniqueness of America is that here for the first time common people could and did make history.

February 11, 1959

Seven hours on a Luckenbach ship at Pier 29. I worked with the bulkhead swampers on the breakup pile. It was steady going all day, yet the feeling at the end was one of pleasure. The pleasantness was due largely to the presence of Jack, the head-up man—a highly competent and soft-spoken person. We did an enormous amount of work yet did not feel driven or frustrated. It made me realize again how a single individual can count in the development of a pattern of life. Yet we are told that it is circumstances and not men that make history. This is an age that saw the fateful role played by Lenin, Stalin, Hitler, Mao Tse-tung and others.

9:30 P.M. What is it that can grip my interest, concentrate my attention, and get my thoughts flowing? Judicious praise? Not quite. Verification of my theories and hunches? More so. Actually, the most durable and effective source of stimulation is a hefty body of manuscript wanting to grow.

I live in a society full of blemishes and deformities. But it is a society that gives every man elbow room to do the things near to his heart. In no other country is it so possible for a man of determination to go ahead, with whatever it is that he sets his heart on, without compromising his integrity. Of course, those who set their heart on acclaim and fortune must cater to other people's demands. But for those who want to be left alone to realize their capacities and talents this is an ideal country. It is incredible how easy it is in this country to cut oneself off from what one disapproves—from all vulgarity, mendacity, conformity, subservience, speciousness, and other corrupting influences and infections.

February 22, 1959

Nine hours on a Luckenbach ship at Pier 29. I am taking the place of a steady hook-on man. All day I had the bay before my eyes. The water was light green speckled with whitecaps. The hills beyond were wrapped in a powder-blue veil through which shimmered the mass of white houses. In the afternoon, over Treasure Island, there was a massing of dark gray and smoky white clouds. One could trace the roots of the white clouds in the gray mass, and the whole thing gave the feeling of a violent reaction out of which something wholly new might emerge.

8:15 P.M. The question of the readiness to work keeps tugging at my mind. My explanation of freedom as an energizer of the masses, and of individual separateness as an irritant which keeps people on the go, is not wholly satisfactory. These are valid causes, but not the main ones. There is, for instance, the fact that there is a greater readiness to work in a society with a high standard of living than in one with a low standard. We are more ready to strive and work for superfluities than for necessities. People who are clear-sighted, undeluded, and sober-minded will not go on working once their reasonable needs are satisfied. A society that refuses to strive for superfluities is likely to end up lacking in necessities. The readiness to work springs from trivial, questionable motives. I can remember Paul Henri Spaak saying after the end of the Second World War that to energize the Belgian workers for the stupendous effort of rebuilding and recovery he had to fill the shops and tease the people with all the "luxuries and vices" they had been accustomed to. Attlee, a better socialist but a lesser statesman, instituted at that time in Britain a policy of "socialist austerity." A vigorous society is a society made up of people who set their hearts on toys, and who would work harder for superfluities than for necessities. The self-righteous moralists decry such a society, yet it is well to keep in mind that both children and artists need luxuries more than they need necessities.

April 17, 1959

Eight hours on the *C. E. Dant*. Finished the job. Had a new partner, a Negro, very conscientious and nice to be with.

Something I read in the *Manchester Guardian Weekly* started me thinking about the attitude of the masses toward the intellectuals. There is no doubt that to most Portuguese and Italian longshoremen a schoolmaster is an important person, almost as much a dignity as the priest. But through most of history the common people resented the educated as exploiters and oppressors. Rabbi Akiba, who started life as a roustabout, recalled how he used to cry out: "Give me one of the learned and I shall bite him like a jackass." During the peasant uprisings the clerks were given short shrift by the mobs. When in the fourteenth century the mob burned the charters and manuscripts of the University of Cambridge an old hag tossed the ashes into the wind crying: "Away with the learning of the clerks, away with it."

April 21, 1959

The fact that I have read a lot and that I think and write has never generated in me the conviction that I could teach and guide others. Even in a union meeting of unlearned longshoremen it has never occurred to me that I could tell them what to do. This reluctance to teach and guide is the result not of a lack of confidence in myself but rather of a confidence in the competence of the run-of-the-mill American.

The important point is that the lack of the conviction that I have the ability and the right to teach others marks me as a nonintellectual. For the intellectual is above all a teacher, and considers it his God-given right to tell the ignorant majority what to do. To ignore this teacher complex is to ignore the intellectual's central characteristic, and miss the key to his aspirations and grievances. I am sure that the passion to teach has been a crucial factor in the rise of the revolutionary movements of our time. In most cases when a revolutionary takes over a country he turns it into a vast schoolroom with a population of cowed, captive pupils cringing at his feet. When he speaks, the whole country listens.

By Milton Himmelfarb

Jewish Class Conflict?

IN NO OTHER American election has the "Jewish vote" ever
been so central to the strategy and tactics of the candidates, or so prominent in the news, commentaries, polls,
and analysis, as in New York in 1969. It was clear that
Mayor Lindsay would get most of the votes at the bottom
and the top: at the bottom the poor—Negroes and Puerto
Ricans; at the top the prosperous and well-educated. In
the middle, it was clear that Lindsay was not going to get
the votes of the Catholics, mainly Italian and Irish, of the
working and lower-middle classes. The question about the
middle was whether he would get enough Jewish votes
to put together a plurality. He did. Or rather, his Democratic opponent failed to get enough. It was less that Lindsay won than that Procaccino lost. (Of the white Protestant minority, most voted for Lindsay: not as the liberal
candidate—they are not extraordinarily liberal—but as the
fellow Protestant, the *landsman*.)

Jews voted more than other whites for the liberal candidate. So what else is new? Jews always vote for the
liberal candidate—notoriously in Presidential elections, as
in 1968, but also locally, as recently in Los Angeles. There

Reprinted from *Commentary*, January, 1970. Copyright © 1970 by the
American Jewish Committee. Used by permission.

they voted not merely more than other whites but actually more than the Mexicans for Bradley, the Negro who was defeated. From one point of view, then, little has changed.

From another point of view, much has changed. Liberalism is comparative. ("How's your wife?"—"Compared to what?") That Jews vote liberal means that dollar for dollar and year of school for year of school, they vote more liberal than others. It does not mean that there are no class differences in the voting of Jews. Prosperous Jews gave Kennedy a higher proportion of their votes than prosperous Christians did, Catholic as well as Protestant, but a lower proportion than less prosperous Jews. And so in all four Roosevelt elections. Now, in New York as in Los Angeles, that has been reversed. Now it is the more prosperous Jews who have been voting more liberal. The reversal began in 1966, in the New York voting on a civilian review board for the police. Then as now, Jews split fairly evenly between what were conventionally regarded as the liberal and the conservative choices, and the well-off made the liberal choice more than the less well-off. (And then as now, as a group the Jews were substantially more liberal than other whites.)

One way of interpreting the reversal is to say that liberalism has new tasks. These require a capacity for sympathetic, imaginative, even abstract understanding. Naturally, the educated, who also tend to be the more prosperous, are better fitted for that understanding than the uneducated. When liberalism was fighting for social security, it was fighting for the bread-and-butter interests of working people, so of course working people supported it, or its party and candidates. Now, the argument goes, the victories of the old liberalism have deprived the new liberalism of programs comparably appealing to its old clientele. Now the old supporters of liberalism—the famous New

Deal coalition—have or think they have an interest in the *status quo.* They have become conservative. They oppose the new liberalism with its new responsibilities, imposed upon it by time and change.

This interpretation is flawed. It may be self-serving, and is self-righteous. In 1969, in New York, the most telling bit of rhetoric was the name the Democratic candidate gave to the prosperous who accused him of conservatism: "limousine liberals." Earlier, in 1966, was it chiefly education that prompted Jews to vote for the civilian review board, and lack of education to vote against it? Perhaps it was prosperity and lack of prosperity. The prosperous could afford their vote. The unprosperous (and elderly), living in apartment houses without doormen and riding subways rather than taxis, may have voted as they did, not because of ignorance but because of concerns explicable by the reality of their lives—a reality against which prosperity shields the prosperous. Similarly with education. Characteristically, in New York, Jews who send their children to private schools have approved for the public schools central educational parks and decentralization, integration, and Black Power—whatever, at any given moment, has been the fashionable liberal thing. In New York, Jews who send their older children to expensive private colleges approve transforming the free municipal colleges.

Less prosperous Jews do not think they are defecting from liberalism. They think they are being made to pay the bill for the limousine liberals' kind of liberalism. And they think that as if that were not enough, salt is rubbed into their wounds. First, the upper class makes the others pay for upper-class notions of liberalism, and then the upper-class liberals are contemptuous. They make jokes. At a rally of Lindsay people, a comedian describes Procaccino—and by implication anyone who would want to support Procaccino—as sitting in his undershirt, drinking beer, and watching Lawrence Welk on television. Presumably Lindsay—and by implication the typical Lindsay voter—is the sort of man who, in dinner jacket, is photographed drinking a martini with Lennie at Lincoln Center, during the intermission of Pierre Boulez's premiere as conductor of the New York Philharmonic.

Italians, especially, must wonder where contempt for a class leaves off and prejudice against Italians begins. People who would not dream of telling Negro jokes regale each other with Italian jokes. Was that a joke against undershirts or against Italians in undershirts? In Washington a political comedian amused his public with something he must have picked up from his set in New York: Mario is so sure of winning that he dropped by the mayor's official residence the other day to measure the living room for linoleum. The jokes that do not get into print are gamier still. If I were Italian, I might imagine that the humorous liberals are not conspicuously partial to Italians. But I am not Italian, so I can understand the undershirt-beer-television-Welk joke to be as much about class and taste as about *italianità*.

In contempt for non-upper whites, many liberals agree with the young ultraradicals, or actually have learned from them. It was the campus revolutionaries from the rich suburbs who first exposed that fascist pig, the average union member—a potbellied oaf, undershirted, swilling beer, staring at the boob tube. Whether or not New York's white clods heard Lindsay's comedian's joke, they got the message, and it did not enhance Lindsay's popularity with them. Since many Jews, too, stare at the boob tube, and even drink beer, they hardly needed specifically Jewish reasons to vote against him.

In fact Lindsay, or his twins—his men on the Board of

Education, that museum director, that university chancellor—had provided in abundance reasons to conclude that he was anti-Jewish: not, or not necessarily, anti-Semitic, but anti-Jewish. For the Jewish members of the pro-Lindsay liberal elite such accusations, or such thoughts, were narrow, tribal, grotesquely passé, not to be entertained privately, let alone uttered publicly, by an enlightened, modern person.

The liberal Jewish politicians, amateur or professional, had their own motives for supporting Lindsay. Though with the same tastes and beliefs as the other top people, yet they more urgently and personally needed him to win. Reform Democrats, they could not afford a Procaccino victory. That would lose them more than the mayor's office, it would lose them control of their party. However liberal and Reform, politicians act on the principle laid down long since by a reactionary, Senator Boies Penrose of Pennsylvania: If you have to choose between losing an election and losing control of your party, you lose the election.

The most interesting voters were that small group of Jews who by education, income, and habit could be thought of as belonging to the liberal elite but who nevertheless voted *against* Lindsay, and that larger group of middling Jews who voted *for* him.

Some of the anti-Lindsay liberal Jewish elite were not especially conscious of themselves as Jews. In general, like their pro-Lindsay brothers, they rarely think about Jewish interests as such. Among these not very Jewish Jews would be some school principals, some professors in the municipal colleges, and a few intellectuals continuing an old, running fight with the kind of middlebrow outlook represented by the editorial columns of *The New York Times*. These were a minority of their minority, because to be anti-Lindsay it helped to be a Jewish Jew. At the municipal colleges, for example, on issues affecting the future of the colleges it was noticeably the Jewish-Jewish professors who took a position that could be translated as anti-Lindsay, i.e., "conservative." (There is a complication. Professors of hard subjects tend to be more "conservative" than professors of soft subjects, and the Jewish Jews seem to bunch in the hard subjects.) Of course, that those professors are "conservative" does not imply that they probably voted for Nixon in 1968. It implies that they were worried about the Jewish future, whether in their colleges or in the city, that they saw a threat, and that they thought the threat came from Lindsay—Lindsay the agent or Lindsay the symbol.

Since, as is well known, parochialism, narrowness, and prejudice are more usual below than above, the conviction that Lindsay and what he symbolized were against the Jews was widespread in the lower-middle and middle-middle class. Lindsay's strategy was to weaken this conviction, to lessen the number of people who held it. In two months he saw the inside of more synagogues than a Jew will see in ten years. He apologized, over and over again: not for having been anti-Jewish—he could not reasonably be expected to concede such a thing explicitly—but for having "made mistakes." If they wished, Jews could interpret that as an apology for acts which had inadvertently injured or offended them. Enough Jews in the middle wished to accept the apology, and to understand it as a promise to mend his ways, for Lindsay to win.

Not that they liked Mordecai, says the Talmud, but that they disliked Haman: not that Lindsay won those Jews, but that Procaccino lost them. If the plurality in the Democratic primary had gone, say, to Wagner—with all his air of fatigue and his redolence of the past—Lindsay would not have had those Jews, or the election. Jews could have voted for Wagner without great enthusiasm but also without feelings of unworthiness, and above all without going against a powerful and still operative Jewish tradition that most are probably not even aware is Jewish. That is the tradition of being attracted by the *edel* (cultivated) Gentile and repelled by the *prost* (common) one.

I can give personal testimony, both to the attraction of the *edel* and to our unawareness that we are attracted because we are Jews. During Kennedy's Presidency I read a newspaper report of something that seemed to me splendidly patrician—the President with elegance and wit welcoming as his guests some artists or scholars, or his wife addressing some gracious words of appreciation, in French, to a visiting ballet company that had danced at the White House. Something like that. I was on the train, and turning to Bill O'Hanrahan, an active Republican despite his name, I told him, more or less: "Bill, forget about politics. Look at this news item. I don't care what your politics are, you've got to admit the Kennedys have class." To which he replied: "Yes, I know that's what you people think." I had thought I knew about the relation between being a Jew and having the tastes and outlooks Jews are apt to have. (I had written about it.) In saying what I said to O'Hanrahan, I had tried to discount that Jewish particularism which likes to regard itself as universalism. He educated me. He was not being anti-Jewish or offensive. He was only saying that my admiration for the Kennedy style was less universal than even I had thought—more Jewish—and less detached from politics. Would I have responded as warmly as he to a newspaper account of Ike enjoying a golf reunion with an old comrade-in-arms?

Lindsay is *edel*—or at any rate urbane. Procaccino is, or increasingly seemed, *prost*. It was so hard for many Jews to vote for Procaccino that Lindsay won. When they entered the booths, numbers of that great majority of Jews who earlier had told the pollsters they detested Lindsay found they could not pull the lever for anyone else. Because Procaccino repelled them, they were prepared to believe Lindsay's apologies and promises. The Jews who stayed with Procaccino were those who found it harder to believe in the new Lindsay.

For the Jewish-Jewish middle-class Lindsay voters, Lindsay had worked hard to appease their resentment. He had eaten crow. Like the emperor Henry IV, he had gone to Canossa—a friend of mine has said that Lindsay went to Canarsie. These Jews concluded that he had apologized enough, that he could be trusted not to backslide, and that his experience would warn him and his successors against making the same mistakes. Other things being equal, they thought, it would be better to vote for someone else, in the Jewish interest; only, as things stood, it was in the Jewish interest to keep New York from the greater chaos into which it would fall with Procaccino. (But if only they had a Wagner to vote for!)

The Procaccino voters asked themselves the same questions but gave different answers—or alternatively, agreed about the factors in the equation but weighted them a little differently. Lindsay would not be that much better, they thought, nor Procaccino that much worse: whoever won would be mayor of an impossible city. And they thought it beside the point to speculate whether Lindsay was or was not a reformed character. Grant what was debatable, that he had truly reformed. It was still necessary to vote against him, as Voltaire said of the British Government's reason for shooting Admiral Byng, *pour encourager les autres.* It is risky for Jews to show that we readily forgive injuries and slights. No other group consciously subordinates its good to the general good. For Jews to forgive, to prefer the general good to our particular good—that is admirable, but also dangerous, and maybe suicidal. Among all the groups in the body politic, if there is only one which shows it is prepared to renounce its interest, which group will go to the wall in the clash of interests? Will a sensible politician hesitate to make such generous, yielding people bear more than their share of the common burden, pay more than their share of the total cost—especially if he knows that later they will not even punish him for it at the polls? Globally, the misfortune of the Jews is that for fifty years we have had no bargaining power. Our enemies have been so intransigent that our friends have not had to be very friendly to be able to count on our support. In New York now, these anti-Lindsay voters could have said: "We do have bargaining power, we are at last free to choose. Let us use our freedom prudently. To vote for Lindsay would be imprudent, so let us vote for Procaccino." (But how much better it would be if there were a Wagner to vote for!)

Only about 10 percent of the Jews voted for Marchi. That is curious, because if any of the three candidates could legitimately be considered as *edel*, it was Marchi. He was superior to his rivals in learning, intelligence, and wit. His personal manner was pleasant. If he had been only the Republicans' candidate, many more Jews would have voted for him. Because he was also the Conservatives' candidate, they could not bring themselves to vote for him.

By now the top people's scorn for the slobs is no secret. The warnings have gone out and a certain amount of literature has even begun to be produced, interpreting the beer guzzlers to their betters. It reminds me of the understand-your-neighbor, one-world, antiethnocentric litera-

212 Overcoming Middle Class Rage

ture that was common twenty and thirty years ago: do not look down on the Singhalese cultivator; he has not had your advantages—that sort of thing. One of the best-known pieces of this new kind is Pete Hamill's "Revolt of the White Lower Middle Class," published in *New York Magazine*. Really, Hamill writes of the Irish and Italian working and lower-middle classes in New York. He takes them seriously, he respects them. He is frightened of what they may do in their rage, and he makes it clear that he will not vote as they will, but he does not condescend to them or poke fun at them. But then, I think Hamill is not a Jew, and he is not writing about Jews. When a man called Rosenbaum writes in *The Village Voice* about the Jewish lower-middle class, he is amused by those vulgar people, expects us superior readers to be amused, and all in all has a fine time telling us how funny their talk and dress are, and how irritable their narrow minds and pinched souls. The very title of his report—an account of Lindsay campaigning in Brooklyn—is a nudge: "When in Brooklyn, Play Gimpel the Fool." Not one of the people Rosenbaum interviewed, unlike one that Hamill interviewed, was quoted as having said he had bought a gun. If we take Hamill's people seriously, as we should, we should take equally seriously Rosenbaum's people. But Hamill wants us to and Rosenbaum does not.

For the first time since 1932, or maybe 1928, the class differences among American Jews are showing signs of emerging as class conflict. The without-a-second-thought Lindsay voters are one class, the Procaccino and the hold-your-nose Lindsay voters the other class. The first is mainly upper and upper middle, the second mainly lower middle and middle middle. (Mainly, not exclusively.) In the second, the proportion of Jewish Jews is higher than in the first. It is members of the first that have dominated the mainstream Jewish institutions and have been prominent in the civic organizations that appeal disproportionately to Jews and rely on their disproportionate moral and financial support, like the civil liberties unions. Until now the absence of a formal mandate has not kept the mainstream institutions from factually representing most Jews—in things like civil liberties, civil rights, separation of church and state—and therefore from having the implicit confidence of most Jews.

Now growing numbers of non-upper Jews have begun to suspect that when it comes to the things that they are most concerned and anxious about, and that affect them most directly, the upper Jews could not care less, or are actually hostile, and contemptuous in the bargain. The split between the two classes would have come more fully into the open in the New York election if in the end enough non-uppers had not felt they must vote for the uppers' candidate (for want of a Wagner). If the uppers want to regain the other Jews' confidence, they will have to be more attentive and respectful than they have seemed to be. They will have to show they care.

By Haskell L. Lazere

Haganah U.S.A.?

Last year James Forman captured national attention when he rose at a Black Economic Development Conference in Detroit to demand that the white religious community pay $500 million in reparations to the Negro community of the United States. Borrowing a page from history, Forman adapted the reparations concept for his own purposes. Just a few days after Forman had disrupted services at the Riverside Church by making his demands from the pulpit, the rumor spread around New York that his next target was Temple Emanu-El on Fifth Avenue—the heartland of the Jewish Establishment. Forman never appeared, but members of the Jewish Defense League did, despite Rabbi Nathan A. Perilman's strong appeal that they stay away.

The press and television dutifully carried the story of the JDL action. A short time thereafter, New Yorkers became even more aware of the JDL presence when *The New York Times* carried a three-column, length-of-the-page advertisement captioned: "Is This Any Way for Nice Jewish Boys to Behave?" Under the question, there was

Reprinted from *Dimensions in American Judaism*, Spring, 1970, published by The Union of American Hebrew Congregations. Used by permission.

a picture of six sun-glassed young men carrying baseball bats, lengths of pipe, and bicycle chains, standing in front of a door leading to a building that could have been taken for Temple Emanu-El.

The ad copy made it very clear the JDL had Forman very much in mind in answering the question about the behavior of "nice Jewish boys."

> Maybe there are times when there is no other way to get across to the extremist that the Jew is not quite the patsy some think he is.
>
> Maybe there is only one way to get across a clear response to people who threaten seizure of synagogues and extortion of money. Maybe nice Jewish boys do not always get through to people who threaten to carry teachers out in pine boxes and to burn down merchants' stores.
>
> Maybe some people and organizations are just too nice. Maybe in times of crisis Jewish boys should not be that nice. Maybe—just maybe—nice people build their own road to Auschwitz.

There is no doubt that the Jewish Defense League exists. It is a physical fact claiming seven thousand members. But physical fact or not, the JDL *is* a state of mind for many in the Jewish community of New York and elsewhere.

The JDL is a creation of Rabbi Meir Kahane, a thirty-nine-year old Orthodox rabbi who until a short time ago was the spiritual leader of the Rochdale Village Traditional Synagogue. Rochdale Village is a middle-income cooperative apartment community in Queens and is an integrated community with the majority of residents being Jewish. Kahane was also a feature writer for the *Jewish Press,* an Anglo-Jewish weekly published in Brooklyn, heavy with articles aimed at the Orthodox community. The *Jewish Press* also sensationalizes stories about anti-Semitic incidents. During the New York City teachers' strikes of 1968–1969, the *Jewish Press* and Meir Kahane had a field day with the black-Jewish confrontations and Mayor Lindsay's role.

There is no doubt that the school strikes which stemmed from Ocean Hill's dismissal of thirteen white teachers, almost all of whom were Jews, led to the formation of the JDL. Other incidents which occurred before and during that time contributed substantially as well: NYU hired (and subsequently fired) John Hatchett, a black man who had written a viciously anti-Semitic article in the Afro-American Teachers' Bulletin; WBAI broadcast an anti-Semitic poem written by a black student and read over the air by Leslie Campbell, one of the black militant teachers who was a ringleader of extremist activities; the Metropolitan Museum issued a catalog in connection with an exhibit, "Harlem on My Mind," in which an essay by a sixteen-year-old black high school girl appeared to be yet another anti-Semitic attack on Jews. (She had lifted a quotation from the Glazer-Moynihan book, *Beyond the Melting Pot.* The editor of the catalog had dropped some key words as well as the quotes and source material reference, so that her words came through both out of context and as yet another example of black anti-Semitism.)

The Mayor's appointments of both black militants and black extremists to high-salaried city posts, the seeming indifference of the black Commissioner of Human Rights to anti-Semitic incidents, and the push for larger numbers of black students in City University by almost any means were yet other factors which gave a push to the growth of the Jewish Defense League. The merit system by which Jews had been able to pull themselves up into responsible positions in the school system and the city government was under concerted attack by black militants. Pressures

for the abolition of standard exams and the substitution
of a system of preferential treatment for nonwhites were
mounting. Article after article began to appear in various
Jewish publications suggesting that the WASP Establishment was either throwing or preparing to throw the Jews
to the Panthers (Black, that is).

The problems of any urban area are multiplied a hun-
dredfold in New York City, where teeming masses are
jammed cheek by jowl into the cramped canyons of the
city. Exploding populations in the ghettos of the city were
pushing outward into previously all-white and mainly Jewish areas. They wanted (and want) in and the insiders
wanted (and want) to maintain the *status quo,* preserving
whatever sense of security and comfort one can have in
the big city.

A Ford Foundation funded study headed by McGeorge
Bundy submitted to the Mayor at his request recommendations that the public school system of New York be decen-
tralized under a system of community control so that the
schools would be more responsive to the needs of the
community and the students. Community control spelled
b-l-a-c-k, because it was the black leadership which was
pushing strongest and most visibly for community control.
This didn't sit well with a community which had not long
before beaten back an effort to establish a Civilian Review
Board for the police because it had been read as b-l-a-c-k.
Crime in the streets meant the Negro, and reports of mug-
gings, purse-snatchings, holdups, and other crimes of violence came through as Negro-committed with or without racial designation by the press.

Gut-reaction and raw emotion fertilized by the hard
realities of New York City life became the roots of the
JDL, and Meir Kahane took full advantage of the opportunity. While national Jewish organizations and leaders

were appealing to reason and balance he was saying their techniques had brought us to where we are. While Jewish moderates and intellectuals were calling for social change which would equalize the opportunities for all, Kahane was speaking in troubled neighborhoods telling troubled people that their interests and immediate concerns came first with the JDL. He was also telling them that the ADL, American Jewish Congress, American Jewish Committee, and other Establishment groups didn't give a damn about them and that the Establishment techniques not only had not worked but had brought the troubles Jews were facing in the big city. He argued that the only way to protect ourselves is to organize a defense force. He illustrated his talks with examples of what the JDL had done: when Gideon Goldberg, dean of boys at Eastern District High School, had been threatened with physical harm by blacks if he came back to school, the JDL provided him with an escort right past two hundred hostile black students and stayed with him all day; when a group of black youngsters approached Montefiore Cemetery intent upon some Halloween fun, a group of JDL members guarding the cemetery told them point-blank that if any desecration occurred, they would strike back tenfold in the black neighborhood, and the black kids went away.

Using the slogan, "Never Again," which doesn't have to be spelled out for any Jew, Kahane has appeared hundreds of times to seek JDL membership and support. He is careful to say that he is not a racist—not anti-Negro— and that he is opposed to extremism, but that what he and the JDL are doing is necessary in these times of crisis and the absence of effective police protection and defense from other quarters. The appeal makes sense to the man in the street.

Kahane has begun organizing in cities outside of New

York—Cleveland, Philadelphia, Boston, and even Miami. "Safe" communities in Connecticut, Long Island, and Westchester have invited him to come as a speaker at synagogues and centers. Kahane has become somewhat of a celebrity. He is also both an embarrassment and a danger to the American Jewish community. Before I get into that, however, I think it important to convey the information I have about the organization of JDL, which I believe to be accurate. There are only two key people in the organization—one is Meir Kahane, the other is Bertram Zweibon, the JDL's general counsel. It was Zweibon who sent telegrams to the Arab legations in New York City following Arab terrorist bombings of Israeli offices in Europe, threatening to retaliate two-for-one against the Arabs here if one Jewish store or institution were bombed.

Kahane is alleged to select the leader of each JDL chapter personally. Whether this is done because he distrusts the democratic election process or whether he is fearful of a security leak I do not know. I would suspect it is the latter. To be sure that he has enough "troops," Kahane opened Camp Jedel near Monticello, New York, this past summer where two hundred teen-agers and others were trained in karate, judo, and marksmanship. Half the day the campers studied Torah and Jewish history and the other half they practiced the arts of self-defense, learned how to fire small arms, and engaged in physical fitness programs. It may be that JDL has seven thousand members, but Kahane has never been able to turn out more than a few hundred for various demonstrations.

During New York's mayoralty campaign, Kahane sponsored a large ad in *The New York Times* saying that "the Jews of New York City cannot afford four more years of John Lindsay." Simultaneously, Kahane held a JDL news conference to say that no one was accusing the Mayor of being anti-Semitic, but, worse than that, he was insensitive to anti-Semitism, which made him far more dangerous. For his political and intemperate attack on Mayor Lindsay, and because he had not been spending the required time on his job, the *Jewish Press* fired Meir Kahane. Sholom Klass, the paper's publisher, ran a front-page editorial explaining why and denounced Kahane as an opportunist. Kahane retorted that the *Jewish Press* had been bought off by the Lindsay people. Kahane had lost his major public outlet when he was discharged from the *Jewish Press*, but he still had the advertising columns of *The New York Times.*

He tried one more shot at Lindsay in the *Times*—a letter to his children, telling them in long, hard-to-read copy why no Jew should vote for John Lindsay. After the election, when Lindsay had won, he tried yet another tack, taken almost from Jim Forman's book; he called upon eight major Jewish organizations to contribute $100,000 to the Jewish Defense League so that it could set up and equip street patrols in troubled Jewish neighborhoods where the crime rate was high and police protection allegedly ineffective. When none of the eight gave him a dime, he took a large ad in the *Times* to appeal for funds for Operation Haganah. The ad was cleverly interspersed with the New York Urban Coalition slogan of "Give a Damn" and urged readers to contribute half of what they would normally give to their organization to the JDL and the JDL would send the contributor's organization a receipt for same in his behalf.

Dishonestly, the JDL ad said, "each and every group turned these poor people down," seeking to show that the organizations were not concerned about unsafe streets in Jewish neighborhoods and masking the fact that it was the *JDL* that was refused—*not Jews.*

The Jewish Defense League is an aberration of American and Jewish life. It is no more acceptable than the Black Panthers or the Minutemen. Its purposes may be different from those of the Minutemen, but its rationale is the same. The Minutemen allege that the law enforcement agencies of our country are infiltrated by the Communists, and when the Communists take over, the only force which can protect the country are the Minutemen, duly armed and trained for that purpose. The JDL says in effect that they are the only ones who can provide protection for Jews by meeting force with force, violence with violence. Either way, it spells vigilantism, be it called Black Panthers, Minutemen, White Citizens Councils, or the Jewish Defense League.

The JDL has been vigorously denounced by every major national Jewish organization as anathematic to American and Jewish traditions. This is not pre-1948 Palestine with organized Arab killers in our midst. It is not the Germany or Poland or Russia of the pogroms. Over three hundred prominent Jews of New York City, led by Arthur Goldberg, signed a statement condemning the Jewish Defense League for its tactics and its unwarranted attack on Mayor Lindsay. One of the rabbis, who appeared at a news conference called for the purpose of denouncing the JDL, read a statement saying that the JDL was neither Jewish nor for defense and quoted Talmud to prove it. Reform, Conservative, and Orthodox rabbis joined in the repudiation of the JDL.

But if the JDL can exist in New York City and other areas in 1970 when Jews are relatively secure from anti-Semitism and discrimination, there have to be some basic reasons which do not simply read "backlash." Some of them have already been listed. They read "fear"—fear of life, security, future. But even that is too simplistic. There

are other more complicated reasons and to attack the JDL
as a vigilante group and to denounce it won't make it go
away or destroy its base.

Somewhere along the way, Jewish agencies have lost
touch with the rank and file of the Jewish community. In
our commitment to a fuller and safer America for all where
the security of the American Jew is an accomplished fact,
Jewish agencies have shown a willingness to accommodate
and adjust to the needs of others, in effect to share and to
make room. They have shown a willingness to be patient
and understanding about excesses. The collective organized Jewish "eye" has been kept on the greater good and
the larger goal because Jews must benefit from an expanded democracy. But the Jewish Establishment has
been dealing with issues at top levels, not in the neighborhoods or the streets. Jewish leadership deals with the
Wilkinses, the Youngs, and the Rustins, and an occasional
extremist. The people in the neighborhoods, especially
transitional ones, are confronted daily with the extremists.

The other day I was told about a meeting in Coney
Island where a group of Jewish and black women had
come together around some community issues. A city-
paid black poverty worker took the floor and began abu-
sively addressing them as "white pigs" and worse. The
Jewish women departed angry and bitter. Jewish teachers
and administrators have been treated in like fashion. Ivy
League and other colleges have bowed to the extortionist
tactics of black students to set up preferential quotas and
black-studies programs. Some of the schools are remembered by Jews for the *numerus clausus* they had not so
many years ago which made it next to impossible for Jews
to get in. And poor Jews, of which there are many in New
York, are watching the blacks and the Puerto Ricans take
control of the poverty programs and get all of the goodies

insofar as paid staff positions are concerned. They are also witnessing big businesses which won't hire *Shomer Shabbat* Jews employing blacks whom they consider to be less qualified, and accommodating to the inconvenience.

I think it is true that the number of extremists in the black community are relatively few, but they are, thanks to the media, visible far above their numbers. I think it is true also that we are undergoing a societal adjustment that will level out as time goes by, but that does not ease the immediate threat or inconvenience and I am not about to assign the cost to one individual or another—or for that matter to any one group as some social engineers seem to be doing. I am sure that what Jews want for themselves as individuals the majority of blacks want also. No Negro in his right mind will want an empty education—at any level—for his children. No one wants to live in an unsafe neighborhood where it's worth life and limb to go out at night. No businessman wants to operate behind locked doors during the day. No one wants to be set upon by street gangs or junkies. A safer city with expanded opportunity and greater economic gains are common goals for all who live in the city. So is good housing and medical care and all the other attainables which lead to a better life. But we've allowed these common goals to be compartmentalized and labeled for "special" groups only. We've forgotten about Newton's Third Law of Motion—that for every action there is an equal and opposite reaction. In the "adjustments" and accommodations we have made, we have neglected to adjust for or accommodate those in our midst. We profess to be acting in behalf of society as a whole and yet we are working on the problems of one segment of it at a time, stating all the while that attaining the objectives for the weakest will assure them for all.

The organized Jewish community has a real image problem. What's coming through to those attracted by the JDL is that we care about others more than we care about our own. That's not so, as any examination of the records will quickly show. But we are engaged in confrontation politics in the United States today. Too often some of the organized Jewish groups practice diplomacy, not politics. We have to be political in times of power redistribution. I don't mean partisan or candidate-centered politics, I mean political in the sense of one hand washing the other —*quid pro quo.*

We don't have to change our agendas, but we do have to change our emphasis. The emphasis has to be on Jewish concerns from a Jewish base. That doesn't mean isolationism or separatism in terms of the general community. It means putting Jewish problems on the agenda as part of the full package to be considered. What happens to Jewish teachers and school administrators should be made an agenda item for black and Puerto Rican leaders even if it would not be made their first priority, just as expanding the number of black and Puerto Rican teachers is an agenda item for Jews. Likewise, the same holds true for the possible displacement of qualified college students by others less qualified. It means that blacks as well as Jews should denounce black anti-Semites or other racists.

It's easy to condemn the Jewish Defense League as a vigilante movement and sorely tempting to characterize the JDL members as racists who are exacerbating polarization of our community. That is an oversimplification. Pious pronouncements are a poor substitute for direct action. Calling people racists who really think their whole system and world are being torn apart and that they are being sold out shows little understanding of the fear and desolation so many feel. We are not facing any simple case of backlash. These people hear the JDL threaten to mount a street patrol in a suburb of Boston and see the police respond immediately with increased protection. The charge of "un-American" or "vigilante" evaporates in the face of what they see. Nor do they think that perhaps the real reason the police came in was to prevent the JDL from precipitating a bloody riot by their presence. They are concerned with their own safety.

Neither troubled blacks nor troubled Jews give much of a damn about polarization. They are concerned about solving their troubles. It is about time that we relegate "polarization" and "depolarization" to the same priority as "brotherhood" and concentrate on the causes of polarization.

Without turning away from the broader community— locally or nationally—we have to turn our attention inward to the troubled neighborhood level. We have to know what goes on in neighborhoods most of us don't live in. For that we cannot rely on the media. The people there have to be consulted and involved. The popular phrase is "community participation." We'd better start using more than just the phrase. We also have to lend some of our "muscle" to the neighborhoods, and when they need more police protection we must use whatever influence we can mount to see that they get it. We have to do these things whether or not there is a JDL.

While we are pushing for equity capital for black businessmen, we should simultaneously be seeking or creating relocation equity for Jewish businessmen who will go under unless it is forthcoming. If we are to set up urban foundations in the Jewish community, they should be as much for the purpose of assisting poor Jews as poor blacks and others.

Social action committees of temples ought to be setting

up "listening posts" or complaint desks so that local problems can be reported and corrective action taken in cooperation with city-wide and national groups. The listening post would perform several functions, not the least of which would be to establish communication where none now exists. It could also be a rumor control center, a resource and referral agency, and perform a coordinating function.

We can send out skilled community organizers to help Jews get together with others to undertake joint action on community problems. Some of that is being done now, but the point of reference is different from what I am suggesting. My point of reference is that the approach should stem from Jewish concern for themselves, not Jewish concern for others. This does not eliminate Jewish concern for others; it gives it a different motivation and a stronger base. What stronger motivation can there be than self-interest? I suggest also that everything we are now seeking to do in terms of the total community would be done quicker and better, for if we can improve the status of one group in a neighborhood, that group will feel compelled to help others maintain the community standard to the common benefit of all.

I am suggesting that we go from the universals to the specifics without giving up our support of the former. I think we have to use our relationships at the universal levels to effect a reconnection for action, to paraphrase the Bundy Report on school decentralization. That means the people we support in achieving broad programs at governmental levels must be asked to support us as they can at the neighborhood levels.

There are probably hundreds of ways in which we can turn our attention to the state of mind or the state of fear which has permitted the rise of the Jewish Defense League.

The JDL for all of its ugliness and public relations embarrassment is of small consequence in contrast to how it was born and how it survives. There is no conspiracy. There is no pogrom. The status of the Jew in the United States is more secure than it has ever been and organized anti-Semitism is at its lowest ebb. There are real problems, though, which involve and confront Jews as individuals. We have to deal with those real problems on a priority basis. Only then will the fears dissolve and with it the paranoia and the Jewish Defense League.

IV | THE "NEW PLURALISM"

To most Americans brought up in a tradition that we are all Americans and nothing more, the recent growth of racial, religious, and ethnic identification is perplexing. Reluctantly it is accepted among blacks as a price this society must pay for its extraordinary treatment of them and their need to achieve greater group cohesiveness to bring about change in their condition. But the tendency among many Americans is to deny the saliency of ethnicity, hope that the current manifestations will be a passing thing, or point out the dangers of tribalism. As we come to accept our dual identities—in being members of the total society and also its smaller, ethnic components—rejection is beginning to give way to a closer examination of the implications of diversity.

This is one of the most exciting explorations currently under way in the social sciences. Involved here is not only a search for a clearer understanding of who Americans are (Consciousness IV?), but clues to resolving some of the most vexing social and political problems confronting us today. The selections in this section illustrate a number of the themes of the "new pluralists." Andrew M. Greeley in "What Is an Ethnic?" examines the reasons that bring and keep groups together. In a somewhat uneven but brilliant paper written in the terminal stages of illness, David Danzig explores the historical evolution of our society to "a pluralist nation with a Protestant tradition." One of the most daring of the "new pluralists," Danzig argues here that "class consciousness is ephemeral and episodic in American history" in comparison with basic ethnic divisions in our society!

Andrew M. Greeley in "'We' and 'They': The Differences Linger" and Irving M. Levine and Judith M. Herman demonstrate the impact of ethnicity in the daily lives of people. Finally, in "Is White Racism the Problem?" I attempt to examine a half dozen recent intergroup relations problems and suggest that conventional "human relations" rhetoric and strategies often exacerbate conflicts that stem from the inevitable clash of groups in American life.

The "new pluralism" has yielded important results in developing approaches for dealing with the problems of low-income white ethnic groups. It is no panacea, however, and opens up as many problems as it sets out to help resolve. We are only at the earliest stages of the serious study of ethnicity in this country. The decision of the Ford Foundation to fund a number of ethnic programs and the possibility that Congress will enact legislation setting up a series of Ethnic Heritage Studies Centers are hopeful signs that, perhaps for the first time in our history, we are beginning to come to grips with our tribal past and present. (Hearings were held before the General Subcommittee on Education of the Committee on Education and Labor, House of Representatives, 91st Congress, 2d Session, on H.R. 14910 [Ethnic Heritage Studies Centers], on Feb. 16, 17, 18, 24, 26; March 4, 5, 19; and May 6, 1970.)

By Andrew M. Greeley

What Is an Ethnic?

IT IS VERY DIFFICULT to speak precisely about what an ethnic group is, but it is possible to develop a wokring definition somewhat empirically and to describe ethnicity by showing how contemporary ethnic groups came into existence. While . . . there is some broad equation possible between ethnic groups and immigrant groups, it is not enough merely to say that the ethnic groups are immigrant groups. Whatever definition we emerge with is likely to leave us with some very embarrassing questions. For example: Does everyone belong to an ethnic group? Is a white Anglo-Saxon Protestant an ethnic? Are Texans or Kentuckians, for example, ethnics? And what about American intellectuals, particularly those who are not Jewish and who seem to be quite cut off from any trace of nationality background? Do they constitute a new ethnic group? Such questions do not admit of quick answers; yet we must address ourselves to them if only because there are a number of Americans who are not prepared to take ethnic issues seriously unless responses to those questions are provided.

The ancestors of the immigrants to the United States were, for the most part, peasants living in the agricultural communities of European postfeudal society. This society was postfeudal in the sense that the peasants either owned some land of their own, or at least had been emancipated from the worst rigors of the feudal system. The peasant villages of Ireland, Germany, Italy, Poland, or the Balkans were not the most comfortable places in the world, and the nostalgia bordering on romance over them that is to be found in the works of some nineteenth-century sociological writers is misleading. Granted that postfeudal peasant society provided a great deal of stability, it did so at the price of stagnancy; and granted also that it provided a great deal of social support, it did so by imposing a great deal of social control. A man was, indeed, sure of who he was and where he stood and what he might become in such societies, but most men were in inferior positions and had no expectation of becoming anything more than inferior.

Nevertheless, there was a warmth and intimacy and closeness in these peasant communities. A person could be sure of the pattern of relationships and be sure that while he might have enemies, he also had friends, and the friends and enemies were defined by historic tradition. Society indeed controlled individual members, but it also rallied support, strength, and resources when help was needed. It was a highly personal world, not in the sense that the dignity of the human person was respected more than it is today, but in the sense that relationships were, for the most part, between persons who knew each other, understood their respective roles, and knew what kind of behavior to expect. Family, church, and community were all fairly simple and overwhelmingly important, and though mankind had evolved beyond the all-pervading intimacy of the tribe or the clan, life was nonetheless quite personal and intimate in a stylized and highly structured way.

Sometime after 1800, European peasant society began to break up, partly because, as the population increased, there were more people than jobs in the agricultural communes, and partly because the emergent industrialization in the cities desperately needed new labor. Those who made the move from commune to metropolis in hope of finding a better life began a number of social trends which actually meant a better life, if not for them, at least for their children or their grandchildren. The pilgrimage from peasant village to city, and later to the cities of America, brought to many the wealth of the affluent society.

But something was also lost: the warmth and intimacy, the social support, of the commune was gone. Gabriel Le Bras, the famous French sociologist of religion, remarked that there was a certain railroad station in Paris which apparently had magical powers, because any Breton immigrant who passed through that station never set foot in a Catholic church again. The church, the family, the commune which had provided the parameters of the ordinary person's life were all either destroyed or so substantially altered as to be unrecognizable. The peasant migrant was forced to spend most of his waking day with people who were strangers. This is an experience which does not seem peculiar to us at all, but to a man who had encountered few strangers ever before in his life, it was frightening and disorienting.

"Our Own Kind"

In the strangeness of the new environment, the individual or his battered and bedraggled family looked around for someone with whom he had something in common—hopefully a place in the big city where previous migrants from his village had settled. Because such settlers were "his kind of people," he could trust them; they knew their obligations to him and would help him to adjust to this new world in which he found himself. Thus, in the Italian neighborhoods of New York's lower east side in the early 1920's it was possible to trace, block by block, not only the region in Italy but also the very villages from which the inhabitants had come. Indeed, it is no exaggeration to say that some of these blocks were nothing more than foreign colonies of Sicilian villages.

If you weren't able to find someone from your own village, then you searched for someone from your area of the country; even though you may never have met him before, you could depend on him to have some of the same values you had, and you shared some sort of common origin. He may not have been from Palermo, but at least he was a Sicilian; he may not have been from Ballyhaunis, but at least he was from County Mayo; and these village or regional groupings, based especially on family and kinship relationships, in their turn sought protection and some power against the strange world in which they found themselves by banding together, one with another. So that for many groups, as Glazer has pointed out, the nationality became a relevant factor only when the necessities of adjusting to American experience forced the village and regional groups to band together.

The ethnic group provided a pool of preferred associates for the intimate areas of life. It was perhaps necessary in large corporate structures to interact with whomever the random possibilities of the economic system put at the next workbench or desk. But when it came to choosing a wife, a poker (and later on, bridge) partner, a precinct captain, a doctor, a lawyer, a real estate broker, a construction contractor, a clergyman, and, later on, a psychiatrist, a person was likely to feel much more at ease if he could choose "my kind of people."

So then, as Max Weber[1] defines it, an ethnic group is a human collectivity based on an assumption of common origin, real or imaginary; and E. K. Francis, supplementing the Weber definition, has argued that the ethnic collectivity represents an attempt on the part of men to keep alive, in their pilgrimage from peasant village to industrial metropolis, some of the diffuse, descriptive, particularistic modes of behavior that were common in the past. The ethnic group was created only when the peasant commune broke up, and was essentially an attempt to keep some of the values, some of the informality, some of the support, some of the intimacy of the communal life in the midst of an impersonal, formalistic, rationalized, urban, industrial society.

That the immigrants tried to associate with their own kind was understandable enough in the early phases of immigration, but we are still faced with the necessity of explaining why ethnic groups have persisted as important collectivities long after the immigration trauma receded into the background. Why was not social class the membership around which American city dwellers could rally, as it was in England? Why have the trade unions rarely, if ever, played quite the fraternal role in American society that they have in many Continental societies? Granted that urban man needed something to provide him with some sort of identification between his family and the impersonal metropolis, why did he stick with the ethnic group when there were other groupings to which he could make a strong emotional commitment?

First of all, one must acknowledge the fact that other

groups have, on occasion, provided the same enthusiasm that ethnic groups do. Some men need more of this enthusiasm than others, and by no means all who need it seek it in a nationality group. As a matter of fact, it is probably likely that for many, at least at the present stage of acculturation, religion is more important than ethnicity as a means of social definition and social support, a means of identifying ourselves in relation to others. However, religion and ethnicity are so intertwined in the United States that it is extremely difficult to separate them; an attempt to sort out this relationship is one of the major challenges facing social theorists who become concerned with ethnic groups.

Pluralism and Group Survival

It seems to me that there were two factors which made for the survival of ethnic communities after the immigration trauma was over. First of all, the United States is a society which has demonstrated considerable ability in coping with religious and racial pluralism, one way or another. A nation which was, in effect, religiously pluralistic before it became politically pluralistic, the United States had to learn a sufficient amount of tolerance for religious diversity merely to survive. It was necessary only to expand this tolerance when the new immigrant groups arrived on the scene with their own peculiar kinds of religious difference. It also seems that, even before the Revolutionary War, nationality differences were important, so the Germans and the Irish (usually meaning the Scotch-Irish) were considered as a group quite distinct from the Anglo-Saxon majority. Furthermore, even though the racial relationship had deteriorated into tyranny and slavery, there was, at least until the invention of the cotton gin, apparently some possibility that even this might be peacefully settled. In other words, by the time the large waves of immigrants came, in the early and middle nineteenth century, America was already acquiring some skills in coping with the religiously and ethnically plural-istic society. The immigrants were not welcome, and con-siderable pressure was put upon them to become Anglo-Saxons as quickly as possible. Yet the pressures stopped short of being absolute; the American ethos forced society to tolerate religious and ethnic diversity even if it did not particularly like it. Under such circumstances, it was pos-sible for the ethnic groups to continue and to develop an ideology which said they could be Irish, German, Polish, or Jewish, and at the same time be as good Americans as anyone else—if not better.[2]

But why is it still important to be an Italian, an Irishman, a German, or a Jew? Part of the reason, I suspect, has something to do with the intimate relationship between ethnicity and religion. But another element, or perhaps another aspect of the same element, is that presumed com-mon origin as a norm for defining "we" against "they" seems to touch on something basic and primordial in the human psyche, and that much of the conflict and strife that persists in the modern world is rooted in such differences. If anything, the separatist nationalisms within the major nation states seem stronger today than they were a quarter of a century ago: Catholics rioting in Londonderry, Ire-land; Scots electing nationalist members to Parliament; the mutterings of Welsh separatism. The Basques, and even the Catalonians, grumble about being part of Spain; the Flemings and the Walloons are at odds with each other over Louvain; the Bretons wonder if it might be possible for them to escape from France; and the French Canadians are not at all sure they want to remain part of the Can-

adian nation, even if they could have their own prime
minister.

Most of these separatist movements make little sense
in terms of economic reality. The Province of Quebec
would be hard put to go it on its own; Wales and Scotland would very quickly have to form a political and economic union with England, not much different from the
one that already exists; and Brittany would have to do the
same with the government in Paris. Maybe tribal loyalties and tribal separatism ought not to continue in a rational, industrial world—but they do, and it is a threat
to the fabric of almost any society large enough to be
made up of different ethnic communities. One is almost
tempted to say that if there are no differences supposedly
rooted in common origin by which people can distinguish
themselves from others, they will create such differences.
I suspect, for example, that if Scotland did become independent of England, there would be conflict between
the Highlanders and the Lowlanders as to who would run
the country. Ethnic diversity seems to be something that
man grimly hangs on to, despite overwhelming evidence
that he ought to give it up.

Edward Shils has called these ties primordial and suggests that rooted as they are with a sense of "blood and
land," they are the result of a prerational intuition. Such an
assumption seems to make considerable sense, but is difficult to prove empirically. It is certainly true, however,
that family, land, and common cultural heritage have always been terribly important to human beings, and suspicion of anyone who is strange or different seems also to
be deeply rooted in the human experience. Ethnic groups
continue, in this hypothesis, because they are a manifestation of man's deep-seated inclination to seek out those in
whose veins he thinks flows the same blood as flows in his
own. When blood is also seen as something intimately re-

lated to belief, and both blood and belief impinge strongly on what happens to a man, his wife, and his children, he is only too ready to fight to protect the purity of that belief, or the purity of his blood, or the purity of his family when it is threatened by some strange outside invader.

This view of ethnicity, it must be confessed, is essentially a negative one. But one can make a more positive case for it. It could be said that the apparent inclination of men, or at least of many men, to consort with those who, they assume, have the same origins they do, provides diversity in the larger society and also creates substructures within that society which meet many functions the larger society would be hard put to service. And while the demons of suspicion and distrust prove very hard to exorcise from interethnic relationships, such suspicion and distrust are not, I am convinced, inevitable. If they can be eliminated, ethnicity enriches the culture and reinforces the social structure.

To sum up, ethnic groups have emerged in this country because members of the various immigrant groups have tried to preserve something of the intimacy and familiarity of the peasant village during the transition into urban industrial living. These groups have persisted after the immigrant experience both because American society was not basically hostile to their persistence and because of an apparently very powerful drive in man toward associating with those who, he believes, possess the same blood and the same beliefs he does. The inclination toward such homogeneous groupings simultaneously enriches the culture, provides for diversity within the social structure, and considerably increases the potential for conflict. It may someday be possible to isolate ethnicity from suspicion and distrust, but no one has yet figured out the formula for doing so.

Notes

1. Max Weber, "The Ethnic Group," in Talcott Parsons, *et al.*, *Theories of Society* (The Free Press, 1961), Vol. 1, p. 305.
2. Daniel Patrick Moynihan summarized the superpatriot syndrome beautifully when he said, "At last the time had come to investigate Harvard men, and Fordham men were going to do the investigating."

By David Danzig

The Social Framework
of Ethnic Conflict
in America

THE RIOTS of three summers and one spring have cut deep wounds across the nation. Between these outbreaks there have been political assassinations and murders inspired by race hate. And yet race conflict shows no sign of abating.

This is happening at a time when the American nation has never been more powerful or more prosperous. It is the oldest nation in existence with a continuous democratic political system. Its record of stability and unity is all the more remarkable for its heterogeneous immigrant population and its rapid industrial development, which has undermined old social institutions and created new ones. It has a history of constantly expanding democracy. Its political and economic institutions have shown themselves to be flexible and capable of great adaptation and expansion. The American nation provides its people with more of the immediate requirements of the good life than does any other nation in the world.

Yet few of us expect a diminishing of violence and a return to the relative domestic tranquillity of yesterday.

A paper delivered at the National Consultation on Ethnic America, Fordham University, June 8, 1968. Reprinted by permission of Mrs. David Danzig.

241

Obviously, great changes have taken place within our society—we apparently have failed to understand them and certainly we have failed to handle them. There can be little doubt that whatever disturbs our community life, its causes lie deep beneath the surface. In the eyes of some people our social disorders are serious but not fundamental; America to them is still the world's outpost of freedom, man's last best hope, morally and politically equipped to lead the so-called free world. To others, our disorders are symptoms of a sick, racist society, ruled by a small power structure whose basic policies—when distinguished from their superficial reforms and populist rhetoric —are dominion abroad and repression at home. . . .

No intelligent person today can have any question that prejudice is widespread in American society—any more than he can question that its eradication is essential to the preservation of political democracy. Yet the heart of the matter today is not the prevalence of prejudice, but its relevance; that is, how it applies in different social situations.

What distinguishes most Americans is not that they are better or worse, or more or less prejudiced than others, but that in some circumstances they recognize and accept the obligation to set aside their prejudices. That they will act upon their prejudices in other circumstances is still a far cry from racism. Few people who live in socially separated ethnic communities, as many Americans do, can be persuaded that because these communities are also racially separated they are morally sick. Having come to accept their own social situation as the natural result of their ethnic affinities, mere exhortation is not likely to convince them—or, for that matter, the public at large—that they are thereby imposing upon others a condition of apartheid.

To pose the issue in this way is to raise the question whether the rights of the individual in these local circumstances are the same as they are acknowledged to be in the national setting.

There can be no question that Americans assume an element of sovereignty in their voluntary group life. The prevalence and diversity of group conflict is some reflection of this. Americans are in conflict today not only over Vietnam, racial violence, and how to deal with the cities and rebellion on the campus, but also because of tensions and differences that arise from their group values and interests.

Controversy among Catholics, Protestants, Jews, and secularists has produced more Supreme Court litigation over the meaning of the First Amendment's "establishment" clause in the twenty years since 1947 than in the previous more than one hundred fifty years since the signing of the Constitution; interracial strife has given rise to more civil rights litigation since World War II than in the entire prior history of the nation; the views of conservatives and liberals on questions of national security and the right of dissent produced a significant body of state and federal Supreme Court decisions affecting civil liberties long before the Vietnam war gave these issues a new urgency. Much the same can be said for the conflicting interests of the core city populations and those of suburbia and the rural upstate people contained in the issue of metropolitan government and the Supreme Court's reapportionment decisions. And this is to say nothing of the conflicting economic interests which have paved the way to the present era, those between business and labor.

Granting the importance of groups, the question remains: Has America substituted for its goal of a unitary integrated community of individuals, a compartmentalized society of groups? This question bears some examination in depth.

Most of us grew up with the idea that a community was made up of individuals. Our picture was usually that of the small town—most ideally the New England small town—its Main Street lined with stately Dutch elms, leading to the wide Common surrounded by austere churches; its public life was based on a shared concern for the common good; its town-hall democracy was characterized by religious freedom and a conscientious expression of sturdy political dissent. In this community there were neither classes, blocs, nor groups conspiring to put self-interest above community welfare. Were temporary groups, cliques, or classes to form, in time they would disappear or they would be put down. This, of course, is the image of James Madison, so clearly put in Federalist No. 10, where he commends the strengthening of the Federal Government as the means to "bridle the power of factions" and protect the integrity of the community as a social contract of discrete individuals.

This picture, of course, suggests a far more negative attitude toward the place of social groups in the civic and political life of the community than as compared to now. Moreover, it strongly implies that the historic American community was far more homogeneous than we now consider it to have been. It is important to hold in mind that for the greatest part of its history America was a nation primarily of small towns and villages which were predominantly white, Anglo-Saxon, and Protestant. Homogeneity may have been affected symbolically, but not practically, by the presence of others of a different race, religion, or nationality. The black people did not count, the Jews were insignificant, and the Germans were predominant only in certain rural areas and a number of

Midwestern towns. Though in time the Irish prevailed politically in some eastern cities, this counted for little in shaping the American ethos, since the cities themselves played so small a part in the national culture. One is reminded that William Jennings Bryan spoke of the eastern cities as "enemy territory," and Truman Douglas, of the Church of Christ, speaking even of the present attitude of much of the population, said: "Anti-urban bias has become almost a point of dogma in American Protestantism." The town, until very recently, was the center of the American nation: in both symbol and reality the American town was the American community.

Not only was it primarily Protestant, each community was usually dominated by one or at most two Protestant denominations. For example, Winthrop Hudson has pointed out that even today, broadly speaking, there are no Presbyterians in New England, no Congregationalists in Pennsylvania, no Lutherans in Mississippi, no Episcopalians in the Dakotas, no Disciples or members of the Churches of Christ in New Jersey, and of the 160 churches in the city of Tulsa more than 100 are one denomination—Baptist—and in more than half the counties of Minnesota the churches are more than 70 percent peopled by members of the Scandinavian Lutheran Church. As well, recall that Quakers, Baptists, and Mormons were unacceptable in many regions; the latter's churches were burned down as late as 1850 and they were driven from a half dozen states. Not until they founded a community entirely their own did they find a place.

The first great threat to this predominantly homogeneous community came with the so-called new immigration, beginning in the 1880's. In place of people from Western Europe there came Slavs, Sicilians, Ukrainians, Poles. Mostly Catholic in religion—except for the Jews among them—and accustomed to a hierarchical social and political life, they crowded into eastern cities. From 1880 to 1914 almost thirty million of these people entered the country.

By the 1920's, foreign stock comprised 40 percent of the population. But, considering that in the eleven southern states those of foreign stock constituted under 5 percent, the percentage in the rest of the nation, particularly in the eastern cities, was considerably higher than the national average. Up to 60 percent of the workers in the packing houses and in the steel and iron industries were foreign-born. Indeed, most manual and dangerous labor such as mining, as well as menial work, was done by the foreign-born.

In consequence of their great numbers and their religious and ethnic differences these immigrants had a profound effect. In a relatively short time ethnic segregation characterized the major American cities and paved the way for ethnic politics, which was strongly resented.

After World War I a wave of antiforeign feeling surged over the nation. In part it was a reaction to the war; in part it was an authentic Kulturkampf. At a time when the nation's population stood in the 120 millions, the Ku-Klux Klan had an estimated membership of over 3 million—its major targets were not only the long-victimized Negro, but also the foreign-born, the Catholic, the Jew, and the Bolshevik labor organizer. The Klan in Indiana, Ohio, and Long Island was as strong as in Alabama. The Sacco-Vanzetti trial and the trial and murder of Leo Frank in Atlanta were threats to the foreign-born. Blue laws, Prohibition, measures against teaching foreign languages in schools, and laws against teaching evolution—the last being only recently rescinded—confirmed the second-class status of Catholics, Jews, and other aliens, and made America safe for a conservative fundamentalism.

By 1924, this attitude of "America for Americans" brought the enactment of restrictive immigration legislation: it reduced the flow of immigrants and wrote into law the preferred status of the Anglo-Saxon peoples. The bill was passed by an overwhelming majority—opposition came only from Congressmen representing ethnic minority districts in the cities. It gave the status of law to the sentiment of most of the people.

The feeling of ethnic nationalism rose to a climax in the Presidential contest between Democratic, Irish Catholic Al Smith and Republican, Quaker, Anglo-Saxon Herbert Hoover. As Sam Lubell has made clear, it was the battle of 1928 with its powerful ethnic implication which began the shift of the big-city vote from the Republican to the Democratic Party. It also started the Democratic Party on its way to becoming the coalition party of the big-city ethnic groups and the Republican Party on its way to being the party of big business.

But the conservatism which had captured America, based on Adam Smith's economics and John Calvin's ethics, was ill suited to a dynamic industrial capitalism and a heterogeneous population. The surge of conservatism that began in the "tribal twenties" did not survive the decade. Franklin Delano Roosevelt, coming on the national scene in the midst of a catastrophic depression, understood fully the economic and ethnic cleavages that cut across the whole of the nation.

While the new liberal coalition that Roosevelt created was economically based, it drew much of its political strength from social groups. It was strongly pro-labor, sympathetic to minorities, concerned about youth and children, supportive of equal rights for the foreign-born and for women, and in favor of aid to the dependent and the unemployed. In 1935 that coalition enacted more social legislation than in any other previous year in American history: the Wagner Labor Relations Act, the Social Security Law, the Public Utilities Holding Act, the WPA, and others.

The New Deal strengthened labor as a countervailing force against management and made the government a third force in the economy. It created the welfare state and in time secured for it the sanction of public policy. It also elevated the political and social status of religio-ethnic minorities and paved the way for the era of civil rights reform.

The New Deal radically enlarged the political community when it engaged America's ethnic groups in national politics. The bloc vote and the balanced ticket graduated from the municipal to the national level. Jews, Catholics, and Negroes pursued their respective and often antagonistic goals within the broad coalition goals set by the New Deal. The stakes which Jews had in a liberal America went far beyond economics. They could not help feeling their very survival hung in the balance when America debated: Who is the greater enemy to democracy, Hitler or Stalin? In some respects, survival was also involved for American Catholics, who saw Left totalitarianism as a threat to Catholic nations. For these and other reasons, both groups sought to be close to the locus of power. Negroes saw in the New Deal the promise that federal power would at last free them from local tyranny as well as provide immediate economic help that was sorely needed. The New Deal, which rewarded minority participation in the national coalition, gave a new relevance to religioethnic groups which was only remotely connected to religion as such.

In 1927, when André Siegfried visited the United States from France, he could still say: "Protestantism is America's national religion; to ignore this is to view it from a false position." But by 1960 this had changed. In those years, the nation had begun to give expression to a profound transformation that had been long under way. When John F. Kennedy took office in 1961, the country over which he presided—whose Presidents until Van Buren had all been born British subjects—had broken sharply with its past in this respect. From a relatively homogeneous Protestant nation with an Anglo-Saxon background, the United States was now acknowledged to be a pluralist nation with a Protestant tradition. Though the election has been rightfully taken as a giant step in the expansion of American political democracy, it was no less important as a public endorsement of pluralism as the national policy. Roosevelt had made the religioethnic group viable and politically relevant; Kennedy made it respectable.

Until the advent of Roosevelt and Kennedy, minority politics was the province of the big machine and the ward heeler. In general, those social practices which stressed the solidarity of minority groups were disapproved while practices that made for their dissolution and led to the assimilation of their members were looked upon with favor. But by the time Kennedy ran for office, group solidarity such as secured for him more than 80 percent of the Catholic vote was generally accepted as natural. His election to the Presidency eliminated second-class status for Catholics and benefited other minorities as well. Minority groups now appeared less an Old World hangover and more an authentic part of the American community. America thereby acknowledged the failure of the melting pot. The answer to ethnic diversity was no longer dissolution and assimilation. The religioethnic group was now seen as a permanent part of the American scene sanctioned by the new doctrine of pluralism.

To be sure, pluralism has yet to be defined in any

comprehensive way. It explains how society is organized and just as often explains why it is disorganized. While in America there has always been a *de facto* pluralism, it has never been justified by a doctrine. In Europe, where pluralism first arose as a theory, it had a quite different thrust from that of our pragmatic approach. There, in the shadow of the monolithic sovereign state, pluralism, which was never much more than a political theory, sought to limit the power of the state, through the countervailing power of autonomous groups. No doubt Germany's aggressive nationalism and belief in the primacy of the state over the individual was a stimulus to European political theorizing. The English Socialists Beatrice and Sidney Webb thus advocated a new society, one that would be composed primarily of autonomous guilds, cooperatives, organizations, and corporations deriving their justification not from the state but from the people whose needs and interests they were created to serve.

As the pluralists on both sides of the Atlantic had recognized, the liberal utilitarianism of Rousseau placed the individual in a social vacuum. The citizen had power only when joining with others, preferably people with whom he cooperated in intimate daily activities of mutual self-interest. Lacking the protective web of associations, the individual was defenseless and his freedom was more abstract than real. Europeans, in a stable—indeed, a quite fixed—society looked to the group as a countervailing force against the power of the state; but Americans in a mobile, dynamic, and atomistic society turned to it for social purposes, a feeling of belonging and communal integration.

In America, the ethnic and religious associations had long formed a stable framework within which people centered a good part of their social activity; group life flourished. But in Britain and Europe where pluralism was projected in quasi-Marxist terms or as an abstract political doctrine and a program, it came to nothing. When, in World War I, totalitarian wartime states demanded and received the total allegiance of the individual, a politically conceived pluralism was no alternative to the overwhelming power of the state. But here, though political needs gave new relevance to social groups (for example, during the New Deal), their existence had long been based on social rather than political functions.

The great changes that followed two world wars underscored this. Mobility, population increases, mass communication, and urbanization greatly modified social relationships in American society. The community which was rooted in proximity, the extended family, and local tradition of a homogeneous population had been rapidly declining. New modes of communal attachment, more attuned to the heterogeneous metropolitanism which characterizes modern life, emerged. Outstanding among these is the religious association initially organized primarily for the pursuit of creedal ends, but which increasingly tends to assume communal functions. As Gerhard Lenski observes in his study "The Religious Factor":

> Religious activity stimulates social interaction and group organization. . . . Religious groups in the modern metropolis are a much more complex form of social organization than has been generally recognized. Far too many American sociologists have regarded them as merely one more type of specialized, formal association—the counterpart of the corporation, the labor union, the Kiwanis Club, or the PTA. . . .
>
> The crucial fact which [this view] ignores is that religious groups are subcommunities as well as religious associations.

Often the communal bonds that evolve in the religious group are further strengthened by ethnic homogeneity. Thus a Protestant community may also be Lutheran and largely German, or Lutheran and largely Scandinavian, or Presbyterian and primarily Scotch; a local Catholic church tends to be either predominantly Irish, Polish, or Italian; and Jewish congregations tend to identify with the local Jewish community. Residential patterns, inter-marriage rates, and voting tendencies show the continued importance of religioethnic loyalties, though the more obvious marks of cultural distinctiveness have diminished. The religioethnic community strengthens the family, and the family in turn replenishes the group. The group medi-ates between the individual and the larger society, and often it becomes the vehicle for social action.

In both obvious and subtle ways the group colors a man's view of himself and what he expects of the world. The culture which it transmits helps or hinders him in the competition he faces from the cradle to the grave. It often provides the auspices for individual activity, and through a network of agencies and organizations it can exert a large measure of control over an individual's life chances. In-deed, what group one is born into is a matter of some im-portance (for example, half of America's first thirty-two presidents were either Presbyterian or Episcopalian).

In the twenty years from 1940 to 1960, fifty million Americans became members of local church or synagogue congregations, making a total membership of more than 65 percent of the total population compared to an esti-mated 10 percent of the population in 1790 when the first census was taken. In the same period nearly twenty million additional young people enrolled in Sunday schools. In one year—1960—over one billion dollars was spent on the construction of new religious buildings. In 1957, a U.S. Census Bureau survey found that 97 percent of the popula-tion over fourteen years of age identified themselves with a religious group. More than 125 million Americans are now affiliated with local congregations.

What this adds up to, then, is this: the widespread existence of such subcommunities and their importance have made our society vastly more complex than our ideas of town-hall democracy would allow us to believe. In one set of circumstances we strive to live up to the principle "regardless of" race, color, and creed; in other circumstances, *race, color,* and *creed* are the very principle by which human relationships are organized. Gunnar Myrdal in my view failed to understand American society when he assumed that this contradictory behavior reflected a moral dilemma. On the contrary, this is the accepted differentiated structure of our social order.

Needless to say, to get acceptance of this and to develop public policies accordingly will not be easy. As the depression showed, our industrialized society, rather than being classless as we liked to think, was quite the opposite. But the organizing of labor, which was opposed for many reasons, was also fought because it would permanently separate America into antagonistic classes; actually, organized labor in time played a major role in reducing industrial strife and reconciling conflicting economic needs and interests of the nation.

It is yet to be recognized how great are the divisions in American society based on race, religion, and ethnicity: Karl Marx notwithstanding, these are turning out to be deeper—and will be perhaps more lasting—than the economic division. Class consciousness has been relatively ephemeral and episodic in American history. But race, color, and creed have plowed a maze of deep furrows across the American nation. This being the case, it is all the more important that we give full credit to our positive achievements and the policies we have arrived at for harmonizing our diverse religioethnic populations to see whether they can also help us in the matter of race barriers.

As has already been pointed out, the election of John F. Kennedy brought changes in the public attitudes toward minorities. In addition to equal rights of individuals, pluralism, which Kennedy's election inaugurated, affirmed the equal rights of groups. The religioethnic group ceased to be a "minority" expected to "wither away" as their members disappeared into the amorphous neutral society or converted to one of the higher-status groups. Where before we had seen only the trees—Catholics, Protestants, and Jews—now we recognized that there was also a forest: the Catholic, Protestant, and Jewish communities.

To be sure, this change had been long in the making. The policies from which it stemmed originated in the earliest days of the nation. Catholics and Jews were simply the belated beneficiaries of policies that had been shaped by the needs of Protestant diversity. For both state and federal governments had long recognized that the religious association was also a corporate entity. As the Wagner Act much later helped to transform an aggregation of workers into a corporate entity, capable of acting on behalf of its members, government support over the years had enabled the religious groups to carry out community responsibilities for their members.

State sanction gave support to the religious group in carrying out many of its communal responsibilities: service to men in the Armed Forces (toward which the state has contributed as high as a hundred million dollars a year in wartime), the right to educate the child, operate hospitals, and provide welfare and other such services. A large part of the resources for conducting these basic community functions came from the public pot. Freedom from taxation for religious institutions as well as for their profit-making enterprises, tax deductions for their contributors, and vast direct and indirect public subsidies provide the means for America's enormous and still growing network of religious-connected voluntary institutions.

The ownership of property gives corporeality to the religious community and links people in time and place. It may well provide both as a symbol and as a reality the urban equivalent of what territoriality gave to the locus community. The performance of social functions gives it relevance and status. The possession of material wealth and power enables it to stand between the individual and family and what is often an indifferent if not hostile society. Though it is the countless acts of self-sacrifice, devotion, and loyalty of its members that bring life to the religious group, public subsidy gives it viability.

These, then, are the policies which have helped bridge the gap between America's religious and ethnic groups, allowing each to go its way or to seek a common ground with others. That the Catholic, Protestant, and Jewish communities have flourished with these policies can hardly be questioned. What, then, does this mean for those who are distinguished from others, not by creed but by that greatest barrier of all, color? . . .

Recognition of the Negro as a valid subsociety need not be on any grounds other than those of other ethnic groups, namely, the constitutional right of free association guaranteed in the First Ammendment. That such recognition would imply a revolution in the scale and the manner in which aid is given to the Negro community goes without saying. Indeed, without such a revolution recognition would mean little. What is called for is assistance on the level given to revive the nation during the depression, or that which transferred more than $150 billion in foreign lands to other needy societies.

But the principle on which such assistance would be given would not be that of collective responsibility or the guilt of racism or preferential treatment. The principle would be none other than that under which the state now transfers vast public funds to other subsocieties, with autonomous institutions capable of performing greatly needed services to its members for the greater benefit of the nation and the entire society.

By Andrew M. Greeley

"We" and "They":
The Differences Linger

WE NOW TURN from speculation and theory about ethnicity to some concrete data about differences among ethnic groups in America. Most of the findings I am about to cite have not yet been published, but I think they help establish the fact that we are not just idly speculating when we say that ethnic groups have survived in the United States and continue to be the bearers of different cultural traditions. In addition, I think they may provide us with some hints as to the problems that ethnic differences seem to portend for American society, as well as some clues to further research that might be appropriate.

The data described stem from three major sources: first, a national survey of American Catholics done in 1963; second, data about the attitudes of June, 1961, college graduates seven years after graduation (collected as part of a long-term study of education and careers by the National Opinion Research Center of the University of Chicago); and finally, information obtained from a study of urban neighborhoods undertaken in 1967, also by the National Opinion Research Center.

The tables documenting these findings are contained in an unpublished set of National Opinion Research Center data entitled "Information About American Ethnic Groups," and the professional sociologist interested in inspecting these tables is welcome to do so. Since most readers, however, will not want to struggle through the statistics, only a few of the tables are reproduced here, while the most interesting and significant findings in all the data are summarized below.

The 1963 Catholic Survey

From the 1963 survey (Table 1) we learn that the Irish, first arrivals among American Catholics, are the most successful group as measured by their education, as well

Table 1. SELECTED ATTRIBUTES
OF CATHOLIC ETHNIC GROUPS IN U.S.

	Irish	Germans	Italians	Poles	French
Have completed high school	77%	62%	51%	46%	42%
Hold prestige jobs	32	31	13	17	22
Earn over $14,000 a year	24	19	17	18	7
Belong to Democratic Party	70	65	67	77	70
Score high on general knowledge	18	9	7	3	5
Score high on open-mindedness	52	48	42	43	40
Consider themselves "very happy"	41	36	35	27	40
Score low on anomie	64	51	47	43	49
Score high on piety	32	31	13	30	22
Score high on religious extremism	19	20	24	34	28
Score high on racism	44	46	54	61	51
Score high on anti-Semitism	29	47	43	52	54
(Number of persons interviewed)	(328)	(361)	(370)	(184)	(177)

as by the prestige of their jobs and their income. They also score highest on measures of general knowledge, are the most open-minded, and the most likely to exhibit high morale, as gauged both by measures of happiness and of anomie, i.e., the state of disorientation, anxiety, and isolation that develops when standards of conduct and belief have weakened or disappeared. They are the most pious and least given to religious extremism, racism, or anti-Semitism.

The Catholic German-Americans are almost as successful as the Irish in occupational status, though not in education or income. They are only slightly less devout than the Irish, slightly more given to religious extremism, somewhat less secure in their personal morale, and somewhat less open-minded.

Italians and Poles, both more recent Catholic immigrants, have yet to achieve the educational, occupational, and financial success of their Irish and German predecessors, and score lower in happiness and open-mindedness. They score higher on measures of racism than the older groups, but while the Poles also score higher on anti-Semitism, the Italians are lower on anti-Semitism even than the Germans. Poles are most likely, and Italians (together with Germans) least likely, to be members of the Democratic Party. And whereas Italians are the least pious of all the Catholic groups, the Poles are almost as devout as the Irish.

Finally, French Americans are among the least pious of American Catholic groups, second only to Poles with respect to religious extremism, and highest of all groups on measures of anti-Semitism. They score almost as high as the Irish in happiness, but they tend a good deal more toward anomie.

Can these differences be explained away, perhaps, by

the fact that some of the Catholic ethnic groups have been in this country longer than others or become better educated? The way to check this is to compare only individuals of the same generation and educational level— for example, those who are at least third-generation Americans and have completed high school (Table 2). We

Table 2. SELECTED ATTRIBUTES OF CATHOLIC ETHNIC GROUPS IN U.S.—HIGH-SCHOOL GRADUATES OF THIRD OR LATER GENERATION ONLY

	Irish	Germans	Italians	Poles	French
Hold prestige jobs	31%	34%	12%	32%	21%
Work as professionals or managers	45	47	37	22	31
Earn over $14,000 a year	26	22	3	21	11
Belong to Democratic Party	67	61	51	62	76
Score high on general knowledge	26	17	20	11	9
Score high on open-mindedness	51	56	51	34	40
Consider themselves "very happy"	47	38	26	32	48
Score low on anomie	74	60	44	61	60
Score high on piety	32	32	10	20	39
Score high on religious extremism	14	15	20	31	26
Score high on racism	39	30	54	61	29
Score high on anti-Semitism	25	38	32	59	43
(Number of persons interviewed)	(131)	(102)	(29)	(24)	(31)

then find that the typical differences between ethnic groups tend to diminish, but that many of them persist at least in some degree.

Thus, in occupational prestige and income the Irish and Germans are still the most successful, though the Poles have just about pulled abreast. The Irish still rank high-

on of, let us say, the Irish Catholic, Italian Cath-
nd Polish Catholic population is such that region
ale cannot account for all of the differences. (Nei-
of course, can social class, since all the respondents
ollege graduates.) The socialization experience of
r education has not eliminated ethnic group differ-
in attitudes and behavior, even among the Scandina-
and the Germans, whose geographic distribution is
r, or among the Irish, Italian, and Polish Catholics,
hare a common religion.

Neighborhood Study

e 1967 study of urban neighborhoods indicates that
are considerable differences in neighborhood be-
r among American groups. The findings show that
most often belong to neighborhood organizations
engage in a considerable amount of socializing, while
oles score lowest on the socializing scale. Italians are
likely to belong to organizations (though they are
likely to describe themselves as very sociable). The
most frequently state that they enjoy everything in
neighborhood and worry little, while both the Ital-
and the Jews score high on measures of worry. But
Italians, while they admit to worrying, also claim
e often than the Jews or any Protestants that they
enjoying themselves. It would seem, then, that the
and the Germans are low worriers and high enjoyers,
le the Italians are high worriers and high enjoyers.
erhaps the most significant findings in the neighbor-
d study have to do with where people live and how
uently they associate with members of their families
ble 4). Of all the ethnic groups Italians most often
in the same neighborhood as their parents and sib-

est in general knowledge, with Italians now in second
place and Germans in third. The Italians now are even
more likely than the Germans to have left the Democratic
Party. Poles again score high on anti-Semitism and racism,
and both Poles and Italians continue to score low on happiness. The Irish and French are again the happiest, putting to rest (forever, I hope) the notion that the Celts are
a morose and melancholy lot. I shall leave to others to
explain why the descendants of sunny Italy seem so
gloomy in this instance—though with only twenty-nine
of them in the table, one could easily argue that the whole
sample must have been made up of somber Milanese.

The findings of the 1963 survey were sorted out according to region as well as generation, with at least one
striking result: The Poles' high scores on measures of
anti-Semitism and racism were limited to the Midwest.
Poles on the East Coast did not differ from other Catholics
in these respects. It seems reasonable to conclude, therefore, that while ethnic differences persist even after three
or four generations and among the better educated, the
shape and direction of these differences is affected by
various other factors—economic, social, or geographical.
In all likelihood, the heavier the concentration of an ethnic group in a given area, the more likely it is to form a
tight ethnic community and to take a negative attitude
toward outsiders.

The Study of College Graduates

The National Opinion Research Center's study of June,
1961, college graduates, and their attitudes seven years
after graduation, was not limited to Catholics; hence, it
provides information about a substantial number of ethnic
groups.

One of the factors touched on was political affiliations. According to the findings, Jews are most likely to belong to the Democratic Party, and Protestants least likely. Polish Jews are more likely to be Democrats than German Jews, and Irish Catholics are more likely to be Democrats than German or Italian Catholics.

The Jews and the Irish score as less likely than any other ethnic group to hold racist ideas, with the Scandinavians and the Poles just behind them. Other groups tend to be substantially more prejudiced, with the Protestant Germans ranking highest among the lot on measures of racism.

As one might expect, Jews score higher on measures of reading and cultural interests than do Protestants, and Protestants score generally higher than Catholics—although Germans, both Protestant and Catholic, are the least likely to report intensive reading habits. German Jews seem to have more intense reading and cultural interests than Polish Jews; the Scandinavians lead the Protestants, and the Irish score highest among the Catholics. Polish Catholics, however, are most likely to plan a career in academia, followed by German Jews, Protestant Scandinavians and Catholic Irish. Protestant and Catholic Germans, together with Italians, are least likely to plan academic careers.

The differences among the college graduates are, in their own way, even more striking than the differences among the general population; for the college graduates are all young, well-educated and (one assumes) thoroughly American. And a college education does indeed seem to change some things—Polish attitudes toward blacks, for example, apparently improve very considerably as the result of higher education. Yet differences of 20 to 30 percentage points persist in many other measure-

ments of attitude and behavior, Fifty-one percent of the Catholi agree with the Kerner Commission racism was the cause of Negro rio while only 34 percent of their Ger vote the same way (Table 3). Thi

Table 3. RACIAL ATTITUDES AMONG OF DIFFERENT RELIGIOUS AND E

(June, 1961, graduates, surve

"White racism is the cause of Neg

	Proportion agreeing	
Blacks	84%	Catl
German Jews	54	Catl
Catholic Irish	51	Prot
Polish Jews	43	Prot
Catholic Poles	43	Prot
Protestant Scandinavians	37	

Protestant Scandinavians could acce mission's conclusions, but only 28 per confreres were willing to agree with

Turning from racism to another me contemporary social problems, an ind student militancy, we find a similar pa the blacks are the most sympathetic; t sympathetic among the Catholics, but of the Poles; and the Scandinavians pathetic of the Protestants—in fact, tians. Germans, both Catholic and Prot sympathetic within their respective re

Regional differences, or differences localities in which the respondents live, of the differences reported here. Yet th lings and visit them every week; together with the Poles and French, they also live most frequently near their in-laws or see them weekly. Protestants as a group are less likely than Catholics to live in the same neighborhood with relatives and to visit them weekly. Jews, though

Table 4. FAMILY RELATIONSHIPS OF RELIGIOUS AND ETHNIC GROUPS

	Live in same neighborhood with			See weekly		
	Parents	Siblings	In-laws	Parents	Siblings	In-laws
Catholics						
Italians	40%	33%	24%	79%	61%	62%
Irish	17	16	16	49	48	48
Germans	10	13	10	48	31	41
Poles	29	25	24	65	46	53
French	15	23	24	61	41	62
Protestants						
English	19	13	12	39	26	35
Germans	12	13	14	44	32	39
Scandinavians	14	11	17	39	26	31
Jews	14	12	14	58	33	58

no more likely than Protestants to live in the same neighborhoods, are more likely to visit their parents weekly than any of the Protestants, or the Irish and German Catholics.

When the same data are sorted out according to social class and the physical distance that separates the respondents from parents and relatives, an extremely interesting finding emerges. Italians are still the most likely to visit both their parents and their siblings. The Jews are now in second place in visits to parents, but at the bottom of the list where visits to siblings are concerned. The Irish, on the other hand, are relatively low on the parent-visiting list, but right behind the Italians in visits to siblings. It would seem that the stereotypes of the tight Italian family, the dominating Jewish parent, and the clannish Irish sib group are, at least to some extent, backed up by hard statistics.

Since relationships with parents and siblings play a major role in the formation of personality, it seems reasonable to suggest that the different patterns experienced by these three ethnic groups in the earliest years of life help make for quite different personality traits. If this be true, we can expect the subtle differences among the various ethnic groups to persist into the future.

Previous studies of Italian Americans, principally by Herbert Gans, indicate that the familial peer group—siblings and other relatives of one's own age—are the most important influence on lower-class Italians. To some extent, data in the surveys cited above confirm Gans's findings. The Italian's relationships with his parents seem to be a function of physical proximity; with his siblings, the bond overcomes even physical separation. However, Gans suggests that this sibling closeness is essentially working-class and not Italian behavior, whereas in our findings the ethnic differences seem to persist even when different social classes are examined separately.

An Overview

It is extremely difficult to tie together the diverse data from the various studies cited into a coherent pattern. But the information summarized above, together with some findings not quoted here, allow us to attempt the following generalizations:

The earlier immigrant groups are both the most socially successful and the most tolerant, but there are enough differences between, say, the Irish and the Germans, or between the Italians and the Poles, to suggest that other factors are at work besides the time at which one's parents washed up on American shores.

Of all the ethnic and religious groups the Jews are politically the most liberal and socially the most active, as well as economically the most successful. They are close to their parents, relatively less close to their siblings, and given to worrying.

Italians are conservative in their child-rearing practices and extremely close to their relatives—to their parents basically because they live close to them, but to their siblings, apparently, because the sibling relationship is very important to them. They are only moderately successful socially and economically, relatively uninvolved in organizational activity (perhaps because of their heavy family commitment) and liberal on some political questions, though more likely to leave the Democratic Party than are other Catholic ethnic groups. Though they think of themselves as very sociable, they are likely to have a lot of worries. They score rather low in measures of canonical religiousness, and fairly high on prejudice, though not as high as the Poles or the French. A college education apparently reduces, but does not completely eliminate, these differences in degree of prejudice.

The Irish are economically and socially the most successful among Catholic immigrant groups and the most liberal politically and socially. They have very strong ties with their siblings, are the most devoutly Catholic, and the least prejudiced, and their view of themselves ranks them as the happiest and most self-confident.

The Poles score lowest, economically and socially, of all Catholic immigrant groups, and those among them who live in the Midwest and have not graduated from college are the most likely to be prejudiced. They are very loyal to the Catholic Church (but in a more "ethnic" way than the Irish or the Germans). They are the most likely to be Democrats and, if they are college graduates, to be liberal Democrats. They are low in morale and sociability, and high on measures of anomie.

The many historical, sociological, and psychological processes that are involved in producing these differences are still frustratingly obscure, but to me they constitute one of the most fascinating questions for social research still open in our culture.

est in general knowledge, with Italians now in second place and Germans in third. The Italians now are even more likely than the Germans to have left the Democratic Party. Poles again score high on anti-Semitism and racism, and both Poles and Italians continue to score low on happiness. The Irish and French are again the happiest, putting to rest (forever, I hope) the notion that the Celts are a morose and melancholy lot. I shall leave to others to explain why the descendants of sunny Italy seem so gloomy in this instance—though with only twenty-nine of them in the table, one could easily argue that the whole sample must have been made up of somber Milanese.

The findings of the 1963 survey were sorted out according to region as well as generation, with at least one striking result: The Poles' high scores on measures of anti-Semitism and racism were limited to the Midwest. Poles on the East Coast did not differ from other Catholics in these respects. It seems reasonable to conclude, therefore, that while ethnic differences persist even after three or four generations and among the better educated, the shape and direction of these differences is affected by various other factors—economic, social, or geographical. In all likelihood, the heavier the concentration of an ethnic group in a given area, the more likely it is to form a tight ethnic community and to take a negative attitude toward outsiders.

The Study of College Graduates

The National Opinion Research Center's study of June, 1961, college graduates, and their attitudes seven years after graduation, was not limited to Catholics; hence, it provides information about a substantial number of ethnic groups.

One of the factors touched on was political affiliations. According to the findings, Jews are most likely to belong to the Democratic Party, and Protestants least likely. Polish Jews are more likely to be Democrats than German Jews, and Irish Catholics are more likely to be Democrats than German or Italian Catholics.

The Jews and the Irish score as less likely than any other ethnic group to hold racist ideas, with the Scandinavians and the Poles just behind them. Other groups tend to be substantially more prejudiced, with the Protestant Germans ranking highest among the lot on measures of racism.

As one might expect, Jews score higher on measures of reading and cultural interests than do Protestants, and Protestants score generally higher than Catholics—although Germans, both Protestant and Catholic, are the least likely to report intensive reading habits. German Jews seem to have more intense reading and cultural interests than Polish Jews; the Scandinavians lead the Protestants, and the Irish score highest among the Catholics. Polish Catholics, however, are most likely to plan a career in academia, followed by German Jews, Protestant Scandinavians and Catholic Irish. Protestant and Catholic Germans, together with Italians, are least likely to plan academic careers.

The differences among the college graduates are, in their own way, even more striking than the differences among the general population; for the college graduates are all young, well-educated and (one assumes) thoroughly American. And a college education does indeed seem to change some things—Polish attitudes toward blacks, for example, apparently improve very considerably as the result of higher education. Yet differences of 20 to 30 percentage points persist in many other measurements of attitude and behavior, despite college training. Fifty-one percent of the Catholic Irish were willing to agree with the Kerner Commission's conclusion that white racism was the cause of Negro riots in cities, for example, while only 34 percent of their German coreligionists would vote the same way (Table 3). Thirty-seven percent of the

Table 3. RACIAL ATTITUDES AMONG COLLEGE GRADUATES OF DIFFERENT RELIGIOUS AND ETHNIC BACKGROUNDS

(June, 1961, graduates, surveyed in 1968)

"White racism is the cause of Negro riots in the city"

	Proportion agreeing		Proportion agreeing
Blacks	84%	Catholic Italians	35%
German Jews	54	Catholic Germans	34
Catholic Irish	51	Protestant English	30
Polish Jews	43	Protestant Irish	28
Catholic Poles	43	Protestant Germans	28
Protestant Scandinavians	37		

Protestant Scandinavians could accept the Kerner Commission's conclusions, but only 28 percent of their German confreres were willing to agree with them.

Turning from racism to another measure of attitudes on contemporary social problems, an index of sympathy with student militancy, we find a similar pattern. The Jews and the blacks are the most sympathetic; the Irish are the most sympathetic among the Catholics, but only slightly ahead of the Poles; and the Scandinavians are the most sympathetic of the Protestants—in fact, of all white Christians. Germans, both Catholic and Protestant, are the least sympathetic within their respective religious traditions.

Regional differences, or differences in the size of the localities in which the respondents live, may explain many of the differences reported here. Yet the geographical distribution of, let us say, the Irish Catholic, Italian Catholic, and Polish Catholic population is such that region or locale cannot account for all of the differences. (Neither, of course, can social class, since all the respondents are college graduates.) The socialization experience of higher education has not eliminated ethnic group differences in attitudes and behavior, even among the Scandinavians and the Germans, whose geographic distribution is similar, or among the Irish, Italian, and Polish Catholics, who share a common religion.

The Neighborhood Study

The 1967 study of urban neighborhoods indicates that there are considerable differences in neighborhood behavior among American groups. The findings show that Jews most often belong to neighborhood organizations and engage in a considerable amount of socializing, while the Poles score lowest on the socializing scale. Italians are least likely to belong to organizations (though they are most likely to describe themselves as very sociable). The Irish most frequently state that they enjoy everything in their neighborhood and worry little, while both the Italians and the Jews score high on measures of worry. But the Italians, while they admit to worrying, also claim more often than the Jews or any Protestants that they are enjoying themselves. It would seem, then, that the Irish and the Germans are low worriers and high enjoyers, while the Italians are high worriers and high enjoyers.

Perhaps the most significant findings in the neighborhood study have to do with where people live and how frequently they associate with members of their families (Table 4). Of all the ethnic groups Italians most often live in the same neighborhood as their parents and siblings and visit them every week; together with the Poles and French, they also live most frequently near their in-laws or see them weekly. Protestants as a group are less likely than Catholics to live in the same neighborhood with relatives and to visit them weekly. Jews, though

Table 4. FAMILY RELATIONSHIPS OF RELIGIOUS AND ETHNIC GROUPS

	Live in same neighborhood with			See weekly		
	Parents	Siblings	In-laws	Parents	Siblings	In-laws
Catholics						
Italians	40%	33%	24%	79%	61%	62%
Irish	17	16	16	49	48	48
Germans	10	13	10	48	31	41
Poles	29	25	24	65	46	53
French	15	23	24	61	41	62
Protestants						
English	19	13	12	39	26	35
Germans	12	13	14	44	32	39
Scandinavians	14	11	17	39	26	31
Jews	14	12	14	58	33	58

no more likely than Protestants to live in the same neighborhoods, are more likely to visit their parents weekly than any of the Protestants, or the Irish and German Catholics.

When the same data are sorted out according to social class and the physical distance that separates the respondents from parents and relatives, an extremely interesting finding emerges. Italians are still the most likely to visit both their parents and their siblings. The Jews are now in second place in visits to parents, but at the bottom of the list where visits to siblings are concerned. The Irish, on the other hand, are relatively low on the parent-visiting list, but right behind the Italians in visits to siblings. It would seem that the stereotypes of the tight Italian family, the dominating Jewish parent, and the clannish Irish sib group are, at least to some extent, backed up by hard statistics.

Since relationships with parents and siblings play a major role in the formation of personality, it seems reasonable to suggest that the different patterns experienced by these three ethnic groups in the earliest years of life help make for quite different personality traits. If this be true, we can expect the subtle differences among the various ethnic groups to persist into the future.

Previous studies of Italian Americans, principally by Herbert Gans, indicate that the familial peer group—siblings and other relatives of one's own age—are the most important influence on lower-class Italians. To some extent, data in the surveys cited above confirm Gans's findings. The Italian's relationships with his parents seem to be a function of physical proximity; with his siblings, the bond overcomes even physical separation. However, Gans suggests that this sibling closeness is essentially working-class and not Italian behavior, whereas in our findings the ethnic differences seem to persist even when different social classes are examined separately.

An Overview

It is extremely difficult to tie together the diverse data from the various studies cited into a coherent pattern. But the information summarized above, together with some findings not quoted here, allow us to attempt the following generalizations:

The earlier immigrant groups are both the most socially successful and the most tolerant, but there are enough differences between, say, the Irish and the Germans, or between the Italians and the Poles, to suggest that other factors are at work besides the time at which one's parents washed up on American shores.

Of all the ethnic and religious groups the Jews are politically the most liberal and socially the most active, as well as economically the most successful. They are close to their parents, relatively less close to their siblings, and given to worrying.

Italians are conservative in their child-rearing practices and extremely close to their relatives—to their parents basically because they live close to them, but to their siblings, apparently, because the sibling relationship is very important to them. They are only moderately successful socially and economically, relatively uninvolved in organizational activity (perhaps because of their heavy family commitment) and liberal on some political questions, though more likely to leave the Democratic Party than are other Catholic ethnic groups. Though they think of themselves as very sociable, they are likely to have a lot of worries. They score rather low in measures of canonical religiousness, and fairly high on prejudice, though not as high as the Poles or the French. A college education apparently reduces, but does not completely eliminate, these differences in degree of prejudice.

The Irish are economically and socially the most successful among Catholic immigrant groups and the most liberal politically and socially. They have very strong ties with their siblings, are the most devoutly Catholic, and the least prejudiced, and their view of themselves ranks them as the happiest and most self-confident.

The Poles score lowest, economically and socially, of all Catholic immigrant groups, and those among them who live in the Midwest and have not graduated from college are the most likely to be prejudiced. They are very loyal to the Catholic Church (but in a more "ethnic" way than the Irish or the Germans). They are the most likely to be Democrats and, if they are college graduates, to be liberal Democrats. They are low in morale and sociability, and high on measures of anomie.

The many historical, sociological, and psychological processes that are involved in producing these differences are still frustratingly obscure, but to me they constitute one of the most fascinating questions for social research still open in our culture.

By Irving M. Levine and Judith M. Herman

The New Pluralism

THE CONTEMPORARY RESURGENCE of interest in blue-collar whites grew from a desire to lessen that group's antagonism to blacks and their goals—that is, to depolarize. Once one begins to look closely at the ethnic factor in blue-collar communities, however, that polarization diagnosis is somewhat weakened and must be replaced, at least at times, with an analysis which includes more groups than the two on opposite sides. Polarization implies mere dichotomy, usually black-white; what we are actually seeing may be much more fragmented, much more highly pluralistic, and much more amenable to a variety of coalitional efforts leading to progress.

The Dissolution of Dichotomy

During the early years of struggle over black needs and demands, blacks and their supporters tended to lump the opposition into one category, "whites" or, after the Kerner Report, "white racists." Similarly, many whites were not adequately sensitive to the range of differences either

From "The Ethnic Factor in Blue-Collar Life," an unpublished paper of the National Project on Ethnic America of the American Jewish Committee, January, 1971. Used by permission.

among blacks or between blacks and such other nonwhite groups as Puerto Ricans, Chicanos, or Indians. Even when there were intensive struggles between blacks and Puerto Ricans in New York's Model Cities program, for example, both groups were seen as "them" by many whites. Similarly, although Irish gangs still attack Italian gangs in South Philadelphia, they are often seen as "all alike" in the eyes of that city's black spokesmen.

The trend toward each large group's accepting the "other side's" definition of themselves—and toward the consequent continuation of a simple black-white split—seems to be dissolving. Especially among the nonwhite groups, who became consciously self-assertive earlier than the still emerging white ethnic groups, there is a growing insistence on the separation between blacks and "others."

The most recent spokesman for this point of view is Deloria, who emphasizes the differences between American Indians and other nonwhite minorities. He says:

> "Intergroup relations" has become synonymous with race relations, which means whites and blacks. There has *never* been an understanding of how groups relate to each other. . . . The whole of American society has been brainwashed into believing that if it understood blacks it could automatically understand every other group.

Most often, Deloria continues to use the category "white," even though he decries the overuse of "black." He does, however, come to recognize the need for finer distinctions among white groups as well:

> We are now watching the dissolution of the very concept of white as the ethnic groups assert their respective identities. Tensions are becoming unbearable because programs, laws, governments, and communications media have been oriented exclusively toward outworn words

and narrow ideas. Yet these very institutions and media are having a tribalizing effect that pulls elements of society farther apart. While the world appears to be shattering, it is in many respects opening the frozen world of white-black relationships and including *others*.

It is certainly true that many white groups tend to coalesce when they feel threatened by what they call a monolithic black advance, and many blacks do the same. How much of that coalescence, though, how much hardening of the lines, is caused by the social definitions of conflicts? Would groups maintain their tendencies toward automatic black-white splits if the prevailing norms of society were not based upon that view of America's groups? In other words, how much is there of the self-fulfilling prophecy in American group relations, with groups acting as they are, in effect, "expected" to act? Furthermore, if we could change those expectations, if we could offer new definitions of group conflict and group interests, could we help open "the frozen world of white-black relationships" and help polarization dissolve into pluralism?

Stereotypes and Fragmentation

While such a change in intergroup relations strategy has many positive possibilities for more fluid relationships between contending groups, more *ad hoc* coalitions, and less escalation of emotion, there are potentially negative side effects to be anticipated and, hopefully, avoided. First, how is a new awareness of diversity and group distinctiveness kept from degenerating into overgeneralization, stereotyping, fragmentation, and destructive separatism? The first tendency of a group which feels it has been forced to repress its identity seems to be a pendulum swing to overidentification before a genuine self-confidence is developed. Ethnocentrism rather than ethnicity can emerge, and might be reinforced by the established generation of ethnic organizational leaders eager to take advantage of their new recognition.

The difficulty of going beyond fragmentation toward a genuine pluralism is illustrated by the current debates over "ethnic studies." The first demands for ethnic studies came from black students and were soon taken up by Puerto Ricans, Chicanos, and other groups. Several white ethnic groups have begun to respond to these assertions with counterproposals for Jewish, Italian, and even Irish studies. In the last session of Congress, Representative Pucinski of Chicago introduced a bill proposing Ethnic Heritage Studies Centers to compile teaching material on individual ethnic groups for public schools. Cosponsored by some twenty colleagues (representing different black and white ethnic groups), Pucinski's bill seemed at first to be a symbolic political item, suitable for newsletters to one's constituency—but the response to it by various ethnic groups and scholars has transformed its chances of passage from remote to serious. While important, the bill's current emphasis on centers which study a single group reflects the difficulty of avoiding fragmentation.

The crucial question is *how* to deal with "ethnic studies" and set up centers. Once all of America's groups clamor for inclusion in textbooks or for separate courses of study, it is not as simple as it originally seemed. Neither the "cameo" theory of history "which lovingly plugs a few feathers, woolly heads, and sombreros into the famous events of American history," nor the "contributions" theory which extols the virtues of groups because of what they have added to American life (from maize to pizza) will work when so many groups are involved. Moreover, both these approaches imply that a group is entitled to acceptance because they have contributed and perhaps even in proportion to that contribution.

What is needed in ethnic studies—and needed to mitigate the problem of ethnocentrism generally—is a more realistic view of the total panoply of "group life" in America. Each ethnic group, privately, will probably continue to teach its own past in its own terms, but the public task is to provide a framework for seeing oneself as a part of a group without the attribution of second-class Americanism which that too often implies.

If ethnic leaders did not feel compelled to compensate for their members' (and their own) low self-esteem, they might find it easier to examine their role in less chauvinistic and more honest terms. Thus, if the government is to enter this area at all, Representative Pucinski's centers should be closer to regional centers on group life and should offer broad approaches to local history, comparative ethnic studies, and general concepts of minority life. . . .

Ethnic Succession

Intimately related to the group self-interest attached to certain occupations is an overlapping ethnic interest in relative power. When many New York schoolteachers are Jews, the Jewish community sees an attack on established teachers' power as an attack on the power of the Jewish community as a whole. Similarly, when the white political domination of Newark was challenged by blacks, the issue became an Italian issue because of the high overlap between "established politicians" and "Italians." Even though "Jewishness" or "Italian-ness" was not specifically attacked except by a few, large segments of both communities felt threatened nonetheless, and not without "legitimate" reason. Where were Jewish teachers or Italian municipal workers to go, and what would be the resulting impact on the ethnic group's status, power, and influence? More important, many informed public officials and other "opinion molders" do not even define the conflicts which arise in terms of group status and power. The result in many cases has been escalating emotions, with the established group attacked as being only "anti" the emerging group and not "pro" their own community's well-being.

There is a scarcity of knowledge or theories dealing with this issue of ethnic succession—the time when a rising group seeks to capture a field of influence from another group.

We need to know much more about how the ethnic succession process has occurred in the past:

What were the instances of succession?

Were the rising groups fought by the established ones, was power ever voluntarily ceded, or was nothing actually given up if the established groups felt it was still a source of power?

What happened to the groups who were succeeded? Did they carry their power with them into new areas? Did they themselves attack still other established groups? Did they actually decline in power?

Has the status hierarchy of groups been maintained even though each group's actual achievements increased?

Is there a line of movement which groups have historically followed?

More important, how were the conflicts which grew out of succession resolved in other historical periods?

Were there new institutional responses which prevented polarization from hardening into decisive combat? Can anything be learned which would make it easier for established groups to give up power in one area while not totally losing their influence? Can we find the "cushions" needed and deserved by individuals who are remnants of their group's power?

For example, in New York's school system, how can we meet the "legitimate" needs of both blacks and Jews—blacks to advance and Jews not to decline? Are there new channels which should be created so that a teacher with twenty years of experience can make that experience useful, even if it is no longer totally relevant in a classroom with a new pupil population? Failing that, can we develop programs to apply to individuals who are "socially displaced" as we have begun to do for those who are technologically displaced? If such benefits were available, would the ethnic group perceive an attack on its occupational area to be as threatening as they do when it seems that the only alternative is to defend themselves or to be cast aside altogether?

"Community" and "Society"

Many of the questions raised regarding the new pluralism are fundamental questions of the relationship between "community" and "society." There is evidence now of a resurging "quest for community," often taking ethnic forms in blue-collar areas—but there is still a need to preserve the total society from fragmenting into disparate and unrelated groups. Moreover, there needs to be some protection for the individual who does not choose to identify with a particular community but opts for an identification which is more universal.

There is a spectrum of ideas concerning the organization of society and the relationship to it of both individuals and groups. At one end there is total reliance upon the individual—legally and socially—and a relegation of intermediate groups to the somewhat anachronistic sphere. At the other end, there are calls for legal recognition of groups and a reorganization of American society around them.

Deloria adopts such a "group rights" position, based on his belief that Indian tribal forms are the most useful forms of social organization and ought to be encouraged. He says:

> It is imperative that the basic sovereignty of the minority group be recognized. This would have the immediate effect of placing racial minorities in a negotiating position as a group and would nullify co-optation. . . . Recognition of new interpretations of the Constitution based on the concept of the group would be the vital step in this process.

In addition, Deloria envisions neighborhoods governed by their own administrative mechanisms containing both public facilities open to all and "enclaves of racial, ethnic, urban, and rural groups that would have a sense of privacy and uniqueness untouched by the outside world." He concludes:

> Alienation would be confined to those times that people stray from their own neighborhood into the world of other peoples. But everyone would have a homeland in which he had an important voice in determining the direction of his community.

This relationship between community and society may seem to some to be extreme, but there have been suggestions for decentralization of governmental bureaucracies which contain this view in their ultimate implications.

Should communities control their own services? What if that control is exercised in order to keep out others? Should a lower-income white ethnic area of Manhattan be entitled to prevent demolition of homes for luxury housing, even though the city's master plan calls for such housing? Should an upper-income suburban community have the same right to exclude apartment house construction because such multifamily structures would interfere with the low density style of life which they enjoy? Does housing for low-income families have priority over local self-determination, or vice versa?

What kinds of guidelines can be developed to take account of both needs, the societal and the communal, and to protect the individual within a community who does not choose to identify himself or does not agree with the majority? Glazer and Moynihan describe two models of group relations, which they call the Southern and Northern models, the former drawing rigid lines between groups, forcing everyone to attach himself somewhere, and operating under a "separate but equal" ideology and reality (i.e., a "polarization" model). The Northern model, a pluralistic one for which they opt, is considerably more visionary:

> There are many groups. They differ in wealth, power, occupation, values, but in effect an open society prevails for individuals and for groups. . . . Each group participates sufficiently in the goods and values and social life of a common society so that all can accept the common society as good and fair. There is competition between groups, as between individuals, but it is muted, and groups compete not through violence but through effectiveness in organization and achievement. Groups and individuals

participate in a common society. Individual choice, not law or rigid custom, determines the degree to which any person participates, if at all, in the life of an ethnic group, and assimilation and acculturation proceed at a rate determined in large measure by individuals.

The difficulties inherent in achieving such a model are immediately evident. It is not easy, for example, to disallow the operation of "rigid custom" and to allow an individual complete freedom in a system of group competition. Still, if American society is to grow in its consciousness of ethnic groups and create new institutions to resolve some of the conflicts which have been identified, we do need some model for which to strive. There has been too little discussion of such models, of the problems inherent in creating a true pluralism in America, and of possible new solutions. If "the frozen world of white-black relationships" is indeed shattering, then new formulas are vitally needed.

By Murray Friedman

Is White Racism the Problem?

ONE OF THE LESS FORTUNATE results of the black revolution has been the development of a by now familiar ritual in which the white liberal is accused of racism and responds by proclaiming himself and the entire society guilty as charged; the Kerner Report was only the official apotheosis of this type of white response to the black challenge of the '60s. No doubt the report has performed a service in the short run by focusing the attention of great numbers of Americans on the degree to which simple racism persists and operates throughout the country, but in the long run its picture of an America pervaded with an undifferentiated disease called "white racism" is unlikely to prove helpful. And even in the short run, the spread of the attitudes embodied in the report may have had a share in helping to provoke the current backlash.

It is, perhaps, understandable that blacks should take phrases like "white racism" and "white America" as adequate reflections of reality. Nevertheless, these phrases drastically obscure the true complexities of our social situation. For the truth is that there is no such entity as

Reprinted from *Commentary*, January, 1969. Copyright © by the American Jewish Committee. Used by permission.

"white America." America is and always has been a nation of diverse ethnic, religious, and racial groups with widely varying characteristics and qualities; and conflict among these groups has been (one might say) "as American as cherry pie." According to the 1960 census, no fewer than 34 million Americans are either immigrants or the children of immigrants from Italy, Poland, Ireland, and a host of other countries. Racially, the population includes not only Caucasians and 22 million blacks, but 5 million Mexican-Americans, and smaller numbers of Indians, Chinese, Japanese, and Puerto Ricans. Membership in U.S. religious bodies, finally, breaks down into 69 million Protestants (who themselves break down into 222 denominations and sects), 46 million Roman Catholics, and 5.6 million Jews.

Neither earlier restrictive immigration laws nor the forces working toward the homogenization of American life have rendered these groups obsolete. While it is true that we have carved out for ourselves a collective identity as Americans with certain common goals, values, and styles, we are still influenced in highly significant ways by our ethnic backgrounds. A number of social scientists, including Gerhard Lenski and Samuel Lubell, have even gone so far as to suggest that these factors are often more important than class. And indeed, membership in our various racial, religious, and ethnic groups largely accounts for where we live, the kinds of jobs we aspire to and hold, who our friends are, whom we marry, how we raise our children, how we vote, think, feel, and act. In a paper prepared for the National Consultation on Ethnic America last June, the sociologist Andrew Greeley reported that Germans, regardless of religion, are more likely to choose careers in science and engineering than any other group. Jews overchoose medicine and law. The Irish overchoose law, political science, history, and the diplomatic service. Polish and other Slavic groups are less likely to approve of bond issues. Poles are the most loyal to the Democratic Party, while Germans and Italians are the least.

Such ethnic differences (including racial and religious differences) are by no means mere survivals of the past, destined to disappear as immigrant memories fade. We seem, in fact, to be moving into a phase of American life in which ethnic self-confidence and self-assertion —stemming from a new recognition of group identity patterns both by the groups themselves and by the general community—are becoming more intense. The Black Power movement is only one manifestation of this. Many alienated Jews suddenly discovered their Jewishness during the Israeli War of Independence and especially the Six-Day War. Italians have recently formed organizations to counteract Italian jokes and the gangster image on television and other media, while Mexican-Americans and Indians have been organizing themselves to achieve broadened civil rights and opportunities. At the same time large bureaucracies like the police and the schools are witnessing a growth in racial, religious, and ethnic organization for social purposes and to protect group interests. (A New York City police spokesman listed the following organizations operating among members of the 28,000-member force several years ago: the Holy Name Society, an organization of Roman Catholics, with 16,500 members; the St. George Association, Protestant, 4,500 members; the Shomrim Society, Jewish, 2,270 members; the Guardian Association, Negro, 1,500 members; the St. Paul Society, Eastern Orthodox, 450 members; and the Hispanic Society, with 350 members of Spanish descent.) To some degree, each of us is locked into the particular culture and social system of the group from which we come.

The myth, to be sure, is that we are a nation of individuals rather than of groups. "There are no minorities in the United States," Woodrow Wilson, a Presbyterian, declared in a World War I plea for unity. "There are no national minorities, racial minorities, or religious minorities. The whole concept and basis of the United States precludes them." Thirty years later, the columnist Dorothy Thompson warned American Jews in the pages of *Commentary* that their support of Israel was an act of disloyalty to the United States. "You cannot become true Americans if you think of yourselves in groups. America does not consist of groups. A man who thinks of himself as belonging to a particular national group in America has not become American, and the man who goes among you to trade upon your nationality is not worthy to live under the Stars and Stripes." And more recently *The New York Times* criticized Martin Luther King, Jr., and James Farmer in similar terms after the two Negro leaders had laid claim to a share of the national wealth and economic power for Negroes as a group. Terming this plea "hopelessly utopian," the *Times* declared: "The United States has never honored [such a claim] for any other group. Impoverished Negroes, like all other poor Americans, past and present, will have to achieve success on an individual basis and by individual effort."

The ideology of individualism out of which such statements come may be attractive, but it bears little relation to the American reality. Formally, of course, and to a certain extent in practice, our society lives by the individualistic principle. Universities strive for more diverse student bodies, and business organizations are increasingly accepting the principle that like government civil service, they should be open to all persons qualified for employment. But as Nathan Glazer has suggested:

These uniform processes of selection for advancement and the pattern of freedom to start a business and make money operate not on a homogeneous mass of individuals, but on individuals as molded by a range of communities of different degrees of organization and self-consciousness with different histories and cultures.

If, however, the idea that we are a nation of individuals is largely a fiction, it has nonetheless served a useful purpose. Fashioned, in part, by older-stock groups as a means of maintaining their power and primacy, it also helped to contain the explosive possibilities of an ethnically hetero-geneous society and to muffle racial divisiveness. Yet one symptom of the "demystification" of this idea has been the recognition in recent years that the older-stock groups are themselves to be understood in ethnic terms. The very introduction of the term "WASP" into the language, as Norman Podhoretz has pointed out, signified a new realization that "white Americans of Anglo-Saxon Protestant background are an ethnic group like any other, that their characteristic qualities are by no means self-evidently superior to those of the other groups, and that neither their earlier arrival nor their majority status entitles them to exclusive possession of the national identity." As the earliest arrivals, the WASP's were able to take possession of the choicest land, to organize and control the major businesses and industries, to run the various political institutions, and to set the tone of the national culture. These positions of dominance were in time challenged by other groups, in some cases (the Irish in city politics, the Jews in cultural life) very successfully, in others with only partial success (thus Fletcher Knebel reports that, contrary to the general impression, "the rulers of economic America —the producers, the financiers, the manufacturers, the bankers and insurers—are still overwhelmingly WASP").

But whatever the particular outcome, the pattern of ethnic "outs" pressuring the ethnic "ins" for equal rights, opportunities, and status has been followed since colonial times and has been accompanied by noisy and often violent reaction by the existing ethnic establishment. There was the growth of the Know-Nothing movement when the mid-nineteenth-century influx of Irish Catholics and other foreigners posed a challenge to Protestant control; there was the creation and resurgence of the Ku-Klux Klan at every stage of the black man's movement toward equal rights; there was the organization of Parents and Taxpayers groups in the North and White Citizens Councils in the South to oppose school desegregation and Negro school gains. Bigotry and racism certainly played a part in these phenomena. Yet they are best understood not as symptoms of social illness but as expressions of the recurring battles that inevitably characterize a heterogeneous society as older and more established groups seek to ward off the demands of newer claimants to a share of position and power.

Even the recent explosions in the black ghettos have a precedent: "In an earlier period," Dennis Clark tells us, "the Irish were the riot makers of America par excellence." They "wrote the script" for American urban violence and "black terrorists have added nothing new." So, too, with some of the educational demands of today's black militants. As late as 1906, the New York *Gaelic American* wanted Irish history taught in the New York City schools!

Racial and ethic conflict takes its toll, but it has frequently led to beneficial results. When pressures mounted by the "outs" have caused widespread dislocation, the "ins" have often purchased community peace by making political, economic, legal, and cultural concessions. As the Irish, for example, became more fully absorbed into Ameri-

can life through better jobs, more security, and recognition
—in short, as the existing ethnic establishment made room
for them—Irish violence decreased, and the Irish have, in
fact, become some of the strongest proponents of the current racial *status quo.* The hope of achieving a similar
result undoubtedly accounts in some measure for concessions which have been made to Negroes in many racially
restive cities today. Thus, when white voters in Cleveland
helped elect a Negro mayor (Carl Stokes), they were not
only recognizing his abilities—which are said to be
considerable—but also acting in the belief that he could
"cool it" more effectively than a white mayor. Nor is it a
coincidence that the Los Angeles city and county school
boards are now headed by Negroes.

In the past, a major barrier to the advancement of black
people has been their inability to organize themselves as a
group for a struggle with the various "ins." Their relative
powerlessness has been as crippling as the forces of bigotry
arrayed against them. As one Philadelphia militant said,
"Impotence corrupts and absolute impotence corrupts absolutely." But some Black Power leaders have recently
emerged with a better understanding than many of their
integrationist colleagues of the fact that successful groups
in American life must reserve a major portion of their
energies for the task of racial or religious separation and
communal consolidation. Divorced from posturing and
provocative language, the emphasis by certain (though
not all) black militants on separatism may be seen as a
temporary tactic to build political and economic power
in order to overcome the results of discrimination and disadvantage. "Ultimately, the gains of our struggle will be
meaningful," Stokely Carmichael and Charles V. Hamilton
wrote in *Black Power*, "only when consolidated by viable
coalitions between blacks and whites who accept each

other as coequal partners and who identify their goals as politically and economically similar."

This is not to suggest that Black Power (or Jewish Power or Catholic Power) is the only factor in achieving group progress, or that "the American creed," of equal rights, as Gunnar Myrdal has called it, is a mere bundle of words. Indeed, the democratic tradition can act as a powerful force in advancing minority claims even when the majority does not accept its implications. Public opinion polls have reported consistently that open-housing laws are unpopular with a majority of Americans, and yet 23 states and 205 cities have enacted such legislation and the Civil Rights Act of 1968 makes it a federal responsibility. Nevertheless, the democratic ideal obviously has never guaranteed full entry into the society to ethnic outgroups. In a pluralistic society, freedom is not handed out; for better or worse, it has to be fought for and won. The "outs" can attain it only by agitation and pressure, utilizing the American creed as one of their weapons.

It is important in all this to recognize that no special virtue or culpability accrues to the position of any group in this pluralistic system. At the moment, the American creed sides with Negroes, Puerto Ricans, American Indians, and other minorities who have been discriminated against for so long. But we should not be surprised when Italians, Poles, Irish, or Jews respond to Negro pressures by rushing to protect vital interests which have frequently been purchased through harsh struggles of their own with the ethnic system. Here is how a skilled craftsman replies to the charge of maintaining racial discrimination in his union in a letter to *The New York Times*:

> Some men leave their sons money, some large investments, some business connections, and some a profession.

I have only one worthwhile thing to give: my trade. I hope to follow a centuries-old tradition and sponsor my sons for an apprenticeship. For this simple father's wish it is said that I discriminate against Negroes. Don't all of us discriminate? Which of us when it comes to a choice will not choose a son over all others? I believe that an apprenticeship in my union is no more a public trust, to be shared by all, than a millionaire's money is a public trust.

Surely to dismiss this letter as an expression of white racism is drastically to oversimplify the problem of discrimination. But if the impulse to protect vested interests accounts for the erecting of discriminatory barriers, no less often than simple bigotry or racism, it is also true that Americans are sometimes capable of transcending that impulse—just as they are sometimes capable of setting aside their prejudices—for the sake of greater social justice. E. Digby Baltzell has pointed out in *The Protestant Establishment* that the drive to gain equal rights and opportunities for disadvantaged minorities has frequently been led by members of older-stock groups. On the other hand, members of minority groups are not necessarily ennobled by the experience of persecution and exploitation. As Rabbi Richard Rubenstein has observed, "The extra measure of hatred the victim accumulates may make him an especially vicious victor."

Nor does the position of a given ethnic group remain static; a group can be "in" and "out" at the same time. While Jews, for example, continue to face discrimination in the "executive suite" of major industry and finance, in private clubs and elsewhere, they are in certain respects becoming an economic and cultural ingroup. To the degree that they are moving from "out" to "in" (from "good guys" to "bad guys"?), they are joining the existing ethnic establishment and taking on its conservative coloration.

Rabbi Rubenstein has frankly defended this change in an article, "Jews, Negroes, and the New Politics," in the *Reconstructionist:*

> After a century of liberalism there is a very strong likelihood that the Jewish community will turn somewhat conservative in the sense that its strategy for social change involves establishment politics rather than revolutionary violence. Jews have much to conserve in America. It is no sin to conserve what one has worked with infinite difficulty to build.

So far so good—though, regrettably, Rubenstein uses this and other arguments to urge Jews to opt out of the Negro struggle. The point, however, is that not all the groups resisting black demands today are "in" groups. Just as in a fraternity initiation the hardest knocks come from the sophomores, the most recently accepted and hence least secure group, so in ethnic struggle the greatest opposition will sometimes come from groups whose interests would seem to make them natural allies.

At the moment some of the hottest group collisions are taking place in the big-city schools. The "outs"—in this case the blacks—see the older order as maintaining and fostering basic inequities. Hence, we are now witnessing the demand for decentralization or "community control" of big-city school systems. The "ins"—in the case of New York, the Jews; in the case of Boston, the Irish—naturally see these demands as a threat. The blacks claim that the existing system of merit and experience tends to favor educators from older religioethnic groups; the latter fear that new and lowered criteria of advancement and promotion will destroy many of their hard-won gains. The result is increasing conflict amid charges of racism from both sides.

The underlying problem, however, is a power struggle involving the decision-making areas controlled by an older educational and ethnic establishment. At the heart of the issue is a group-bargaining situation whose handling calls for enormous sensitivity and the development of procedures that will protect the interests of the conflicting groups. A similar confrontation in the nineteenth century which was badly handled was a major factor in the withdrawal of Catholics from the Protestant-dominated public schools and the creation of their own school system.

In the meantime, struggles among other groups persist, often also involving the schools. Frequently, these result from differences in group values and styles as well as interests. An example is the school board fight in Wayne Township, New Jersey, which attracted national attention in February, 1967. The Jewish, and total, population of Wayne, a suburb of Paterson and Newark, had grown sharply since 1958, when it was a homogeneous Christian community with only fifteen Jewish families. With a changing community came new pressures—burgeoning school enrollment and school costs, and anxiety over court rulings banning prayer and the reading of the Bible in public schools. There was one Jew on Wayne's nine-member school board in 1967 when two others decided to run. The vice-president of the board, Newton Miller, attacked both Jewish candidates, noting, "Most Jewish people are liberals, especially when it comes to spending for education." If they were elected, he warned, only two more Jewish members would be required for a Jewish majority. "Two more votes and we lose what is left of Christ in our Christmas celebrations in the schools. Think of it," Miller added.

Subsequently, the Jewish candidates were defeated amid widespread condemnation of the citizens of Wayne. The incident was cited by sociologists Rodney Stark and Stephen Steinberg as raising the "specter of political anti-Semitism in America." In their study, they concluded, "It couldn't happen here, but it did."

Miller's statements may indeed have appealed to existing anti-Semitic sentiment in Wayne. But this was not the whole story. After all, the Jewish member already on the board had been elected by the same constituency that now responded to Miller's warnings. And it must be admitted, furthermore, that by and large Jews *are* "liberals," willing to spend heavily on the education of their children just as they are desirous of eliminating religious practices from the public schools—attitudes shared, of course, by many non-Jews. Miller appealed to group interests above all: to an interest in preserving traditional religious practices in the schools and in holding down education expenditures. There was in this case genuine concern by an older religio-ethnic establishment that its way of life and values were in danger of being swept away. The votes against the Jewish members were of course illiberal votes, but that was just the point. In Wayne, charges of anti-Semitism obscured the real problem: how to reconcile differences in group values in a changing, multigroup society.

All this is not, of course, meant to deny the existence of racism as a force in American life, nor to underestimate the cruel and pervasive conflicts which it engenders. But it must be recognized that the crucial element in much of intergroup conflict is not how prejudiced the contending parties are, but what kinds of accommodations they are capable of making. For many years, a federal aid to education bill has been tied up in Washington, in part because of a Roman Catholic veto. The Catholic hierarchy, whose schools have been undergoing financial crisis, and a number of Orthodox Jewish groups who also want government assistance for their schools are ranged on one side of the issue. On the other side are most Protestant and Jewish groups, along with civil-liberties and educational organizations, who are suspicious of the motives of the Catholic Church and fear that financial assistance by government to parochial schools will lead to an abandonment of the separation of church and state principle embodied in the federal and state constitutions, with the resultant destruction of the public schools. Debate now ranges in many states over providing free busing of pupils to parochial schools, supplying textbooks, auxiliary services, and equipment to nonpublic school students, and financing construction of buildings at church-related colleges and universities. The result has been an intensification of religious tensions.

In this controversy, however, the problem is not, as many seem to believe, mainly one of constitutional law. In spite of the First Amendment, American public education throughout our history has reflected the values and goals of a Protestant society—until, that is, Catholics and other groups began to press for, and finally obtained, a more neutral posture. The problem here is rather one of adjusting to the reality of the Catholic parochial school system—to the public service it performs and to the political power it represents. When the Constitution was adopted, Catholics numbered less than 1 percent of the total population. Today they are the largest single religious group and they support a parochial school system which, in spite of criticism inside and outside the church, continues to educate large numbers of Americans. (A study by Rev. Neil G. McCluskey in 1963 reported that 26 percent of the children in New York, 34 percent of those in Chicago, 39 percent in Philadelphia, 23 percent in Detroit, 28 percent in Cincinnati, 30 percent in Boston, and 42 percent in Pittsburgh attend Roman Catholic parochial schools.)

It seems likely that this controversy will be resolved through a redefinition of the American public education system. Thus, secular and other aspects of parochial education that benefit the general community—subjects such as foreign languages, mathematics, physics, chemistry, and gym—will in all probability receive some form of public assistance. Indeed, this is already happening in the form of shared time or dual enrollment (parochial school children spend part of the day in public schools), aid to disadvantaged children under the Elementary and Secondary Education Act of 1965, and various other measures.

It is a tribute to our social system, proof of its workabilty, that the inexorable pressures of pluralistic confrontation do result in shifts in power and place. WASP control of political life in the nation's cities was displaced first by the Irish and later by other ethnic groups. The newest group moving up the political ladder is the Negro, with mayors now in Gary and Cleveland. The Negro press predicts that by 1977 there may be twenty-one black mayors.

There are, of course, many real differences between the Negro and other groups in this country, including the Negro's higher visibility and the traumatic impact of slavery. He is, nevertheless, involved in much the same historical process experienced by all groups, with varying success, in attempting to "make it" in American life. The idea that he faces a monolithic white world uniformly intent for racist reasons on denying him his full rights as a man is not only naïve but damaging to the development of strategies which can lead to a necessary accommodation. It does no good—it does harm—to keep pointing the finger of guilt either at Americans in general or at special groups, when what is needed are methods for dealing with the real needs and fears of all groups.

As David Danzig has written: "Few people who live in socially separated ethnic communities, as many Americans do, can be persuaded that because these communities are also racially separated they are morally sick. Having come to accept their own social situation as the natural result of their ethnic affinities, mere exhortation is not likely to convince them—or, for that matter, the public at large— that they are thereby imposing upon others a condition of apartheid." Nor is exhortation likely to convince the twenty million families who earn between $5,000 and $10,000, a year that they are wrong in feeling that their own problems are being neglected in favor of the Negro. It is clear that intergroup negotiation, or bargaining, with due regard for protecting the interests of the various groups involved, is one of the major ingredients in working out racial and religious adjustments. In other words, power has to be shared—in the schools, on the job, in politics, and in every aspect of American life.

The time has come to dispense with what Peter Rose has called the "liberal rhetoric . . . of race relations." There can be no effective intergroup negotiation or bargaining unless due regard is paid to the interests of all groups. Nor will effective bargaining take place until we learn to go beyond simplistic slogans and equally simplistic appeals to the American creed.

V | THE POLITICS OF MIDDLE AMERICA

BY AND LARGE, POLITICIANS ARE THE OLDEST OF THE "NEW pluralists." They have always had to have a firm grasp of the "ethnics" of American politics to develop winning issues and tickets. The emergence of Middle America has produced a number of efforts to understand the political implications of this phenomenon; and of these Kevin P. Phillips' analysis is perhaps the most penetrating. While a number of his predictions went awry in the 1970 elections, his account of the long-range political trends among the various racial, religious, ethnic, and geographic groups —as summarized in the selection here—contains important insights.

Two speeches reprinted here contrast both in content and style the varying approaches made by national figures to winning the affections of Middle America. Vice-President Agnew's address at a Republican dinner during the 1970 elections (slightly abridged to exclude plugs for local candidates) was one of his sharpest attacks on intellectuals and was meant clearly to widen the gap between them and the broad body of Americans. In his nationally televised speech on the eve of the election, Senator Edmund S. Muskie sought to allay fears, to reconcile Americans and, of course, to win votes. It is significant that the two figures who have emerged most prominently from recent political wars are persons of clearly identifiable and recent ethnic origins.

The success of a liberal, Adlai Stevenson, III, in his bid for election to the U.S. Senate from Illinois backed by the Daley machine and the "old politics," raises some interesting questions for those seeking political clues to Middle America. In his essay, "Take Heart from the Heartland," Greeley suggests, hard as it may be to believe, that the ethnic politician continues to remain a reliable guide to understanding and reconciling the diverse and explosive social forces that make up our communities today. In this respect, Bayard Rustin calls for "Mobilizing a Progressive Majority" of blue-collar whites and blacks into a new political coalition for social progress.

By Kevin P. Phillips

The Future
of American Politics

THE LONG-RANGE MEANING of the political upheaval of 1968 rests on the Republican opportunity to fashion a majority among the 57 percent of the American electorate which voted to eject the Democratic Party from national power. To begin with, more than half of this protesting 57 percent were firm Republicans from areas—Southern California to Long Island's Suffolk County—or sociocultural backgrounds with a growing GOP bias. Some voted for George Wallace, but most backed Richard Nixon, providing the bulk of his Election Day support. Only a small minority of 1968 Nixon backers—perhaps several million liberal Republicans and independents from Maine and Oregon to Fifth Avenue—cast what may be their last Republican Presidential ballots because of the partisan realignment taking place. The third major anti-Democratic voting stream of 1968—and the most decisive—was that of the fifteen million or so conservative Democrats who shunned Hubert Humphrey to divide about evenly between Richard Nixon and George Wallace. Such elements stretched from the "Okie" Great Central Valley of California to the mountain towns of Idaho, Florida's space centers, rural South Carolina, Bavarian Minnesota, the Irish sidewalks of New York, and the Levittowns of Megalopolis. . . .

Although most of George Wallace's votes came from Democrats rather than Republicans, they were conservatives—Southerners, Borderers, German and Irish Catholics —who had been trending Republican prior to 1968. The Wallace vote followed the cultural geography of obsolescent conservative (often Southern) Democratic tradition. There was no reliable Wallace backing among blue-collar workers and poor whites as a class; industrial centers in the Yankee sphere of influence from Duluth to Scranton, Fall River, and Biddeford shunned the Alabama ex-governor with a mere 2 percent to 3 percent of the vote. Areas of eroding Democratic tradition were the great breeding grounds of Wallace voters.

In the South, Wallace drew principally on conservative Democrats quitting the party they had long succored and controlled. Generally speaking, Wallace's Southern strength was greatest in the Democratic Party's historic (pre-1964) lowland strongholds, while the Alabaman's worst Southern percentages came in the Republican highlands. White voters throughout most sections of the Deep South went two-to-one for Wallace. In the more Republican Outer South, only one white voter out of three supported the third-party candidate. In the South as a whole, 85 to 90 percent of the white electorate cast Nixon or Wallace votes against the realigning national Democratic Party in 1968, an unprecedented magnitude of disaffection which indicates the availability of the Wallace vote to the future GOP.

Four of the five Wallace states had gone Republican in 1964, and although the Alabaman greatly enlarged the scope of Southern revolt by attracting most of the (poor white or Outer South Black Belt) Southerners who had hitherto resisted Republican or States' Rights candidacies, much of his tide had already been flowing for Goldwater. Nor does the Nixon Administration have to bid much ideologically for this electorate. Despite his success in enlarging the scope of white Southern revolt, George Wallace failed to reach far enough or strongly enough beyond the Deep South to give his American Independent Party the national base required for a viable future. Republican Nixon won most of the Outer South, establishing the GOP as the ascending party of the local white majority. Having achieved statewide success only in the Deep South, and facing competition from a Southern Republicanism mindful of its opportunity, the Wallace movement cannot maintain an adequate political base and is bound to serve, like past American third parties, as a way station for groups abandoning one party for another. Some Wallace voters were longtime Republicans, but the great majority were conservative Democrats who have been moving—and should continue to do so—toward the GOP.

The linkage of Wallace voting to the obsolescent Democratic loyalties of certain areas and groups can also be proved far beyond the old Confederacy. Wallace support in the Ohio Valley, instead of standing out in backlash-prone industrial areas, followed rural contours of traditional Democratic strength, moving farthest north along the Scioto River, central Ohio's roadway of Virginia and Kentucky migration. And in New York and Pennsylvania, certain levels of Wallace support probed farthest north along the Susquehanna, Delaware, and Hudson valleys, outliers of traditionally Democratic non-Yankee rural strength. Out West, Wallace percentages were greatest in the Oklahoma- and Texas-settled towns of California's Central Valley, the populist mining and logging counties of the Rocky Mountains, the traditionally Democratic Mormon reaches of Idaho, and in Alaska's long-Democratic sluice and sawmill districts.

In addition to Western or Southern Democrats of conservative or populist bent, Wallace also scored well among Catholics, but only in certain areas. From Maine to Michigan, across most of the belt of Yankee-settled territory where local cleavage, though changing, still pits Protestant Republicans against urban Catholic Democrats, the Catholic trend away from the Democrats was slight. However, in the greater New York area, as well as Gary and Cleveland, where minority group (Negro and/or Jewish) power has taken control of local Democratic machinery, Catholic backing of Wallace was considerable. Here, Catholics are leaving the Democratic Party.

The common denominator of Wallace support, Catholic or Protestant, is alienation from the Democratic Party and a strong trend—shown in other years and other contests—toward the GOP. Although most of Wallace's votes came from Democrats, he principally won those in motion between a Democratic past and a Republican future. In the last few weeks of the campaign, labor union activity, economic issues, and the escalating two-party context of October, 1968, drew many Wallace-leaning Northern blue-collar workers back into the Democratic fold. Only those fully alienated by the national Democratic Party stuck with Wallace in the voting booth. Offered a three-party context, these sociopolitical streams preferred populist Wallace; a two-party context would have drawn them into the GOP. Three quarters or more of the Wallace electorate represented lost Nixon votes.

A few states—Mississippi or Alabama—may indulge in future third-party or States' Rights efforts. The Wallace party itself, however, has dubious prospects, being not a broad-based national grouping but a transient 1968 aggregation of conservative Democrats otherwise trending into the Republican Party. Generally speaking, the South is more realistic than its critics believe, and nothing more than an effective and responsibly conservative Nixon Administration is necessary to bring most of the Southern Wallace electorate into the fold against a Northeastern liberal Democratic Presidential nominee. Abandonment of civil rights enforcement would be self-defeating. Maintenance of Negro voting rights in Dixie, far from being contrary to GOP interests, is essential if Southern conservatives are to be pressured into switching to the Republican Party—for Negroes are beginning to seize control of the national Democratic Party in some Black Belt areas.

Successful moderate conservatism is also likely to attract to the Republican side some of the Northern blue-collar workers who flirted with George Wallace but ultimately backed Hubert Humphrey. Fears that a Republican administration would undermine Social Security, Medicare, collective bargaining, and aid to education played a major part in keeping socially conservative blue-collar workers and senior citizens loyal to the 1968 Democratic candidate. Assuming that a Nixon administration can dispel these apprehensions, it ought to be able to repeat—with much more permanence—Eisenhower's great blue-collar success of 1956. Sociologically, the Republican Party is becoming much more lower middle class and much less establishmentarian than it was during the 1950's, and pursuit of an increasing portion of the Northern blue-collar electorate— an expansion of its 1968 Catholic triumph in greater New York City—would be a logical extension of this trend.

Although the appeal of a successful Nixon Administration and the lack of a Wallace candidacy would greatly swell the 1972 Republican vote in the South, West, Border, and the Catholic North, the 1972 GOP may well simultaneously lose a lesser number of 1968 supporters among groups reacting against the party's emerging Southern, Western, and New York Irish majority. Yankees, Megalopolitan silk-stocking voters, and Scandinavians from Maine across the Great Lakes to the Pacific all showed a distinct Democratic trend in the years between 1960 and 1968. Such disaffection will doubtless continue, but its principal impact has already been felt. Richard Nixon won only 38 percent of the total 1968 presidential vote on Manhattan's rich East Side; he took only 44 percent of the ballots in Scarsdale, the city's richest suburb; New England's Yankee counties and towns produced Nixon majorities down 10 percent to 15 percent from 1960 levels; fashionable San Francisco shifted toward the Democrats; and Scandinavian Minnesota and Washington State backed Humphrey, as did the Scandinavian Northwest of Wisconsin.

All of these locales shifted *toward* the Democrats during the 1960–1968 period. Because the local realignment pivoted on liberal Republicans rather than conservative Democrats, these areas evidenced little or no support for George Wallace. Beyond the bounds of states that went Democratic in 1968, the Yankee, silk-stocking, establishmentarian and Scandinavian trends predominate only in Vermont, New Hampshire, and Oregon. Although Northern California, Wisconsin, Ohio's old Western Reserve, central Iowa, and parts of the Dakotas are likewise influenced, other conservative trends—those of Southern California suburbanites, German Catholics of the upper Farm Belt, and the quasi-Southern Democrats of the Ohio Valley —should keep those states Republican. Yankee, Northeastern silk-stocking, and Scandinavian disaffection with the GOP is concentrated in states which the party has already lost, and it menaces only a few states which the GOP won in 1968.

The upcoming cycle of American politics is likely to match a dominant Republican Party based in the Heartland, South, and California against a minority Democratic Party based in the Northeast and the Pacific Northwest (and encompassing Southern as well as Northern Negroes). With such support behind it, the GOP can easily afford to lose the states of Massachusetts, New York, and Michigan—and is likely to do so except in landslide years. Together with the District of Columbia, the top ten Humphrey states—Hawaii, Washington, Minnesota, Michigan, West Virginia, New York, Connecticut, Rhode Island, Massachusetts, and Maine—should prove to be the core of national Democratic strength. The new battlegrounds of quadrennial Presidential politics are likely to be California, Ohio, and Pennsylvania.

Unluckily for the Democrats, their major impetus is centered in stagnant Northern industrial states—and within those states, in old decaying cities, in a Yankee countryside that has fewer people than in 1900, and in the most expensive suburbs. Beyond this, in the South and West, the Democrats dominate only two expanding voting blocs —Latins and Negroes. From space-center Florida across the booming Texas plains to the Los Angeles–San Diego suburban corridor, the nation's fastest-growing areas are strongly Republican and conservative. Even in the Northeast, the few rapidly growing suburbs are conservative-trending areas. Because of this demographic pattern, the South and West are gaining electoral votes and national political power at the expense of the Northeast. The conservative Sun Belt cities are undergoing a population boom

—and getting more conservative—while the old liberal cities of the Northeast decline. And the Northeast is steadily losing relative political importance to the Sun Belt.

One of the greatest political myths of the decade—a product of liberal self-interest—is that the Republican Party cannot attain national dominance without mobilizing liberal support in the big cities, appealing to "liberal" youth, empathizing with "liberal" urbanization, gaining substantial Negro support, and courting the affluent young professional classes of "suburbia." The actual demographic and political facts convey a very different message.

The big-city political era is over in the United States. With Negroes moving into the cities, whites have moved out. Moreover, white urban populations are getting increasingly conservative. Richard Nixon and George Wallace together won 40 percent of the vote in liberal New York City. Perhaps more to the point, leading big-city states like New York, Michigan, and Massachusetts are no longer necessary for national Republican victory.

Youth is important, but voters under twenty-five cast only 7.4 percent of the nation's ballots in 1968. And while many Northeastern young people are more liberal and Democratic than their parents—especially the affluent and anarchic progeny of the Establishment—the reverse seems to be true in Southern, Border, Rocky Mountain, Catholic, lower-middle-class and working-class areas. In these locales, the young electorate's trend against local political tradition helps the GOP, as does resentment of the blithe nihilism of the children of the affluent society.

While urbanization *is* changing the face of America, and the GOP must take political note of this fact, it presents the opposite of a problem. A generation ago, the coming of age of the working-class central cities condemned the Republican Party to minority status, but the new "urbanization"—suburbanization is often a better description—is a middle-class impetus shaping the same ignominy for the Democrats. All across the nation, the fastest-growing urban areas are steadily increasing their *Republican* pluralities, while the old central cities—seat of the New Deal era—are casting steadily fewer votes for Democratic liberalism. No major American city is losing population so rapidly as arch-Democratic and establishmentarian Boston, while the fastest-growing urban area in the nation is Southern California's staunchly conservative Orange County, and the fastest-growing cities are conservative strongholds like Phoenix, Dallas, Houston, Anaheim, San Diego, and Fort Lauderdale.

Substantial Negro support is not necessary to national Republican victory in the light of the 1968 election returns. Obviously, the GOP can build a winning coalition without Negro votes. Indeed, Negro-Democratic mutual identification was a major source of Democratic loss—and Republican or American Independent Party profit—in many sections of the nation.

The liberal and Democratic 1960–1968 shifts of a few (now atypical) silk-stocking counties were dwarfed by the conservative trends of the vast new tracts of middle-class suburbia. Actually, the Democratic upswing in a number of rich suburban areas around New York, Boston, and Philadelphia is nothing more than an extension of the liberal establishmentarian behavior of Manhattan's East Side, Boston's Beacon Hill, and Philadelphia's Rittenhouse Square. Typical suburban behavior is something else again.

Centered in the Sun Belt, the nation's heaviest suburban growth is solidly middle-class and conservative. Contemporary suburban expansion in the Northeast pales next to the spread of the Florida, Texas, Arizona, and

Southern California suburbs. Rapid, although less spectacular, suburban growth is occurring in the areas around Camden (New Jersey), Washington, D.C., Richmond, Atlanta, Memphis, St. Louis, Chicago, Oklahoma City, Tulsa, and Denver. These suburbs are also conservative, often highly so. And even the few fast-growing Northeastern suburban counties—Suffolk, New York; Burlington, New Jersey; Prince Georges, Maryland—are conservative-trending, middle-class sections. The principal exception is Maryland's rich but fast-expanding Montgomery County, liberal seat of the upper echelons of Washington's federal bureaucracy.

From a national perspective, the silk-stocking liberal suburbs of Boston, New York, Philadelphia, San Francisco, and (to a lesser extent) Chicago and Washington cast only a minute fraction of the ballots wielded by the preponderance of unfashionable lower-middle- and middle-income suburbs. And because more and more new suburbanites come from lower-middle-income backgrounds, this gap should widen.

The National Commission on Urban Problems, chaired by former Illinois Senator Paul Douglas, has drawn attention to the increasingly powerful shift of blue-collar and lower-middle-class population to suburbia, but suprisingly few Establishment liberals understand or admit these demographic facts of life. Instead, they typically portray the large conservative majority of Americans as a mere obsolescent and shrinking periphery of society, meanwhile painting their own peer group as the expanding segment of the nation committed to cosmopolitan thinking, technological sophistication, and cultural change.

This myopia has considerable precedent. Since the days of Alexander Hamilton and the Federalists, the United States—and the Northeast in particular—has periodically supported a privileged elite, blind to the needs and interests of the large national majority. The corporate welfarists, planners, and academicians of the Liberal Establishment are the newest of these elites, and their interests —for one thing, a high and not necessarily too productive

Central City–Suburban Apartheid:
The Demographic Projections of the President's National
Commission on Urban Problems, July, 1968

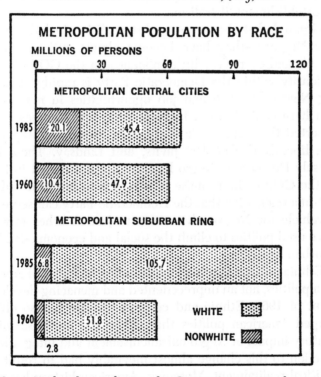

Note—As the chart indicates, the Commission expects the nation's growth over the next twenty years to ignore the cities and focus on suburbia. Indeed, only the urban growth of the South and West will prevent a sharp decline in the nation's central city population based on the steady shrinkage of northeastern central cities.

rate of government social, educational, scientific, and research spending—are as vested as those of Coolidge-
Hoover era financiers and industrialists. The great political
upheaval of the 1960's is not that of Senator Eugene
McCarthy's relatively small group of upper-middle-class
and intellectual supporters, but a populist revolt of the
American masses who have been elevated by prosperity
to middle-class status and conservatism. *Their* revolt is
against the caste, policies, and taxation of the mandarins
of Establishment liberalism.

Granted that the new populist coalition includes very
few Negroes—they have become almost entirely Democratic and exert very little influence on the GOP—black
solidarity within the Democratic Party is rapidly enlarging Negro influence and job opportunities in many old
Northern central cities. In New York, few Negroes have
deserted the Democratic Party even to support Republican liberals Rockefeller, Javits, and Lindsay. These in-
tensely Democratic Negro loyalties are not rooted in fear
of the GOP or its promise of a return to law and order,
but in a realization that the Democratic Party can serve as
a vehicle for Negro advancement—just as other groups
have used politics to climb the social and economic ladder
of urban America.

Ethnic polarization is a long-standing hallmark of American politics, not an unprecedented and menacing development of 1968. Ethnic and cultural division has so often
shaped American politics that, given the immense mid-
century impact of Negro enfranchisement and integration,
reaction to this change almost inevitably had to result in
political realignment. Moreover, American history has another example of a persecuted minority—the nineteenth-
century Irish—who, in the face of considerable discrimination and old-stock animosity, likewise poured their ethnic
numbers into the Democratic Party alone, winning power,

jobs, and socioeconomic opportunity through local political skill rather than the benevolence of usually Republican national administrations.

For a half century after the Civil War, the regular Democratic fidelity of the unpopular Irish city machines helped keep much of the nation Republican, and it seems possible that rising Negro participation in (national) Democratic politics from Manhattan to Mississippi may play a similar role in the post-1968 cycle. Growing Negro influence in—and conservative Southern, Western, and Catholic departure from—the Democratic Party also suggests that Northeastern liberals ought to be able to dominate the party, which in turn must accelerate the sectional and ideological realignment already under way.

To the extent that the ethnic and racial overtones of American political behavior and alignment are appreciated, they are often confused or misstated. For example, far from being opposed by all nonwhites, Richard Nixon was strongly supported by one nonwhite group—the Chinese. San Francisco's Chinese electorate was more Republican in 1968 than the city's white population. Nor is today's Republican Party Protestant rather than Catholic. In New York City, the party is becoming the vehicle of the Italians and Irish, and in the Upper Farm Belt—Wisconsin, Minnesota, and North Dakota—German Catholics are moving to the fore. From the first days of the Republic, American politics have been a maze of ethnic, cultural, and sectional oppositions and loyalties, and this has not deterred progress or growth. The new popular conservative majority has many ethnic strains, and portraits showing it as a white Anglo-Saxon Protestant monolith are highly misleading.

The emerging Republican majority spoke clearly in 1968 for a shift away from the sociological jurisprudence, moral permissiveness, experimental residential, welfare, and ed-

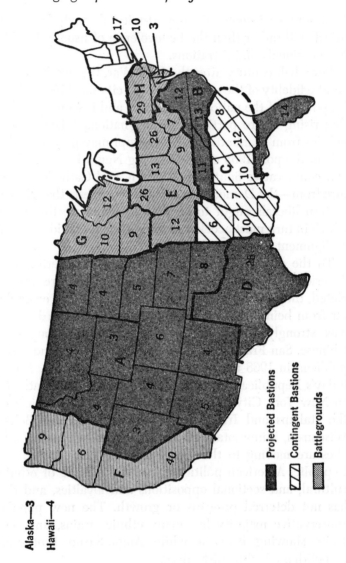

Explanation of Map

A. *Plains and Mountain States*—With 61 electoral votes, these constitute the conservative geographical heartland of the emerging Republican majority.

B. *The Outer South*—The states of Florida, Virginia, North Carolina, and Tennessee are not only conservative but ever more reliably Republican in Presidential elections. Their 50 electoral votes are vulnerable only to Republican Administration policies which keep alive third-party sentiment.

C. *The Contingent South*—The conservative Deep South and Arkansas (totaling 53 electoral votes) will join GOP ranks—by default—against Northern liberal Democrats, provided simply that Republican policies pay sufficient attention to conservative viewpoints to undercut third-party movements and create a national Republican vs. national Democratic context.

D. *Texas*—Without third-party interference, Texas (25 electoral votes) will support moderate conservative national Republicanism against Northern Democratic liberalism.

The South and rock-ribbed conservative sections of the Heartland have 189 of the 270 electoral votes needed to elect a President. *Moderate* conservatism will forge its emerging Republican majority in several battleground areas: The Ohio-Mississippi Valley (93 electoral votes); the Pacific (60); the Upper Mississippi Valley (31); and the non-Yankee Northeast (59).

E. *The Ohio-Mississippi Valley*—The erosion of Civil War–rooted German and Border Democratic fidelity, together with growing white urban Catholic conservatism from Cleveland to St. Louis should put most of the key 93 Missouri, Illinois, Indiana, Kentucky, Ohio, and West Virginia electoral votes into the GOP column.

F. *The Pacific*—California, which casts 40 of the 60 Pacific electoral votes, is becoming more Republican than the nation as a whole in response to the middle-class population explosion of Southern California.

G. *The Upper Mississippi Valley*—The GOP is not on the upswing in Iowa, Minnesota, and Wisconsin—old Yankee-Scandinavian party strongholds—but it remains likely to win Iowa's and Wisconsin's share of 31 electoral votes.

H. *The Non-Yankee Northeast*—Of Pennsylvania, New Jersey, Delaware, and Maryland, the latter three (30 electoral votes), all pushing below the Mason-Dixon Line, are particularly likely to participate in the emerging Republican majority.

ucational programming and massive federal spending by which the Liberal (mostly Democratic) Establishment sought to propagate liberal institutions and ideology—and all the while reap growing economic benefits. The dominion of this impetus is inherent in the list of Republican-trending groups and potentially Republican Wallace electorates of 1968: Southerners, Borderers, Germans, Scotch-Irish, Pennsylvania Dutch, Irish, Italians, Eastern Europeans, and other urban Catholics, middle-class suburbanites, Sun Belt residents, Rocky Mountain and Pacific Interior populists. Democrats among these groups were principally alienated from their party by its social programs and increasing identification with the Northeastern Establishment and ghetto alike. Except among isolationist Germans, resentment of the Vietnamese war, far from helping to forge the GOP majority, actually produced *Democratic* gains among the groups most affected: silk-stocking Megalopolitans, the San Francisco-Berkeley-Madison–Ann Arbor electorate, Scandinavian progressives, and Jews. As for the Republican trend groups, nothing characterizes their outlook so much as a desire to dispel the Liberal Establishment's philosophy of taxation and redistribution (partly to itself) and reverse the encroachment of government in the social life of the nation.

Shorn of power, stripped of vested interests in misleading and unsuccessful programs, the Liberal Establishment may narrow its gap between words and deeds which helped to drive racial and youthful minorities into open revolt. So changed, Democratic liberalism will once again become a vital and creative force in national politics, usually too innovative to win a Presidential race, but injecting a needed leavening of humanism into the middle-class *Realpolitik* of the new Republican coalition.

Because the Republicans are little dependent on the Liberal Establishment or urban Negroes—the two groups most intimately, though dissimilarly, concerned with present urban and welfare policies—they have the political freedom to disregard the multitude of vested interests which have throttled national urban policy. The GOP is particularly lucky not to be weighted down with commitment to the political blocs, power brokers, and poverty concessionaires of the decaying central cities of the North, now that national growth is shifting to suburbia, the South, and the West. The American future lies in a revitalized countryside, a demographically ascendant Sun Belt and suburbia, and new towns—perhaps mountainside linear cities astride monorails two hundred miles from Phoenix, Memphis, or Atlanta. National policy will have to direct itself toward this future and its constituencies; and perhaps an administration so oriented can also deal realistically with the central cities where Great Society political largesse has so demonstrably failed.

When new eras and alignments have evolved in American politics, the ascending party has ridden the economic and demographic wave of the future: with Jefferson, a nation pushing inland from the Federalist seaboard and Tidewater; with Jackson, the trans-Appalachian New West; with Lincoln, the free-soil West and industrial North; with McKinley, a full-blown industrial North feeding from a full dinner pail; and with Roosevelt, the emergence of the big cities and the coming of age of the immigrant masses. Now it is Richard Nixon's turn to build a new era on the immense middle-class impetus of Sun Belt and suburbia. Thus, it is appropriate that much of the emerging Republican majority lies in the top growth states (California, Arizona, Texas, and Florida) or new suburbia, while Democratic trends correlate with stability and decay (New England, New York City, Michigan, West Virginia, and San Francisco-Berkeley).

The map sketches the emerging Republican majority.

The GOP core areas are the Mountain, Farm, and Outer South states. The Deep South will become a GOP core area once it abandons third-party schemes. The Democratic stronghold is obvious: New York and New England. Most of the upcoming cycle's serious Presidential campaign strategy will relate to three battleground areas: (1) the Pacific; (2) the Ohio-Mississippi Valley (Ohio, Indiana, Illinois, Kentucky, and Missouri); and (3) the non-Yankee Northeast (New Jersey, Pennsylvania, Delaware, and Maryland). Overall trends favor the Republicans in each of these battlegrounds.

It is doubtful whether either party could turn back the clock, but neither has attempted to do so. The 1968 election returns were barely final before Richard Nixon announced that he was transferring his voting residence from New York to Florida, and picked a cabinet notably short on representatives of the Northeastern Establishment. And the Democrats waited only a little longer to replace Louisiana's Earl Long with Massachusetts' Edward Kennedy as their Senate Whip. A new era has begun.

By Spiro Agnew

Address,
Delaware Republican Dinner,
Wilmington, October 14, 1970

LADIES AND GENTLEMEN: I can't stress too much the importance of this election to Delaware and our country in carrying out the mandate you gave our President in 1968.

We do *not* need more big spenders who will drive the cost of living ever upward.

We need a responsible Congress to help complete the job of curbing the runaway inflation that we inherited.

When I hear the leading radical liberal Democrats trying to pin responsibility for that inflation on us, it reminds me of germs complaining about disease.

We need a responsible Congress to back up the President's successful policy of a viable South Vietnam and a peace with honor in Southeast Asia. We do *not* need more Congressional irresponsibles who would abandon our ally to the invader and forsake a heavy investment in American lives.

We need a Congress that will respond to the Administration's efforts to curb the crime rate and restore respect for law in this country. We do *not* need a continued indulgence of disorder.

We need a Congress that will help bring about a reform

Reprinted with the permission of Vice-President Spiro Agnew.

of the federal bureaucracy and create a new working partnership with the states. We do *not* need more obstruction of every innovative program offered. . . .

As some of you may know, I've been moving in a low-key way around the country these last few weeks, quietly encouraging the people to remove from Congress a band of obstructionists I have referred to as the radical liberals.

I have discussed these radical liberals from almost every angle. I have carefully defined the characteristics of a radical liberal. I have named a few of them—and I've been explicitly bipartisan about it. I've told of some of the things these people have tried to do that would be bad for the country—and some of the things they have blocked the President from doing that would have been good for the country.

Tonight I would like to discuss one of the radical liberal's chief afflictions, the reason he acts as he does. In a word, it's "elitism."

The elite, Webster tells us, is "a minority group or stratum that exerts influence, authority, or decisive power." Let me repeat those words: *"influence, authority, power."*

And elitism is defined as "belief in and advocacy of leadership or rule by an elite."

Now, you don't have to be elected to office to be part of this elite or ruling class. In fact, most of the elite are not officeholders. You can direct the news policies of a TV station or write editorials or columns, or you can take over a college classroom and influence young minds, or you can be an author, or an entertainment personality, or a businessman.

The occupation doesn't really matter too much—just as long as you don't get your hands dirty—because there's just no room for blue collars among the elite.

The most basic qualifications are that you dabble in

politics. Read the same things your peers read, go to the same cocktail parties, share the same beliefs, support the same causes, and repeat the latest "in" word or phrase of the group. This week it might be "crisis of confidence," next week it might be "isolation of the President."

There was a time when you could not belong to the elite unless you attended their prep schools and select universities. But not now. Eastern formal schooling is still preferred, but it is by no means mandatory. The important thing is that you mouth the group opinion and deprecate any other. You are expected to fawn on the opinion leaders of the group. You must believe, of course, in their infallibility, and in your own infallibility as a member of the elite. Above all, cleave to the elite line; don't be an individual.

The Wall Street Journal editorialized a while ago about how the elite had swapped its traditional custodial role for one of attacking the Establishment from which it sprang. Said the *Journal:*

> In any society the task of the elite is to supply the bonds that hold together diverse and potentially competing factions. It's up to the elite to articulate and defend the values through which society judges what behavior is appropriate, or inappropriate, how redress is properly sought, what decisions must be accepted as legitimate. . . .
>
> Over the past decade—and this is the new factor—the American elite has not been protecting these social bonds but systematically assaulting them.

The elite consist of the raised-eyebrow cynics, the anti-intellectual intellectuals, the pampered egotists who sneer at honesty, thrift, hard work, prudence, common decency, and self-denial. In their lust to divorce themselves from the ordinary mortals, they embrace confrontation as a substitute for debate and willingly wrench the Bill of Rights to cloak criminal and psychotic conduct it was never intended to cover. They consider this self-alienation to be true sophistication.

Innocently or not, this haughty clique has brought on a permissiveness that in turn has resulted in a shockingly warped sense of values—for instance, the criminal who throws a bomb at a bank is hailed as a hero in some circles for destroying a "capitalist institution." The policeman killed trying to stop him is derided as a "pig." And the "in" thing is to hold a fund-raiser for the Black Panthers or one of their backers.

Let's look at how this sense of self-righteousness develops among these elitists. I recently received a letter from a college student who took me to task for supporting the so-called "straights" who constitute the majority of college students and working people who believe in the values and principles that have made America strong.

Said my young correspondent: "Students and young people are the ones who love their country the most. They wish to change the system so something can be done to stop the war, not give some company another defense contract; or stop pollution, not keep General Motors in business."

And he says of the workingman: "The 8 to 4 man making a living is your hero, but what does he care about when elections come, if he cares then? He is looking for self-benefits."

And he says that the silent majority of students is really interested only in attending classes, drinking, and going to ball games.

There we have a youth who is the conventional paragon of a concerned American. I suppose he is concerned, but I think he is in great danger of becoming intellectually snooty. First, he says in effect that only he and his peers truly love this country because they want to do it over. Those reasonably proud of America, with all her faults— the workingman and most students—just don't understand. I maintain this young man has underrated both the workingman and his fellow students—that they are far more interested in constructively working to solve the problems of America, and are more capable of doing so, than this fledging elitist.

Herbert Marcuse, godfather of the New Left, who in my opinion is responsible for many problems on our campuses today, attacks American democracy as a deceitful and repressive form of popular government which actually enslaves. He looks to students to become the "revolutionary force" that will eventually lead us out of this system into a new socialist society, since workers have so many material benefits they don't realize how bad off they are.

Professor Marcuse finds violence not unacceptable if it comes from those he calls "the oppressed" and breaks what he considers "injustices." But he is intolerant of an opposite opinion. Words used so often today such as "repression" and "alienation" are sprinkled through his writings.

The elitist or self-styled intellectual simply discards anything that does not fit his own stereotyped order of how things should be.

Recently in Las Vegas, Nevada, I was greeted by an editorial in the local paper which compared me with Joseph McCarthy, Hitler, Stalin, and Mussolini. It went on to say *I* should watch *my* rhetoric!

The editorial concluded: "The young intellectual people must never again permit a demagogue to so capture the hearts of the unthinking masses that the very foundations of the nation will be toppled."

Here we have the essence of elitism, or snobbery, this
time by a publisher-journalist. Anyone who stands up and
speaks out for principles not accepted by the elitist is
automatically a demagogue. The people are "unthinking
masses" who have to be controlled by "young intellectuals."

Fortunately, the great majority of the American people
see right through such flimsy thinking. Unfortunately,
however, the word "demagogue" has become a popular
epithet with editorialists who don't share one's viewpoint
on a particular issue or issues, and it is a byword with the
elite. In any event, it is just as hot as my rhetoric they
criticize so much.

Professor Andrew M. Greeley, writing in *The New York
Times Magazine* about self-styled intellectuals as an
"ethnic group" in their own right, observes this characteristic of the elitists:

"Rarely, if ever, does one encounter the slightest hint
that anyone thinks he might not have all the information
or be mistaken in his judgments or that his opponents,
either inside the group or outside of it, might possibly be
men of intelligence and sincerity."

Professor Greeley says that one reason for contempt
directed at other ethnic groups is that they don't show
the required amounts of guilt—for racism in America, for
example, or for the massacres at Song My.

He said the intellectuals enthusiastically embraced the
militant minorities of the black and youthful populations
and denounced Middle America as morally inferior.

"Historians of the future," says Professor Greeley, "may
look on the 1960's as a time not when Middle America
deserted the intellectual ethnic group, but rather as a
time when the intellectual ethnic group deliberately
turned its back on its own mass population support and

began a flirtation with radical groups whose ability to bring about social change was dubious, but whose moral rectitude—at least from the intellectual elite's viewpoint—was beyond question."

My friends, for the past few minutes, I have been quoting sensible, articulate sources who have long been pointing out the danger to this country of a paralyzing elitism. The fact is, however, that these sources have not been heard. Why not? Because of an Elitist Protective Society in much of the media, which ignore and bury attacks on themselves.

But they could hardly ignore a senior official of the United States Government when he called elitists "impudent snobs," as I did last fall. That may be why I am credited with leading the attack against elitism in America, despite the excellent previous work done in the field.

Perhaps there is someone in this audience tonight who wonders if he or she is an elitist. Let me suggest a test. Here are ten questions to ask yourself:

1. Do you walk around with an expression on your face that seems to say that the whole world smells a little bit funny?

2. Do you wish those great masses of people would stop questioning your right to determine public morals and public policy?

3. Do you think that a college education makes you not only intellectually superior, but morally superior as well, to those who did not have your opportunity?

4. Do you think that blue-collar work—like fixing an automobile or driving a truck—is not nearly as dignified or significant as pushing a pencil at a tax-exempt foundation?

5. Does the very thought of a silent majority fill you

with revulsion, while a phrase like "power to the people" appears to you as the essence of the revealed wisdom?

6. Does it make you feel warm and snugly protected to read the *New York Review of Books?*

7. Do you think it is awkward and demeaning for United States senators to have to submit themselves for reelection to a group you call the great unwashed?

8. Do you tune in a Presidential speech at the end just to get your opinions from the instant analysis?

9. Did you ever go to sleep and dream of J. William Fulbright's becoming Secretary of State—without waking up screaming?

10. Do you support a constitutional amendment to abolish the office of Vice-President of the United States?

My friends, if your answer to even two or three of these questions is "yes," you may regard yourself as a full-fledged elitist, and you can treat yourself to two seats on the aisle for *Oh! Calcutta!*

But if your answer to each of these questions is a ringing, indignant "No!"—then welcome to the silent majority.

In all seriousness, ladies and gentlemen, an arrogant and aloof elitism has no place in a democracy. Indeed, the greatest invitation to anti-intellectualism in American life today comes from those narrow-minded, big brains who are giving real intellectualism a bad name. Outright snobbery—and reverse snobbery—drive a people apart and slam the door to intelligent inquiry and productive debate.

Of course, some people are smarter than others. Of course, some people are richer than others, or more powerful than others, or more talented than others. We are not created the same, but we are created equal—and that means equal rights in our system. It means that no one and no group has any more rights than any other.

The danger to the life of the mind today comes not so much from the know-nothings, but from the know-it-alls. Fortunately for this nation, public policy is made neither by the know-nothings nor the know-it-alls. Our future is shaped by the people who know enough to trust the good sense and generous nature of the common man.

Opinion leaders make a terrible mistake when they high-hat the public. And this is why: presented with a choice between the high-hat and the hardhat, the American people will come down on the side of the hardhat every time.

The breakup of the old elite and the rise of the silent majority augur well for democracy and equal justice in this nation. With the passing of the old elite will come an end to arrogance and the beginnings of mutual respect in a nation that prizes a unity of purpose and a diversity of opinion.

By Edmund S. Muskie

Election Eve Television Address, November 3, 1970

FELLOW AMERICANS:

I am speaking from Cape Elizabeth, Maine—to discuss with you the election campaign which is coming to a close.

In the heat of our campaign, we have all become accustomed to a little anger and exaggeration.

Yet, on the whole, our political process has served us well—presenting for your judgment a range of answers to the country's problems . . . and a choice between men who seek the honor of public service.

That is our system.

It has worked for almost two hundred years—longer than any other political system in the world.

And it still works.

But in these elections of 1970, something has gone wrong.

There has been name-calling and deception of almost unprecedented volume.

Honorable men have been slandered.

Faithful servants of the country have had their motives questioned and their patriotism doubted.

This attack is not simply the overzealousness of a few local leaders.

Reprinted with the permission of Senator Edmund S. Muskie.

It has been led . . . inspired . . . and guided . . . from the highest offices in the land.

The danger from this assault is not that a few more Democrats might be defeated—the country can survive that.

The true danger is that the American people will have been deprived of that public debate, that opportunity for fair judgment, which is the heartbeat of the democratic process.

And that is something the country cannot afford.

Let me try to bring some clarity to this deliberate confusion.

Let me begin with those issues of law and order . . . of violence and unrest . . . which have pervaded the rhetoric of this campaign.

I believe that any person who violates the law should be apprehended . . . prosecuted . . . and punished if found guilty.

So does every candidate for office, of both parties.

And nearly all Americans agree.

I believe everyone has a right to feel secure . . . on the streets of his city . . . and in buildings where he works or studies.

So does every candidate for office, of both parties.

And nearly all Americans agree.

Therefore, there is no issue of law and order . . . or of violence.

There is only a problem.

There is no disagreement about what we want.

There are only different approaches to getting it.

And the harsh and uncomfortable fact is that no one—in either party—has the final answer.

For four years, a conservative Republican has been governor of California.

Yet there is no more law and order in California today than when he took office.

President Nixon—like President Johnson before him—has taken a firm stand.

A Democratic Congress has passed sweeping legislation.

Yet America is no more orderly or lawful—nor its streets more safe—than was the case two years ago . . . or four . . . or six.

We must deal with symptoms—strive to prevent crime, halt violence, and punish the wrongdoer.

But we must also look for the deeper causes in the structure of our society.

If one of your loved ones is sick, you do not think it is soft or undisciplined of a doctor . . . to try and discover the agents of illness.

But you would soon discard a doctor who thought it enough to stand by the bed and righteously curse the disease.

Yet, there are those who seek to turn our common distress to partisan advantage—not by offering better solutions—but with empty threat . . . and malicious slander.

They imply that Democratic candidates for high office in Texas and California . . . in Illinois and Tennessee . . . in Utah and Maryland . . . and among my New England neighbors from Vermont and Connecticut—men who have courageously pursued their convictions . . . in the service of the Republic in war and in peace—that these men actually favor violence . . . and champion the wrongdoer.

That is a lie.

And the American people know it is a lie.

And what are we to think when men in positions of public trust openly declare—

that the party of Franklin Roosevelt and Harry Truman which led us out of depression . . . and to victory over international barbarism;

the party of John Kennedy who was slain in the service of the country he inspired;

the party of Lyndon Johnson who withstood the fury of countless demonstrations in order to pursue a course he believed in;

the party of Robert Kennedy, murdered on the eve of his greatest triumphs—

How dare they tell us that this party is less devoted or less courageous . . . in maintaining American principals and values . . . than are they themselves.

This is nonsense.

And we all know it is nonsense.

And what contempt they must have for the decency and sense of the American people to talk to them that way —and to think they can make them believe.

There is not time tonight to analyze and expose the torrent of falsehood and insinuation which has flooded that unfortunate campaign.

There is a parallel—in the campaigns of the early fifties—when the turbulent difficulties of the postwar world were attributed to the softness and lack of patriotism of a few . . . including some of our most respected leaders . . . such as General George Marshall.

It was the same technique.

These attacks are dangerous in a more important sense, for they keep us from dealing with our problems.

Names and threats will not end the shame of ghettos and racial injustice . . . restore a degraded environment . . . or end a long and bloody war.

Slogans and television commercials will not bring the workingman that assurance—of a constantly rising standard of life—which was his only a few years ago . . . and which has been cruelly snatched away.

No Administration can be expected to solve the difficulties of America in two years.

But we can fairly ask two things: that a start be made and that the nation be instilled with a sense of forward movement . . . of high purpose.

This has not been done.

Let us look, for example, at the effort to halt inflation.

We all agree that inflation must be arrested.

This Administration has decided it could keep prices down by withdrawing money from the economy.

Now I do not think they will ever control inflation in this way.

But even if their policy was sound, the money had to come from someone.

And who did they pick to pay?

It was the workingman . . . the consumer . . . the middle-class American.

For example, high interest rates are a part of this policy.

Yet they do not damage the banks which collect them.

They hardly touch the very wealthy who can deduct interest payments from their taxes.

Rather, they strike at every consumer who must pay exorbitant charges on his new car or house. And they can cripple the small businessman.

Their policy against inflation also requires that unemployment go up.

Again, it is the workingman who pays the price.

In other fields the story is the same.

They have cut back on health and education for the many . . . while expanding subsidies and special favors for a few.

They call upon you—the working majority of Americans—to support them while they oppose your interests.

They really believe that if they can make you afraid enough . . . or angry enough . . . you can be tricked into voting against yourself.

It is all part of the same contempt . . . and tomorrow you can show them the mistake they have made.

Our difficulties as a nation are immense, confused, and changing.

But our history shows—and I think most of you suspect —that if we are ever to restore progress, it will be under the leadership of the Democratic Party.

Not that we are smarter or more expert, but we respect the people.

We believe in the people.

And indeed we must, for we are of the people.

Today the air of my native Maine was touched with winter . . . and hunters filled the woods.

I have spent my life in this state . . . which is both part of our oldest traditions and a place of wild and almost untouched forests.

It is rugged country, cold in the winters, but it is a good place to live.

There are friends . . . and there are also places to be alone—places where a man can walk all day . . . and fish . . . and see nothing but woods and water.

We in Maine share many of the problems of America and, I am sure, others are coming to us.

But we have had no riots or bombings, and speakers are not kept from talking.

This is not because I am Senator, or because the Governor is a Democrat.

Partly, of course, it is because we are a small state with no huge cities . . . but partly it is because the people here have a sense of place.

They are part of a community with common concerns and problems and hopes for the future.

We cannot make America small.

But we can work to restore a sense of shared purpose and of great enterprise.

We can bring back the belief—not only in a better and more noble future—but in our own power to make it so.

Our country is wounded and confused, but it is charged with greatness and with the possibility of greatness.

We cannot realize that possibility if we are afraid . . . or if we consume our energies in hostility and accusation.

We must maintain justice—but we must also believe in ourselves and each other—and we must get about the work of the future.

There are only two kinds of politics.

They are not radical and reactionary . . . or conservative and liberal. Or even Democrat and Republican. There are only the politics of fear and the politics of trust.

One says: You are encircled by monstrous dangers. Give us power over your freedom so we may protect you.

The other says: The world is a baffling and hazardous place, but it can be shaped to the will of men.

Ordinarily that division is not between parties, but between men and ideas.

But this year the leaders of the Republican Party have intentionally made that line a party line.

They have confronted you with exactly that choice.

Thus, in voting for the Democratic Party tomorrow, you cast your vote for trust—not just in leaders or policies —but for trusting your fellow citizens . . . in the ancient traditions of this home for freedom . . . and, most of all, for trust in yourself.

By Andrew M. Greeley

Take Heart
from the Heartland

I don't like ethnic campaigning; I think it's kind of cheap.
—Arthur Goldberg, candidate for governor of New York, to an audience of Italian-Americans.

If you are humble in victory and courageous in defeat, you'll always get along in politics. Tonight is a night for great humility.—Richard J. Daley, November 4, 1970.

BOTH KEVIN PHILLIPS and the team of Richard Scammon and Ben Wattenberg are agreed that the Middle West is crucial in American politics. Whether it be called the "Heartland" or the "Quadracali," it is the "swing region" in Presidential elections; and as the elections of 1970 quickly become an unpleasant memory, one is forced to say that the heartland has moved to the left. In the massive block of America between the Ohio River and the Rocky Mountains, Democrats managed to hold almost all of their supposedly tenuous Senate seats, score most of their House gains, send a bright new liberal face to the United States Senate, and grab just about every governorship in sight.

Reprinted from *The New Republic*, December 12, 1970, © 1970 by Harrison-Blaine of New Jersey, Inc. Used by permission of *The New Republic*.

How can this be? What happened to the silent majority? Where is the backlash? What became of the crime issue? Apparently, they've all migrated east of the Hudson River.

And, if the heartland has become liberal once again, its capital is the despised Second City on the shores of Lake Michigan, for the hated Daley organization won what may be its greatest victory. Adlai Stevenson, III, now holds the Senate seat his father always wanted, having obtained 2,065,154 against his opponent's 1,519,718 votes. Two other attractive Democratic candidates—Alan Dixon, the new state treasurer, and Prof. Michael Bakalis, the superintendent of public instruction—joined with Stevenson in leading the first major success for the organization in previously solid Republican suburbs of Chicago; the Republicans find themselves with almost nothing left in Cook County, and the Democrats dominate the state legislature in Springfield for the first time in the twentieth century. Not bad at all for the last hurrah.

While Democrats and liberals in New York and Connecticut were busily engaged in committing suicide, Richard J. Daley was picking up every marble on the playground. While progressive New York was helping Mr. Agnew put James Buckley in the United States Senate, benighted, hardhat Illinois was giving an overwhelming victory to a man whose family name symbolizes all that was supposedly dear in American liberalism. Is it possible that those who do most of the thinking and writing about American politics, who shape the issues and campaigns, who author the columns and the articles in the liberal journals have missed something critical about American politics?

One of my colleagues remarked the day after election that "of course you can elect a liberal in Illinois if his name happens to be Adlai Stevenson." Leaving aside the fact that there was a liberal called Paul Douglas and another called Charles Percy, the question remains why a name which symbolizes the "liberal permissiveness" that Mr. Agnew so cheerfully denounced is political magic in a state supposedly dominated by the silent majority and, to use a term bandied about at a meeting of the American Sociological Association in 1968," shanty Irish bigots"?

I am contending that the Chicago system deserves a fair investigation in the wake of November 3 to see what it may tell us about the operation of the political process. Martin Meyerson, Edward Banfield, and James Q. Wilson have made such investigations on the scholarly level, but their investigations are systematically ignored, even by their sometime colleagues at the University of Chicago. And the journalists from the East—to say nothing of their alienated imitators from Chicago—are interested only in telling it like they knew it was before they bothered to investigate it in any depth. Let me illustrate.

An Eastern paper the day after the election wrote of a "deal" by which Stevenson agreed to support Daley candidates in return for Daley's support of his senatorial candidacy. The article added that while Stevenson had won easily, the Daley machine had not done well. The facts are that such "deals" do not exist in Chicago politics (they are not necessary), that Stevenson *was* a Daley candidate, and that the Daley organization *had* won the greatest victory in its history.

The normally fair Howard K. Smith lumped Stevenson (though not by name) with Agnew on the night before the election as an example of campaign demagoguery because Adlai wore an American flag on his lapel, emphasized the crime issue, and put a famous prosecutor on his campaign staff. The facts are that Stevenson had authored crime legislation before it was fashionable to do so and that the prosecutor in question, Thomas Aquinas Foran, receives more hate mail for prosecuting a school integration case in a Chicago suburb, indicting police for the convention disturbances, and pushing faculty integration in the public schools.

Roy Newquist, writing obviously for non-Chicagoans in Fielding's *Guide to Chicago,* observes, "The political complexion of Chicago seems to be undergoing a change. The 1968 Democratic Convention riots upset the natives more than anything else that has happened in decades, and citizens of all colors are taking harsh second and third looks at the regular Democratic (or Daley) machinery." Newquist is right, of course, that the natives were upset by the convention demonstrations, but the slightest glance at the public opinion polls ought to have indicated that it was not the organization at which they were angry.

A prizewinning Chicago journalist has quoted several times a sentence from a speech of Foran's after the conspiracy trial in which the prosecutor said, "Our children are shocked when they hear us saying 'wop' and 'nigger.' " He never bothers to add that the next sentence was, "And they are right to be shocked." Nor does he point out that on racial and economic matters Foran has always been a liberal. Indeed, one of the most fascinating interludes of the campaign was Foran—an impressive TV personality— upstaging Jesse Jackson on a TV talk show with ploys like, "I agree with you completely, Reverend Jackson, but I'd want to go further and take an even more radical stand."

A New Yorker once observed to me, "Everyone knows that Julius Hoffman is the most corrupt judge who ever bought a seat on the bench from Dick Daley." Hoffman is a Republican appointed by Dwight Eisenhower before Daley was mayor of Chicago, and judgeships are not "bought" in Chicago. They *are* frequently a reward for loyalty, but Chicago has no monopoly on this method of judicial selection.

The ordinary explanation for the "machine's" triumphs implies that in part the votes are bought or stolen, and that in part they are cast by a patronage army. One gets the picture of vast, unthinking Slavic hordes marching in tight discipline to the polls. The facts are that you cannot steal or buy a half million votes, and that the patronage army is tiny compared to the size of the city. Furthermore, the black and Slavic voters of Chicago are no less intelligent than voters elsewhere. The blacks have had alternative candidates to the Daley candidates and have, with one or two exceptions, soundly rejected them. Nor are the Polish voters who overwhelmingly endorsed Adlai Stevenson unaware of his racial stand. To explain the organization's ability to get more than three fourths of the Polish vote and three fourths of the black vote in terms of fraud, fear, and theft is to turn the voters of Chicago into dull, stereotypical automatons. Such a strategy is useful for those who don't want to face the possibility that there may be some extremely important political truth that the organization has discovered. But it is also prejudice in the strict sense of that word.

One moderately militant black summarized the position of many of his colleagues when he told me, "We're loyal to the organization because it works, because we know of no better way of improving our position in Chicago, and because, while it can't give everyone everything he wants, it can give most Chicago groups enough to keep them happy." Such a comment may sound cynical and, from a black, even treasonable. But, from the point of view of Chicago Democrats, it represents the essence of the political process.

The masters of ethnic politics are not intellectuals;

they are not given to articulating abstract ideas; only
Foran and one or two others look good on TV; their insight into the city and what makes it tick is not phrased
in slick social science terminology, but is concrete and instinctual. Any attempt to state their model of the political
process in formal terms—such as I will shortly engage in
—is bound to lose something of the vigor and flavor of
the original. On the other hand, while intellectual types
may find the poor diction and malapropisms of some of the
ethnic politicians vastly amusing, their amusement should
not blind them to the fact that the best of politicians have
an intuitive grasp of the city that would make the most
skillful social scientist look naïve.

The first assumption of ethnic politics is that the city is
composed of various groups—national, racial, economic,
religious. It is the politician's role to act as a broker among
these groups, arranging and rearranging power and resources in such a way as to prevent one group from becoming so unhappy with the balance that they will leave
the system. He arranges, usually indirectly and informally,
and almost always gradually, compromises among the various power elements within the city which these elements
could not achieve by direct negotiation among themselves.
Thus, Irish aldermen or congressmen are slowly phased
out to be replaced by Poles and then blacks (there are
three Polish Democratic congressmen, two blacks, two
Jews, one Irishman, and one Italian from Chicago, and
in the next aldermanic elections about 30 percent of the
city council seats will be held by blacks); but there is no
great fanfare accompanying such changes. Does the organization slate a black congressman to represent Cicero
and Berwyn? It surely does; but it doesn't issue press re-
leases claiming that it is engaged in a revolution.

The "balanced ticket" is a symbol of this power brokerage game. To exclude a group its "place" on the ticket is to insult and offend them. If you should tell an ethnic politician that in one state (New York) the Democratic slate was made up of three Jews and a black and that the party still expected to get the Irish and Italian vote, he will simply not believe you. And if you tell him that in another state (Connecticut) a Unitarian minister with an Irish name and a liberal background led a slate on which, for the first time in many years, there were no Irish Catholics, he would assume that the Irish vote would go Republican and wonder who was responsible for such an inept decision.

Nor would he be able to understand why some would consider piece-of-the-pie demands to be immoral. The model of the new politics—enthusiastic college students from "out of the neighborhood," vigorous ideological liberalism, passionate moral self-righteousness—would baffle him. The ethnic politician knows that in most of the districts of his city this model will not win elections.

In his frame of reference you can't afford to lose one economic or racial or ethnic group. If you win an election at the price of turning off one such segment of the city and setting the others against this scapegoat group, you're simply asking for trouble. No political leader can afford to lose a major group from his consensus, for he will find it difficult to govern without this group and even more difficult to be reelected.

The ethnic politician also realizes that most people are not ideologues. He knew long before Amitai Etzione's brilliant article in *Transaction* that most people are quite "inconsistent" in their political attitudes; they are "liberal" on some issues, "conservative" on others. Furthermore, the ethnic politician realizes that for all the attention they get on the media, self-appointed "spokesmen" usually represent only themselves and a tiny band of friends. Most citizens are not interested in ideology but are moved by more concrete and pressing matters—jobs, sidewalks, garbage removal, streets, transportation, housing, access to the government to get assistance when needed. The vast network of precinct captains is not merely, or even principally, a downward channel of communication designed to convey voting instructions. It is also a technique—frequently more effective than public opinion polling—for determining what is on people's minds and providing them with a feeling of access to the system.

Why do you slate an obvious liberal like Adlai Stevenson at a time when the pundits are all persuaded that there is a "shift to the right"? Partly, you may do it because you don't read the pundits, but partly because your instincts and your organization say that Adlai is a winner. Why are you undismayed when a smooth advertising firm, relying on poll data and White House advice, turns out clever ads suggesting your candidate is "soft" on student radicals? Mostly because your instincts and your organization tell you that the student issue is not all that important and that Adlai is still a winner. And why do you rejoice when the Vice-President arrives on the scene as part of the "realignment" strategy and accuses Adlai of disgracing his father's name? Because you know your voters well enough to know that they are not going to be "realigned" by such foolishness and will certainly resent such an attack on someone about whom they have already made up their minds.

The ethnic politician is also free from the pundit's uncertainty about the nature of the electorate. Before the election, there was much fear that the voter was a narrow, frightened, easily swayed member of the silent majority, and maybe a hardhat to boot. After the election, he looked more like a responsible, discriminating, and sophisticated person. But from the ethnic politician's viewpoint, both images are incomplete. He is well aware of the unpredictability, the strain toward bigotry, the extreme sensitivity to slights, the fear, the impatience with all politicians. But he also realizes that their is a strain toward rationality, openness, and trust, and a sympathy for social reform, and that, in his better moments, John Q. Voter is capable of civility, intelligence, and generosity. Thus, the ethnic politician is not too surprised when he rises to heights. In other words, you appeal to both the voter's fears and his idealism, his selfishness and his integrity; and, after a while, you hope that you have become skillful in the art of blending the two kinds of appeals.

The ethnic politician's slogan that social progress is good politics is neither phony nor cynical but simply a statement of political reality as he sees it. He knows that if he is too "conservative," the balance he has established will not shift rapidly enough to keep up with the changing state of his city; and if he is too "liberal," he may attempt to force change on the city before there is a broad enough consensus to support it. In the thirties he supports the trade unions and in the sixties the black demand for power, but he supports both such demands in ways that will not drive other groups out of his coalition. There may be a tendency in such an approach to move too slowly, especially if the organization has poor communication links with a minority group. But the political leader is much less sanguine that his academic critic about the ability of any leadership to correct most social problems in a brief period of time.

The two Stevensons, Paul Douglas, Otto Kerner (who presided over the extremely liberal report on civil disturbances), and the present lieutenant governor, Paul Simon, represent a liberal tradition of which any state might be proud. Michael Bakalis, a thirty-two-year-old university professor (of Greek origin, conveniently enough), and U.S. Congressman Abner Mikva are liberal enough to please Professor Galbraith. The ethnic politician knows that there is a strong liberal strain in his electorate and that an articulate and intelligent liberal can have strong voter appeal. The liberal must, of course, be able to win, he must want to win (frequently a difficulty for many American liberals), and he must not forget who helped him to win—or run the risk of not winning again. Furthermore, he must realize that he and his fellows cannot claim a monopoly on all offices. From the point of view of the ethnic politician, liberalism is good politics, especially when he can find a liberal who is willing to admit that politics can be good liberalism.

While his critics contend that it is patronage which holds the organization together, he knows himself that "loyalty" is more important than jobs. As one young Irish lawyer put it, "A man who is not loyal to his friends will never be loyal to an idea." The mockery to which Arthur Goldberg was subjected by those who thrust him into the political limelight would be unthinkable to an ethnic politician. You stand by your own, even if they have made mistakes, or if they have perhaps grown a bit too old. You wait patiently in line until it's "your turn" to be slated. You accept the decisions of the organization with good grace and work for the success of the ticket, even though you are personally disappointed. You do so because you're convinced that there is no other way to engage in politics and that the alternative is what New York Democrats are currently calling Balkanization.

In his book *The Irish and Irish Politicians,* Edward Levine tells the story of Nineteenth Ward Committeeman John Duffy who supported Martin Kennelly against Daley in 1955 because of the loyalty that Duffy's mentor, Thomas Nash, felt for Kennelly. According to Levine, Daley is reputed to have said, "If I were Duffy, I would bolt." Later, Duffy became the organization's president of the county board and worked closely with the Mayor. There is a nice etiquette required of those who must balance loyalties, but the phrase "Do what you have to do" is fully understood by the ethnic politicians. When he hears that this is "clannishness" the ethnic politician is puzzled. What are the alternatives? To quote one of Levine's informants: "The only thing you have in politics is your word. Break your word and you're dead. The most successful politician is the politician who kept his word." But if he is puzzled by the failure of the "liberal" to understand this truism, the ethnic politician would probably be astonished that such New Left political theorists as John Schaar are demanding the same kind of personal fealty from their political leaders. The ethnic leader and the hippie guru may have more in common than they know.

There are obvious faults in such a political model in addition to those which are inevitable in any political model. Its very flexibility and amorphousness may make dishonesty and corruption somewhat easier than the so-called Reform models of politics, but ethnic systems are much less corrupt in most American cities than they have been in the past, and ethnic politicians have no monopoly on corruption. Nor is the charge that the ethnic system is not open to the major forces of social change a valid one; quite the contrary, if the system is working properly, social change is precisely what it is open to, though it distinguishes between actual social change and that announced by academic theorists.

There are three critical weaknesses, however. First, the responsiveness of the system to groups depends to some extent on how well organized and articulate a given group is. The ethnic politician does not readily spot a situation where a given group may need his help in organizing itself and articulating its demands.

Second, small but potentially explosive groups can be missed. The basic problem at the root of the 1968 turmoil was that the organization had had little experience with the youth culture and was unprepared to deal with it. It learned quickly, and there has been no repetition of the scene in front of the Conrad Hilton, but the mistake of playing into the hands of the radicals was a function of the fact that until the convention, youth culture was not seen as a serious problem to cope with.

Finally, while the ethnic politician is not likely to be swayed by the moralism, the dogmatism, and the perfectionism of the academic, his own proclivity to a concrete and instinctual style makes it hard for him to communicate with the intellectual and make use of the intellectual's important contribution to the political process—and, in particular, the intellectual's ability to spot long-range trends and problems.

It is difficult to write such an article for non-Chicago readership. The mere mention of "Chicago politics" or "Richard Daley" or "Irish politicians" erects a barrier in certain segments of American society which is hard to pierce. The system is immoral and corrupt or, to use Mr. Goldberg's word, cheap.

But the "liberal" may want to ponder the thought that the alternative is Nelson Rockefeller and James Buckley till the year 2000. And the "radical" may feel that ethnic politics are part of the "establishment" which must be overthrown in "the revolution"—whether it be the peaceful revolution of Consciousness III or something more bloody. But the "radical" may want to ponder the fact that even after the revolution he will have to contend with the same social groups in the large city with which the ethnic politician must cope, and that if he does not come up with a better method, he will either have to fall back on the ethnic strategy or maintain a very efficient secret police and a very large system of concentration camps.

By Bayard Rustin

Mobilizing a Progressive Majority

PORTRAITS of the ancient Roman god Janus show a creature with back-to-back faces, one looking to the past, the other to the future. The god of gates, he has come down to us in our literature as a symbol of the termination of one segment of time and the commencement of another. We meet him at the beginning of every year and also at the beginning of a historical period.

We are now at the beginning of such a period. Although powerful emotions and discontents still trouble us, there are signs that the siege of protest and passion this country has been living through is giving way to fatigue and reevaluation. What this will lead to is not entirely clear, for the character of the new period remains to be determined by the actions of those involved in social and political movements. Character is not predetermined. Thus we can play a role in shaping the future, but we can do so only if we turn from the past and base our judgments on the conditions that are unfolding. In the process we should be wary of what is fashionable, for it is not likely to be relevant, as the saying goes, for very long. Much of

Reprinted from *The New Leader*, January 25, 1971. Copyright © by the American Labor Conference on International Affairs, Inc. Used by permission.

what was "new" in the last decade is now frayed by the passage of time and by too many encounters with hard realities. The New Left, the New Politics, and the new modes of activity by young Negroes have not produced, to say the least, a millennium. If anything, they have disoriented many people and, I suspect, contributed to the growth of the Right. Clearly, a reassessment is necessary if we are to know how to proceed.

Having always been a protester, I have always felt the need to protest against injustices not only in our society but throughout the world. Anyone who feels himself to be oppressed, or empathizes with others who are oppressed, shares this need. Indeed, the existence of exploitation, prejudice, inequality, and, most basically, man's inhumanity to man can drive someone who believes in justice into a frenzy of outrage. Yet if there is one thing I have learned, it is that protest alone is inadequate. Under certain conditions it can be a useful tactic for eliminating specific injustices, as the carefully conceived, effectively executed protests against Jim Crow demonstrated during the late '50s and early '60s. But even then I thought the civil rights movement had to go beyond protest. It was important, I felt, to adopt a strategy that could deal in a comprehensive way with the causes of domestic tension, and I urged a turn to politics.

There are some people, especially many young people, who do not understand the vital role of politics. It is the most democratic form of expression I know of, and the most powerful means of achieving social change. In fact, it is the one means of doing what must be done to bring about justice in America. If the problem were simply racism, we could proceed merely by calling each other names, psychoanalyzing each other, beating our breasts, and moralizing. But the problem runs much deeper. It is rooted in our social institutions, and its solution requires a broad, well-planned, massively financed social program. We need government action, and for that we need politics.

I use the term "politics" here in the broad democratic sense of mobilizing a majority that has power, durability, and a commitment to social change. Negroes by themselves, of course, do not constitute such a force; a minority does not have the strength to carry through a basic reform of our social and economic system. Negroes can initiate change and provoke a reaction, as they have on several occasions with great effectiveness, but the decisive factor will be the direction of the majority. The political objective of the black struggle must, therefore, be the creation of a progressive majority in the form of a coalition. And the most powerful social institution in the country that can be enlisted for this purpose, with which Negroes must ally, is the American trade union movement.

Much has happened since I first set forth this strategy. To be very honest, I did not foresee all the obstacles that have complicated its achievement. Nevertheless, I think the essential idea has proved out.

One obstacle was the rise of black nationalism and the growing tendency on the part of Negroes to advocate and engage in violence. I am fully aware of the causes of these tendencies: the terrible frustrations, the deep and bitter resentments, the dramatic quest for identity. It would seem self-evident, though, that if one wants to quicken the pace of reform, one should not take an approach that will strengthen the enemies of change. Separatism, for example, is simply a black version of Jim Crow, and we know the history of oppression that is associated with this kind of segregation. It is tragic and shocking, but alas inevitable, that the head of the Congress on Racial Equality turned to some of the most reactionary Southern governors to enlist support for a separatist school proposal. Who else is in such total agreement with his basic philosophy?

Then came the advocates of violent revolution. Where are they now? Some are dead, others are in jail, and the rest are scattered all over the world—people without countries or constituencies. In their wake, and in the wake of the violence of the past six years, there has been nothing more than a trail of martyrs, gutted buildings, and political reaction. Haven't we had enough martyrs? Haven't we had enough aimless violence? Toward what end are these futile gestures of anger and despair?

If I read the mood in the black community correctly, the answer is: "Yes, we have had enough of violence and extremism. We have no use for guerrilla tactics imported from Algeria and ideologies imported from China, North Korea, and even Stalin's Russia. We need program, politics, and power. Not the false power of empty slogans and loaded guns, but the real power that comes with holding public office, having jobs, sending one's children to schools that educate, living in decent homes and safe communities, being full and equal citizens in the country where we and our parents and their parents were born—in America."

I do not mean to imply that this is a new feeling among Negroes. These have always been the goals of the overwhelming majority. And throughout recent years, when voices arose to repudiate these goals and to deny the possibility of ever gaining equality in America, the largest and most representative organization in the Negro community, the NAACP, firmly adhered to a program of democratic social reform; it refused to compromise its faith in integration and nonviolence.

So there has been consistent opposition to the separatists. But today this opposition is getting stronger; the tide is turning in its favor. The separatists have failed, and now a new period is at hand. Look at the 1970 election. Negroes made greater gains than in any campaign since Reconstruction, with some of the most important victories scored in majority white areas: Wilson Riles, Superintendent of Education in California; Richard Austin, Secretary of State in Michigan; and three Democratic Congressmen—Ronald Dellums in Oakland, California, George Collins in Chicago, and Parren Mitchell in Baltimore. These men know the folly of separatism, and they are part of an expanding trend in the black community toward electoral political action.

The A. Philip Randolph Institute voter registration groups, organized in cities across the country by Norman Hill, represent the kind of political involvement we will be seeing more and more of in the years ahead. And make no mistake about it: this is militant political involvement. It is not militant to talk about killing pigs, though that may tingle the spines of some New Leftists. It is militant to go out and mobilize the black community so that it can have an impact on the electoral process. The 1970's, I predict, will mark the Negro's full-scale entrance into American politics—to change the society and to control his own destiny.

Yet as I have already noted, we cannot do this alone. Without allies we can accomplish nothing of significance. In this regard, I think one of the brightest developments throughout the lean years of the late '60s was a strengthening of the bonds between the civil rights and labor movements.

I cannot emphasize too strongly the importance of this alliance to the black struggle. Ask anyone who had anything to do with the legislative battles in Congress and he will tell you that none of the major civil rights acts could have been passed without labor's support. Newspaper reports about their being divided notwithstanding, the civil rights and labor movements combined to block the appointments of Clement Haynsworth and G. Harrold Carswell to the Supreme Court, too. While this is well known, it is worth repeating because some people have short memories.

It is also worth repeating something Martin Luther King, Jr., said a decade ago that remains equally relevant today: Negroes are overwhelmingly a working people. We have never been able to develop much in the way of a capitalist class. We are workers, and as workers we have the same needs as our white counterparts—full employment, decent wages, job security, pensions, a safe workplace, quality public education, livable cities.

In other words, we share with white workers a common interest in labor's program. Alliances are not based on mutual affection, as some people might think. Affection may bring individuals together, but common interest is the stuff of social movements and it is what binds the Negro-labor alliance. That is important for us to realize in our coalition, because obviously there is much wrong with the trade union movement; obviously there is much wrong with black people in the United States; obviously there is much wrong with white liberals; obviously wherever we look we can find fault. But the only result of endless fault-finding is that you end up in a corner with the few people who are as good and pure as you are. It renders impossible the building of a political movement capable of directing its attention to the most basic task of all—the redistribution of wealth.

Workingmen, blue-collar as well as blacks, must be brought together in support of a mutually beneficial platform if we are to have any social progress—or register any political gains at the polls in 1972. And I think the key to accomplishing this is having as much compassion for the blue-collar worker as we have for the people in the ghetto. They appear to be better off, and they are. Remember, though, that they are the ones who cannot get scholarships for their children because they earn too much, yet do not earn enough to afford the tuition; they are the ones who do not receive medical assistance, yet suffer virtual bankruptcy when plagued by long illness; they are the ones—not the rich and not the very poor—who have been hit hardest by President Nixon's tax policy.

Blue-collar people work hard and long for what they have, and they are fearful. They may have two cars, but these are probably not paid for and the second car, far from being a luxury, more likely enables the wife to hold a job. We must address ourselves to them no less than to blacks in the ghetto. For unless we get rid of black rage and white fear simultaneously, we shall not get rid of either. That brings me back, more or less, to where I started from: The only independent institution in this country with the mechanism for eliminating black rage and white fear at the same time is the trade-union movement. When labor speaks of free medical care, it is saying we need it for blacks who do not have it and whites who are concerned that they will have to pay for giving it to them. When labor calls for full employment, it is talking about blacks who are without jobs and whites who want to protect the ones they have. When labor says we must build more homes, it is seeking to create a society where the black brother need not be enraged because he does not have a home and the white need not fear for the home he has.

There are those who would deny this, who say the trade-union movement is the enemy of the Negro's struggle for equality. Usually they are the same people who blame the workingman for inflation, the conservative backlash, and war. You can be sure they are not workers themselves, struggling to make ends meet on $7,000 to $8,000 a year. Usually they live sheltered lives in sheltered, affluent communities, far from the cutting edge of social change. Their children have not died in Vietnam. They do not understand and show no signs of wanting to understand the difficulties a worker must face on as well as off the job. This being the case, it is not surprising that they dismiss out of hand the one organization the worker can turn to for assistance in coping with his problems—his union.

The views held by these people, many of whom consider themselves liberals, are not only wrong, but threaten serious harm to the coalition upon which we all depend for social progress. Labor is not the black man's enemy, and to keep insisting otherwise is to help the conservative elements with an interest in weakening their relationship. This is not to suggest that where there is discrimination in the labor movement it should not be vigorously opposed and rooted out. Action, not mere words, is required to correct inequities where they exist; action that will strengthen the bonds between Negroes and the unions. Ernie Green's rapidly expanding Joint Apprenticeship Program is an example of such action. It has scored a major breakthrough by increasing minority participation in the building trades, and has the full backing of the AFL-CIO leadership.

The Joint Apprenticeship Program has received little recognition from labor's critics. Those heading it do not engage in the fashionable practice of making sweeping moral judgments, and do not advocate confrontations with white workers. Instead, they base their approach on a fundamental political principle: that social change cannot come about through conflict between the have-nots and the have-littles; that, in fact, such a conflict would benefit not the poor but the rich and the reactionary.

We saw what happened in 1968 when the two groups were divided. We had Wallace, and we are left with Nixon. But we also learned how to fight this problem. The entire trade-union movement, the AFL-CIO and its affiliates and the United Auto Workers and the Teamsters, undertook a massive educational program that appealed to workers not to sacrifice their economic self-interest to the "law and order" demagoguery of the Right. It was almost enough to defeat the conservatives.

In 1970, the trade-union movement launched another tremendous political effort. The working class was supposed to be moving to the Republicans on "the social issue," and President Nixon played this one for all he thought it was worth. The unions, meanwhile, kept drumming home the economic issues—unemployment, inflation, high interest rates. These are the things that are hurting workers, that are hurting blacks, and that resulted in the coalition frustrating Nixon's strategy. Now, in addition to full employment, the Administration must be pressed to meet the needs of the cities and the rural slums.

We have lived through a decade in which race was the focal point of our domestic politics, and we have entered a decade in which the spotlight is shifting to economic justice. Foreign policy, to be sure, cannot be neglected. Not while the crisis in the Middle East threatens the survival of one of the bravest democracies in the world; while the Vietnam war continues; while there are nations in Africa, Asia, and Latin America struggling to develop; while the stability of international relations is in constant flux. We cannot withdraw into a neoisolationist shell.

But it would be self-defeating at this time to let differences over foreign policy become the overriding issue in our coalition; we should emphasize what unites us. I have in mind how labor in the last elections backed candidates because they supported progressive domestic policies, not on the basis of their Vietnam position. This kind of political activity strengthened the coalition and was an important factor in the GOP setback. It underlined, too, the error many liberals made in 1968 when they sat out the election because of Vietnam and, in so doing, helped elect Richard Nixon. If the 1970 elections are a model for the future, it will be possible to rebuild the coalition and reverse the country's political direction.

Just as it was appropriate to get millions of people into the trade-union movement in the '30s, and just as it was appropriate in 1963 to get hundreds of thousands of people to Washington to march for racial justice, today it is appropriate to get millions upon millions of people to march into voting booths and cast ballots for those who will carry out the kind of programs we need. There is no other way to change America, there is no better way to change America. It is the way we can build a just society, not on the ruins of the present society, but out of the aspirations of a majority of the people—the poor people, the working people, the common people, black and white, who together can and should determine the destiny of this nation.

OVERCOMING
VI MIDDLE CLASS
RAGE

THERE IS A NEED TO DEVELOP A CLEARER ETHNIC POLICY AND
for programs aimed at overcoming middle-class rage. This
is necessary not only to alleviate racial tensions and to
achieve a greater measure of social progress but because
it is right and necessary to begin to deal constructively
with the problems of lower-middle-class white ethnic
groups. In "For the Present," from the 1970 Introduction
to *Beyond the Melting Pot,* Glazer and Moynihan suggest eight approaches to living in multiethnic New York
and for making such a society work which they believe
are "applicable in major degree in every large city in
the country." My article "Overcoming Middle-Class Rage"
lays out a number of programs and policies. They range
from tax relief, day-care centers for working mothers and
special assistance to neighborhoods undergoing racial
change to an appeal to our cultural leadership to demonstrate greater empathy for the legitimate problems and
values of Middle Americans.

In a conference on group life recently, Andrew Greeley
suggested a number of rules for "intergroup ecumenism"
which provide a fitting note on which to close this discussion. Summarized briefly, they are:

1. Don't turn other groups into scapegoats in seeking
your own group's interests and purposes.

2. Try to learn about other groups from the inside—

that is, from the vantage point of how they feel and act.

3. Leadership should strive to resist moralistic righteousness.

4. Don't feel all morality and virtue is on one side or the other of an issue or group.

5. Leadership should support only people who offer rational and moderate solutions to problems.

6. Don't let the other group be totally defeated. (The defeat of the Irish and Italians in New York by John Lindsay proved to be a Pyrrhic victory as subsequent events were to prove.)

By Nathan Glazer and Daniel Patrick Moynihan

For the Present

POLICY, of course, in most areas, cannot wait on research, however enlightening research might be. What proposals for an ethnic policy—a policy conscious of the reality of the distinctive ethnic and racial groups, with distinct interests, with specific and general conflicts, some reaching to the foundations of the society—can one give? We orient our suggestions to New York City, though they are applicable in major degree to every large city in the country. They are offered in humility, but actions will be taken, and these considerations, we suggest, should guide action.

First, we must be aware that all policies in the city *are* inevitably policies for ethnic and race relations. This is inevitable, because the ethnic and racial groups of the city are *also* interest groups, based on jobs and occupations and possessions. Nor are they interest groups alone; they are also attached to symbols of their past, they are concerned with the fate of their homelands, they want to see members of their group raised to high position and

357

respect. But, aside from all this, owing to the concrete nature of their jobs (or lack of jobs), their businesses, and their professions, they are also defined by *interest.* And since they are interest groups, and since all policies affect interests differently, they also affect group relations. This is the first thing one must be aware of. If one does something that affects the position of organized teachers, one does something that affects the attitudes of the Jewish community, for half the teachers are Jews, and they have relatives. If one does something that affects policemen, one affects by that token the attitudes of the Irish, for a substantial part of the police force is Irish, and they have relatives. (How many is impressive: the study of Brooklyn voting on the police civilian review board shows that 54 percent of Catholics in Brooklyn have relatives or close friends on the police force. Even 21 percent of Jews have relatives or close friends on the police force!) If one affects the position of people on welfare, one immediately touches one third of the Puerto Ricans and Negroes in the city. If one affects the interests of small homeowners, one touches the Italian community. If one affects the interest of small shopkeepers, one has touched the Jews and Italians. And so it goes. Thus, a policy that affects race relations for the city must be a policy that affects all policies in the city. Each of them must be judged from the point of view of its impact on race relations. This impact must be a criterion, not the sole criterion, in every policy one undertakes. It should not be possible for a political leadership ever again to find itself in the position of pressing for a major policy, such as school decentralization, without at least considering in advance its impact on race relations, and how it might be moderated.

Second, policies must be based on the reality that the great majority of the people of the city are workers, white-collar workers, businessmen, and professionals, white and black, who are not aware that their position in life is based on massive governmental assistance. The great majority do not believe that they subsist on the basis of the exploitation of the black and the poor. And their interests and morality must serve as major limits to policy. Many people believe if the interests and morality of these groups are determinant, then nothing can be done for the poor and the black, and, therefore, the interests and morality of the workers and the middle class must be attacked in head-on and destructive conflict. Thus, one often hears the argument that one reason that the people on welfare have such a hard time is that whites and middle-class people refuse to see that work is not superior to nonwork, a point which is presented as an essential insight for the better society of the future. If, indeed, the progress of the poor and the black depends on such a change of values, then we will have to wait a long time for progress. Or we will have to devise means, in a democracy, by which policies can be carried out in the face of the opposition of the great majority. But to say that policies must take into account the interests and morality of the workers and the middle class is not to say that no decent policies are possible. The people of the city do support strongly policies to root out discrimination and prejudice. They do support policies to increase the number of jobs, income from jobs, security from jobs. Policies along these lines, which, of course must involve state and federal as well as city government, would do much to make jobs more attractive and, by the same token, welfare less attractive.

Third, policies must accept the reality, at least for some time to come, of ethnic communities with some distinctive social concerns, and of people who prefer living with other members of their group. The positive aspects of ethnic attachment should be recognized; the general approval of efforts to build up black pride and self-confidence and self-assertiveness will encourage this. This is perhaps the most difficult point to make, for we believe it would be a disaster for the city if ethnic divisiveness is fostered. But we can *accept* the reality of group existence and group attachment, yet not allow it to become the sole basis of public decisions. The city should not be a federation of nations, with protected turfs and excluded turfs. The organization of the groups should be, as it has been in the past, voluntary. Public action should operate not on the basis of group membership but on the basis of individual human qualities. It has been the curse of this country for so long that this did not happen in fact, and that Negroes—and other groups, in lesser degree—were excluded from evenhanded public action. We must not now move to another extreme, in which the sense of injustice is implanted in other groups.

A subtle mix of policies has emerged in the city, in which group existence is recognized and tolerated, in which groups move upward, economically, politically, socially, in which individuals are free to associate with ethnic groups or not as they will, in which groups are given recognition informally but not in formal and fixed procedures. In other words, New York City is neither Lebanon, where Moslems and Christians have formal and fixed constitutional roles, nor Malaysia, where, again, the groups are recognized in public policy and their place and privileges fixed. Nor should it be. How to maintain respect for group feeling and identity while maintaining the primacy of individual rights and responsibilities is perhaps the most difficult task of government, yet the history of New York City gives us some insight into this difficult task, and should not be ignored.

Fourth, one of the chief problems of race relations in

this city is the disproportionate presence of Negroes and Puerto Ricans on welfare. As long as one third or more of the members of these groups are on welfare, as long as welfare remains, as it has become, the largest single item of expenditure in the city, it is hard to see how race relations in the city will not be basically and deeply affected. (One could say the same of the disproportionate Negro role in street crime and crimes of violence.) We know this is a national problem, but it is in even larger measure a New York City problem, for no other city, even those with higher proportions of Negroes and equally generous welfare provisions, shows such huge numbers on welfare. Obviously, this is a problem in its own right, and it is not easy to know what one might do about it. The solution to this problem, if there is one, lies more at the federal than the city level. The Nixon Administration has moved strongly to propose a radical revision of the welfare system, one which would tie it in more closely to work, encouraging those requiring government aid to work on the one hand and giving government aid to those who work at low wages on the other, while providing assistance to city and state governments suffering under the strains of increasing welfare needs. This is not the place for an analysis of the problem of welfare in its own right. But there is a role for city government in this respect. As long as the great majority of the population is a working population and a tax-paying population, and as long as welfare aid goes disproportionately to certain ethnic and racial groups, the city government must not place itself in the position of appearing to encourage welfare or of actually encouraging it. Aid to the deprived is a right and an obligation of government. But, as Tocqueville pointed out long ago, rights vary in dignity and virtue. The right to welfare should not be endowed with the same dignity and virtue as the right to work. This can only exacerbate racial and ethnic tensions in the city. Meanwhile, the amelioration of the problems of welfare, which must be sought at many levels both of government and policy, should be pursued.

Fifth, a higher level of civic amenity must be attained to reduce the frustrations and miseries of the poor and the indignation of Negroes and Puerto Ricans. It is easy to say this, impossible to prescribe within present budgetary limits. The mayors are already a powerful lobby demanding more help from the Federal Government for this purpose. The streets should be cleaner, the subways less of a misery, the parks and playgrounds more numerous, policing—including local constabularies—more effective, and so on. If more money can regularly flow to such urban needs, one hopes that, in some measurable degree, anger will decline.

Sixth, one must beware of encouraging and supporting purely divisive groups and philosophies. The difficult question that we face today is whether black groups that insist—rhetorically or not, who is to tell?—on armed revolution, on the killing of whites, on violence toward every moderate black element, should be tolerated. Even if they are, however, they should not receive public support and encouragement. Intellectuals in New York have done a good deal to encourage and publicize this kind of madness.* The strong corporate feeling today in black com-

---

* Not just in New York. The president of a Middle Western university, prominent in civil rights activities, learned of this phenomenon in a most direct way. He recruited to his campus a young Negro law professor and gave him special responsibilities to deal with minority students. Before many months had passed, the professor submitted his resignation. His life had been threatened. The president was indignant: he asked for the name of the student and vowed he would be off the campus in twenty-four hours. The professor was not moved. Not just

munities makes actions against even the least representative and most dangerous groups difficult. Persecution will probably make these groups stronger and will gain them sympathy from moderate blacks, not to mention white liberals. Perhaps the most that can be said at this point is that they should not be encouraged. More positively, this means that every element in the Negro community that *does* believe an integrated, democratic society is possible should be encouraged. There are many such people, and many of them are now cowed by the verbal (and not only verbal) violence of black militants and the unthinking and dilettantish support they now receive from such wide strata of white intellectuals and liberals. Those elements which do believe there is hope for American society should be given recognition and support. They have organizations: these should be given important roles to play in the economic and political improvement of the Negro communities. They have leaders: they should be recognized. They have ideas: they must have the opportunity and power to carry them out.

Seventh, all institutions that wield great power—we think primarily of government, business, labor unions, universities and colleges, hospitals—must be constantly aware of the need to place significant numbers of blacks and Puerto Ricans in posts of responsibility and power. To prescribe how this is done in each area is beyond the confines of this article. Government has been perhaps most active in this respect. Labor unions have been among the more backward, yet owing to the large numbers of

---

his life had been threatened, but that of his wife and child. He had no choice but to leave. The incident is worth reporting because the university president in question had earlier been thoroughly resistant to the idea that such things were taking place. In truth, white liberals have come close to sacrificing the interests of black moderates in order to sustain their own threatened ideology of race relations.

Negroes and Puerto Ricans who now make up the working population of New York, and who will make up ever larger proportions in the near future, they have a particular responsibility to develop Negro and Puerto Rican leadership more rapidly. They should have more black and Spanish-speaking business agents, organizers, representatives, union presidents. One can envisage the New York City labor council conducting a serious leadership training for young blacks and Puerto Ricans, both in and outside the labor movement with a guarantee of jobs to successful graduates. This might provide one kind of constructive channel for the driving energy of so many young blacks today, and it might help to provide new vigor to an institution in American life that has done more than any other to raise the position of the poor and the worker. Obviously, similar programs would be a good idea in other major institutions too.

Eighth, a good deal still devolves upon the complex public and private machinery that has been built up in the city to promote good race relations. We think in particular of the Jewish defense organizations, which have substantial resources and staffs, and which represent the largest single group in the city, the traditional Negro organizations (NAACP, Urban League), the City Commission on Human Rights, and the state agency with parallel responsibilities to fight discrimination and promote good race relations. Obviously, as we argued in our first point, race and ethnic relations are no longer specialized functions for specialized groups. They are issues that must be in the consciousness of public and civil leaders, no matter what area of policy they deal with. Yet there is one major area of tension and conflict in which these specialized agencies can play an important role, and that is the area of Negro-Jewish relations. We discussed the reasons for this tension in *Beyond the Melting Pot* in 1963, and they remain the same. The ironies of history have placed Jews disproportionately in positions of landlord, merchant, doctor, teacher, and social worker; and Negroes, disproportionately, in the positions of tenants of these landlords, customers of these merchants, patients of these doctors, pupils of these teachers, and clients of these social workers. These primary reasons for conflict have existed for a long time, and they have by now, in large measure, effaced the strong alliance that, in the forties and fifties, made New York State and New York City a leader in the passage of civil rights legislation and the development of programs for integration. New sources of tension have been added, in particular, the alliance between American black militants and the revolutionists of the third world. This turns many black leaders into stated enemies of Israel, even if this is not a particularly salient part of their political outlook.

There is no easy way to get at the sources of the conflict. Changes are occurring. Tenement landlords are, owing to varied developments, rapidly abandoning many of their properties, and small businessmen are abandoning theirs. The American Jewish Congress has been instrumental in launching a program to transfer Jewish business properties in black areas to blacks. There are programs to increase the number of Negro doctors. There has been a huge increase of Negroes and Puerto Ricans in the City Colleges, which will increase the number of teachers and social workers. One can think of many other programs that will perhaps more rapidly increase the number of Negro and Puerto Rican landlords, merchants, doctors, teachers, and social workers. All these will have a potential for increasing conflicts between groups, but in the long run we believe they must reduce them.

The voluntary organizations and the city and state

agencies can play important roles in all these areas. The voluntary agencies in particular can and should continue the efforts they have carried on throughout the years to promote more direct discussion and meeting between people of different groups. In the end, a good deal must depend on the political intelligence of Jews and Negroes, the two chief groups in conflict. Leaders on both sides can inflame passions. The voluntary organizations that have worked together in the past should be in the best position to educate members of both groups to the enormous dangers in such a path, to spread sound information, to promote tolerant and understanding attitudes.

This is a small budget of suggestions, indeed, for a big problem. Certainly, we are now living through the severest test that New York as a multiethnic society has ever experienced. As we see how other multiethnic and multiracial societies solve or, rather, do not solve their problems, we cannot be too encouraged. And yet, in some respects, the United States, and in particular the great cities, have developed unique approaches to a multiethnic and multiracial society. They may be sufficient for the test.

By Murray Friedman

Overcoming Middle Class Rage

IN HIS ATTACK on television commentators, school bussing to achieve integration, "so-called intellectuals," and critics of the Administration's Vietnam policies, Vice-President Agnew has been hailed as "telling it like it is" and denounced for opening "a Pandora's box of reaction, backlash, and repression." Whatever the view, he has emerged overnight as the spokesman of many working- and middle-class Americans who have been discovered, recently, by national news media and described as troubled, angry, and in revolt.

The complex phenomenon of Agnew and the mood he so clearly represents is a growing and enormously significant social and political factor in American life. Magazines like *The New Republic* and *Newsweek* have warned in recent months that the revolt of "The Troubled American" threatens progress in civil rights, personal liberties, and educational reform. Some see even the emergence of a protofascist movement built around the police and the rising demand for law and order. With the exception of the work of urbanologist Irving Levine and a few others, there has been little public discussion of new strategies

Reprinted from *La Salle*, a quarterly La Salle College magazine, Vol. 14, No. 2 (Spring, 1970). Used by permission.

for reversing these trends, concrete programs for dealing with the very real problems of middle-class America and how to build a new political base for effecting change.

Clearly, there is a need for the development of measures for overcoming middle-class rage, admittedly a fuzzy category. I am referring to large numbers of working Americans, including blacks, many of them union members, whom former Undersecretary of HUD Robert C. Wood described several years ago as earning between $5,000 and $10,000 a year, which inflation has pushed somewhat higher. According to the AFL-CIO, 50 percent of all union members and as many as 75 percent of those over age thirty live in suburbs. In addition, there are those with higher incomes and first- and second-generation ethnic groups whose values and style of life can be described generally as middle class.

Middle America is in revolt because it is experiencing many severe problems and tensions which it finds difficult to handle and the broader society is ignoring. Economically, these Americans have often made little progress and some have moved backward in an "age of affluence." S. M. Miller notes that if we divide white families into five groups ranked by income from 1956 to 1966, only the bottom and top layers advanced economically while the second and third levels actually declined during this period. As of February, 1969, the average worker's purchasing power was 13 cents less than it was a year before. His position is threatened further by inflation, work slowdowns and high and regressive taxes. It is significant that backlash voting developed recently after a period of intense industrial strife. The number of man-hours lost in strikes in 1967–1968, for example, was higher than that of any comparable period since World War II. These are people above the poverty level but deeply in trouble.

Moreover, many of the foundations and values on which middle-class Americans have built their lives—neighborhood and friendship associations, national pride and patriotism, sexual reticence in a period of greater openness and permissiveness, an orientation of reward based on work and reasonable order in their lives and the society around them—have become unstable.

George Kennan has written with great insight, "Whenever the authority of the past is too suddenly and too drastically undermined—whenever the past ceases to be the great and reliable reference book of human problems —whenever, above all, the experience of the father becomes irrelevant to the trials and searchings of the son— there the foundations of man's inner health and stability begin to crumble, insecurity and panic begin to take over, conduct becomes erratic and aggressive."

The focus of much of middle-class anger tends to come to rest on the Negro who stands as a symbol of its discontent and alienation. While a number of ethnic groups have long histories of friction with black people, racism is only part of the problem. In their recent study of working-class youth, William Simon, John H. Gagnon, and Donald Carns note: "Change itself becomes the enemy. . . . The Negro community now represents the most powerful symbol of disruptive change in their lives. Moreover, this symbol is perceived by working-class youth as being endorsed or at least tolerated by the major institutions of the society." Another group of social scientists who examined the defeat of liberal forces in the 1966 New York City referendum on civilian police review concluded, "There is little evidence that the Brooklyn respondents [to a special poll] were expressing attitudes of blatant bigotry."

The core of any strategy to reduce middle-class rage might be built around programs that benefit broad group-

ings of Americans, not blacks alone. Whether stated or
not, the thrust of many of the programs for the poor and
disadvantaged in recent years has been based on a "black
strategy." Poverty and Model City efforts, ineffective or
at least underfinanced as many have been, nevertheless
are seen as for Negroes only. The emphasis on the latter
is only natural, since blacks have been the most discriminated against and disadvantaged in our society. But they
are not the only ones. Many poor whites and working
Americans feel left out. In a pluralistic society, those who
feel passed over attempt to neutralize or veto the gains of
seemingly more favored groups. A better strategy is "something for everyone."

Such broadly based programs may be found in income
maintenance plans such as child allowances, negative income tax, guaranteed annual income, and improvement of
social security allowances for the increasingly large elderly
population. Congressional moves to raise social security
allotments for the elderly and liquidating the bankrupt
system of welfare payments by replacing them with a
federal income maintenance floor for unemployed and
working poor as recommended by President Nixon and
the Heineman Commission are moves in the right direction.

Inadequate as the President's income proposals are, they
have made the idea of a guaranteed annual income respectable. Representatives John Conyers (D., Michigan),
Jonathan Bingham (D., New York), and Charles Whelan
(R., Ohio) have introduced legislation calling for a
broader, less restrictive program for a "national living income program" which provides a much larger guaranteed
annual allowance. These programs will benefit blacks more
than any other group but will be available and acceptable
to all Americans. It is significant that while welfare spend-

ing is generally assumed to be anathema to many Americans, the Harris Survey reports the President's income proposal is supported by a margin of 44 to 32 percent.

An effort should be made, also, as S. M. Miller, professor of education and sociology at New York University has suggested, to universalize services such as day-care centers for working AFDC mothers, legal-aid services, and Head Start. Many blue- and white-collar wives work and have makeshift arrangements for their children. A day-care service for all would help them. So would Head Start programs and pocket money and the experience of the Neighborhood Youth Corps.

It is important to understand, also, that tax reform or tax relief has important consequences to working- and lower-middle-class whites and is not simply a conservative ploy to gain more at the expense of the have-littles.

Congress voted recently to raise social security benefits and the standard income-tax deduction from $600 to $750, but only after two years, and has plugged some loopholes that benefit the more affluent. These reforms, however, are really quite small. (The AFL-CIO had recommended that the tax paid by a married worker with two children be cut by 42.1 percent if he makes $5,000 a year and 15.9 percent if he earns $15,000. Senators Harrison Williams (D., New Jersey) and Fred Harris (D., Oklahoma) had earlier introduced bills which would make completely deductible medical expenses, and provide exemptions for daily transportation expenses to and from work.) They put comparatively little cash into the pockets of embittered workers and Middle Americans, thereby failing to curb an underlying cause of middle-class rage.

Tax relief might also be a means of making available to families of working- and lower-middle-class whites greater opportunities for improving the education of their children thereby raising their economic level and status. During the Congressional debate on the tax bill, the Senate enacted a proposal offered by Senator Peter Dominick (R., Colorado) to allow parents to subtract up to $325 from their taxes for any child's education, and there has been public discussion of introducing legislation to amend property tax laws and to provide funds for a multibillion-dollar community college program to allow children from less advantaged homes to gain the education necessary for mobility.

In this respect, as Irving Levine, Urban Affairs Director of the American Jewish Committee, has pointed out, too many workers reach a dead end employmentwise by the age of thirty-five or forty. We need programs which will encourage working Americans to broaden their educations for the possibility of second careers. These might be modeled after the GI education bill and include government support for on-the-job training, upgrading skills and changing job categories thereby making white workers more sympathetic to similar programs for hard-core unemployed.

The education of many working-class whites in this country is as much a national scandal as the generally inadequate education endured by blacks in the slums of our cities. The public focus has been on black schools and here the discussion and educational interest has often centered on racial balance and bussing to achieve greater desegregation rather than the broader educational needs of white and black children. Desegregation is important—in fact vital—but bringing disadvantaged blacks into nearby disadvantaged white schools hardly seems to offer improvement educationally or racially. Levine has suggested that some of the most fruitful possibilities for change lie in advanced educational technology and organization including educational parks and campus arrangements which offer greater possibilities for desegregation than most integration plans. He writes:

> The possibilities opened up by effective decentralization and community participation, by computer technology, and by a widening of the choice of educational options should be disseminated throughout ethnic America and held up as models for new programs. The granting of a per pupil stipend might encourage new, competing educational systems, relieve the failure-oriented public-school apparatus of the total burden, and satisfy parents of parochial school children (most of whom are ethnic whites) that their special financial problems are not totally disregarded.

The latter suggestion coincides with the recommendation for subsidized private education for blacks recently made by Christopher Jencks which would pluralize American education further.

If private education is to play a greater role in relieving some of our educational problems, especially those of middle-class whites, we need to come to grips with the issue of aid to children in parochial schools. These educate as many as 30 percent to 40 percent of the children in major metropolitan centers of the country. This problem has become a major source of anger among many Roman Catholics who possess the most extensive private-school system and, to a lesser degree, orthodox Jews. Catholics number approximately one out of four Americans today and more than any other group are the backbone of middle-class rage. They are deeply disturbed that their schools are falling behind in educational improvement and, in effect, they are supporting two school systems. A report released last spring estimated that 301 Roman Catholic elementary schools in the United States were about to shut down and 111 more were phasing out classes due to rising costs.

Despite some "give" on the part of liberal and civil libertarian groups which resulted in passage of the Elementary and Secondary Education Act of 1965 authorizing certain limited forms of aid to nonpublic schools, we have been largely unresponsive to the plight of these schools. Many liberals fear new forms of aid will weaken public schools further and destroy the constitutional separation of church and state. A number of suggestions have been advanced to provide various forms of assistance which may not generate constitutional issues such as tax credits, tax deductions, and block grants for parents and shared time or dual enrollment. The "purchases of services" bill passed by the Pennsylvania legislature has opened the door to financial aid for certain secular subjects taught in parochial schools but it remains to be seen if the U.S. Supreme Court will accept such aid as constitutional.

In the meantime, many Catholic politicians and voters have been dragging their feet on school bond issues and other methods of improving the public schools, in part, because they see no aid coming to their own schools. In spite of constitutional and other problems that stand in the way, adoption by liberals of a "something for everyone" strategy and cooperation between the two school systems in permissible areas might well tamp down anger here and move us away from the current impasse in which public and parochial school education finds itself today.

One difficulty we have had in recognizing the need for special help to various religious and racial groups—we have accepted doing this for economic or class groups such as trade unions and farmers—is that we are just beginning to study and attempt to understand how an ethnically and racially pluralistic society works. A body of scholarly data has begun to appear which suggests that group identification, values, styles, and special needs are tenaciously maintained in spite of the emphasis on the common American nationality. We have become conscious of this as we watch the race revolution unfold, but America is going through a period of re-ethnization in which being Jewish, Polish, Italian, and members of other groups is "beautiful" as well. The reasons for this are quite complex, but the result is that we are witnessing a series of collisions between and among racial, religious, and ethnic groups who are, themselves, at different stages of integration in American life.

We have tended to view the bitter struggles over desegregation of recent years, for example, as moral issues—which they are—but there is another dimension: Which group or groups will have to pay the costs of major social change? There has always been a class basis to desegregation confrontations beginning with the Little Rock, Arkansas, school crisis in the late 1950's. (Little Rock is divided into working-class white and black central city and the rolling uplands of Pulaski Heights where upper-class, affluent whites live. Desegregation was begun at Central High School while the brand-new high school in Pulaski Heights remained lily-white.) As Negroes have sought desegregation in housing, education, employment, and other areas of American life, they are most frequently encountering working- and lower-middle-class Irish, Italians, Jews, and Poles rather than more affluent WASP's, upper-class Jews, and other groups whose liberal convictions are sincere, but who as individuals are often physically removed from the scene of the action.

Andrew Greeley in his perceptive analysis, *Why Can't They Be Like Us?* points out that ethnic and working-class groups that are reacting so violently to Negro move-ins or efforts to bus to achieve desegregation are often those who are still completing their own integration into American life. For them, a move-in by a black family represents a threat not only to the value of their property (although overwhelming evidence contradicts this) but to friendship patterns, homogeneous ethnic churches, familiar landscape and shopping areas, "all those things a man has come to value in that particular area he thinks of as his own." When this is added to the other anxieties felt by Middle America, we are better able to understand why desegregation has been so difficult.

S. M. Miller and Frank Riessman in their book *Social Class and Social Policy* have urged that society as a whole should help assume the burden and costs of desegregation rather than permit them to fall on "vulnerable individuals whose recalcitrance and anger reflect the risk and costs they have to bear as individuals, unsupported by any over-all programs." They suggest that neighborhoods experiencing such change should be provided with more money for their schools, expanded recreational facilities, improved police protection, and insurance for homes which may suffer temporary loss in value because of the new residents. Last spring, the U.S. Conference of Mayors called for federal compensation for homeowner victims of "block-busting" real-estate tactics in changing neighborhoods. Obviously, such efforts will only go part of the way in spreading the burden of social change but they would help convince many middle-class whites that we are concerned about their problems and willing to try to do something about them.

Broadening black admissions at colleges and universities through the use of quotas and preferential treatment has also been an issue that has stirred up middle-class rage. This was seen most dramatically last spring in the confrontation at City College in New York when the latter considered an arrangement to admit half of its entering class by regular standards and half according to special procedures for impoverished blacks and Puerto Ricans. Lowering standards and allocating scarce places disproportionately to the latter may be more acceptable to upper-class and WASP students at elite colleges such as Harvard or Columbia who are relatively secure, can identify more easily with the aspirations and needs of the black poor, and have other options generally open to them.

At City College, which has traditionally served as an educational ladder by which lower-middle-class Jews, Italians, and other groups have moved up in our society, such procedures led to violent confrontation and the temporary closing of the institution. Many white students were worried about opportunities for admission for their younger brothers and sisters and feared that lowered standards would depress the quality and prestige of the institution thereby marring their chances to get ahead. It is not hard to predict that if the rules of college admissions are changed to favor blacks, at the expense of working- and lower-middle-class whites, the City College experience of black-working white confrontation will develop at other public campuses throughout the country.

The human problem here is terribly complex and can only be met by mounting a program of universal and free higher education for *all* those who desire it. California has introduced such a system by expanding its community college facilities. Open enrollment is scheduled to go into effect next September in the City University's fifteen senior and community colleges. The Carnegie Commission on Higher Education headed by Clark Kerr has recommended a multibillion-dollar federal program be set up, by 1976, to finance the college education of students who cannot afford it. This could do for Americans what the free municipal colleges in New York did for children of immigrants in the first half of this century. In this way, everyone benefits. A bill largely embodying this recommendation has been introduced by Ogden R. Reid (R., Westchester), but has not been passed. Provision can also be made for special tutoring and other arrangements for those not up to standards; abandoning or sharply compromising standards, however, will tend to lock middle-class America into a posture of permanent intransigence.

One of the most inflammatory issues that has enraged Middle America and made it less amenable to traditional appeals to social progress and change has been the growing fear of violence and personal safety. A character in Jules Feiffer's play, *Little Murders*, describes this fear.

> You know how I get through the day? . . . in planned segments: I get up in the morning and I think, O.K., a sniper didn't get me for breakfast, let's see if I can go for my morning walk without being mugged. O.K., I finished my walk, let's see if I can make it back home without having a brick dropped on my head from the top of a building. O.K., I'm safe in the lobby, let's see if I can go up in the elevator without getting a knife in my ribs. O.K., I made it to the front door, let's see if I can open it without finding burglars in the hall. O.K., I made it to the hall, let's see if I can walk into the living room and not find the rest of my family dead. This Goddamned city!

In the first six months of 1969, violent crimes in the United States increased 13 percent. Armed robbery was up 17 percent; forcible rape 15 percent; aggravated assault 10 percent; and murder 8 percent. We have not been sufficiently sensitive to the anxieties this situation has created. Obviously, a number of politicians have capitalized on these fears for electoral gains but it is not enough to dismiss appeals to law and order as code words for racial bigotry or to talk about getting at the underlying forces that make for crime and violence, necessary as this is. It is undoubtedly true, as Irving Levine has pointed out, that "to preach continually that we must eliminate the cause of crime foolishly leads only to a generalized rejection of progressive social programs as encouraging violence."

We need new and creative programs of law enforcement that will deal with these problems *right now* while expanding efforts aimed at more fundamental change. This is not the place to spell out a comprehensive safer community program. Many of the ideas are described in the recommendations of the President's Crime Commission and the Kerner Commission. In essence, these call for greater use of advanced technology and neighborhood and community participation in cooperation with the police. They include utilization of neighborhood people in security roles such as escort services for women, storefront police stations and direct home-to-police burglar systems. If such advanced programs were put into effect and began to have some effect, we might well make inroads on increased gun-purchasing and other forms of vigilantism that have been marked in recent months.

In this respect, the liberal community needs to develop new relationships with the police. Some have engaged in day-to-day harassment and physical violence with regard to slum dwellers and overreacted to black and campus militance and demonstrations as the Walker Commission reported in its study of the 1968 Democratic Convention confrontation. These excesses need to be corrected, but there has been a tendency on the part of liberals to ascribe to the police, unexamined, the stereotypes and conventional wisdom of the Left. There has been little understanding of the sense of alienation of the police, the feeling that *they* constitute an underprivileged group —drawn, not incidentally, largely from lower-middle-class white ethnic groups—who are under continuous criticism and danger as they patrol society's frontiers of racial anger, poverty, and youthful revolt. By our failure to attempt to develop lines of communication with the police and support for their legitimate needs, we have, in effect, left them no one to fall back on except groups like the John Birch Society.

A more effective approach to dealing with the police might recognize that they have an extraordinarily difficult job to perform and require our assistance in doing it simultaneous with efforts to raise salaries thereby attracting and keeping a higher caliber of officer. Federal Judge George Edwards, former police commissioner of Detroit, reports that the median salary of policemen in cities over 25,000 is $5,843 and in smaller cities it is even less. He has recommended that a fully trained and qualified officer should command a salary of $10,000. He has suggested also, establishment of a National Police College—a West Point for police—and other measures which would raise the professional level of police and provide them with greater status and self-respect. If we begin to identify with the legitimate aspirations of police, we would be on firmer grounds in pressing for necessary reforms in the law enforcement process including a greater degree of community participation. . . .

In a fundamental sense, middle-class America is the very cement that holds our society together. "If all the Ph.D. sociologists go on strike, no one would notice," Barbara Mikulski, a Baltimore ethnic intellectual, said recently, "but let the Polish bus drivers do it, and the whole city falls apart." Even the traditional conservatism of middle-class America represents a visceral understanding of the importance of order and stability in society.

E. Digby Baltzell, the University of Pennsylvania sociologist, has pointed out that important as is the need for reform and change, those forces which hold a community together must also be carefully preserved. Campus revolts against unquestionable inequities, a general decline in traditional morality, and the testing of the outer limits of freedom by youths and adults alike have had, undoubtedly, liberating and progressive significance. But they have helped also to destroy our sense of continuity with the past and led to many of the present difficulties we are having in handling the present. Has the time come when we can give two cheers for the middle class?

There is reason to believe that many of us who have long credited ourselves with being sensitive to the needs of the disadvantaged and the masses of Americans in our society have in fact lost contact with large numbers and perhaps the majority of Americans. One of the great failures in recent political life has been the inability to develop liberal leaders who can speak for the needs, values, and interests of middle-class America while at the same time advancing programs for racial and social progress for the more disadvantaged. This has made even more tragic the death of Robert Kennedy. Campaigning across America just before his assassination, he called for law and order, coupled this with attacks upon bureaucracy and repeated assertions that violence in the cities was unacceptable. (This brought from Senator Eugene McCarthy the rejoinder that Kennedy was offering "a kind of jigsaw arrangement" that sought "combinations of separate interests or separate groups." This was true, although Kennedy and his staff had done considerable creative thinking about the causes and cures of racial disorders.) When the votes were counted in Indiana, for example, Kennedy had won the support not only of the blacks of Gary and Indianapolis by huge totals but carried the

Southern-oriented counties along the Ohio River, scored a clear majority among the Slavic minorities in the industrial cities, and won first place in 51 of Indiana's 92 counties, carrying rural and urban alike.

We are moving into a period of vast social and political change only part of which is visible or understood. The revolt of angry blacks and the new politics symbolized by campus youth and the McCarthy movement are quite clear. Working Americans and blue-collar youth, who are considerably more numerous than the campus and McCarthy youngsters, are less articulate but they represent a third and growing revolutionary force. Social scientists are just beginning to probe the significance of this, but already we have learned that blue-collar youth who have no memories of the depression voted twice as heavily for Wallace as they did for Goldwater in 1964.

A preliminary report by the University of Michigan's Survey Research Center reports that the McCarthy movement was a considerably more complicated affair than is commonly believed. Widely seen as a manifestation of widespread public dissatisfaction with the war in Vietnam and a desire for peace, it was, in part, also a "no confidence" vote for the Johnson Administration and the conventional values of the Democratic Party's liberal wing. The report notes, "Among his [McCarthy's] supporters in the [New Hampshire] primary those who were unhappy with the Johnson Administration for not pursuing a harder line against Hanoi outnumbered those advocating a withdrawal from Vietnam by nearly a three-to-two margin." At the outset of his campaign, the report indicates, McCarthy drew racial bigots, Vietnam hard-liners, and those who were demanding "law and order."

What is urgently needed is for some of the brilliance which has gone into fashioning the New Deal and race revolutions to be developed to speak to and for middle-class America. This should not be seen as bowing to a reactionary mood now extant in the land. Nor should it be based purely on practical politics, since the aspirations and needs of working Americans are as legitimate as any other group in our society. The growth of political reaction today is as much due to liberal loss of contact with troubled Americans over the past two decades as to any resurgent right-wing movement. We have gravitated to a politics of gesture and confrontation rather than a politics of depolarization in which we choose issues and work for those programs which are commonly seen as benefitting large groupings of Americans including, of course, the most disadvantaged.